The Families' Civil War

The Families' Civil War

Black Soldiers and the Fight for Racial Justice

HOLLY A. PINHEIRO JR.

The University of Georgia Press *Athens*

Athens, Georgia 30602
www.ugapress.org

Set in 9.75/13.5 Baskerville 10 Pro Regular
by Kaelin Chappell Broaddus

Most University of Georgia Press titles are
available from popular e-book vendors.

Printed digitally

Library of Congress Cataloging-in-Publication Data

Names: Pinheiro Jr., Holly A., 1983– author.
Title: The families' civil war : black soldiers and the fight for racial justice / Holly A. Pinheiro Jr.
Other titles: Black soldiers and the fight for racial justice
Description: Athens : The University of Georgia Press, [2022] | Series: Uncivil wars | Includes bibliographical references and index.
Identifiers: LCCN 2021052512 | ISBN 9780820361956 (hardback) | ISBN 9780820361963 (paperback) | ISBN 9780820361970 (ebook)
Subjects: LCSH: Philadelphia (Pa.)—History—Civil War, 1861–1865—Social aspects. | African American soldiers—Pennsylvania—Philadelphia—History—19th century. | African American families—Pennsylvania—Philadelphia—Social conditions—19th century. | African American soldiers—Family relationships—History—19th century. | United States. Army. Colored Infantry Regiment, 3rd (1863–1865) | United States. Army. Colored Infantry Regiment, 6th (1863–1865) | United States. Army. Colored Infantry Regiment, 8th (1863–1865) | Free African Americans—Pennsylvania—Philadelphia—Social conditions—19th century. | Philadelphia (Pa.)—Race relations—History—19th century. | United States—History—Civil War, 1861–1865—Participation, African American.
Classification: LCC F158.44 .P85 2022 | DDC 305.8009748/1109034—dc23/eng/20211103
LC record available at https://lccn.loc.gov/2021052512

To all of the families of USCT soldiers

CONTENTS

ACKNOWLEDGMENTS ix

INTRODUCTION 1

CHAPTER 1
The African American Family in the Free North 13

CHAPTER 2
The United States Needs African American Men 34

CHAPTER 3
The Idealism versus the Realism of Military Service 52

CHAPTER 4
Familial Hardships during the Civil War 73

CHAPTER 5
Reconstructing the Northern African American Family 88

CHAPTER 6
USCT Families in an Industrializing Nation 115

EPILOGUE 143

APPENDIX I
Methodology 147

APPENDIX II
Philadelphian-Born United States Colored
Infantry (USCI) Soldiers 150

NOTES 157

INDEX 217

ACKNOWLEDGMENTS

First and foremost, I want to give all glory to Jesus Christ. Nothing in my life, including this book, would be possible without you. I sincerely thank you for your sacrifice, love, and grace you have shown me over the years. Through the joys and hardships, I have always felt your support. You have always been and will always be there. I am forever grateful that you continue to shine your light on me.

To my family, it would honestly take an entire book to properly thank everyone, so please accept this portion as an example of my gratitude. In terms of coming to history, I remember my uncles—Darrell and Stephen—strongly encouraged me to learn about African American history at a young age. Furthermore, I owe my uncle Darrell everything it took to finance my undergraduate education when I was depressed and doubted my future. I will never forget the advice and time you gave me. Meanwhile, randomly interjecting Glory into conversations with my uncle Peter will never get old. I am indebted to my siblings for how they inspire me, and it is a joy to see how we have grown even closer as adults. I hope that seeing this book come to fruition brings the same excitement and tears of fun (like when I called my grandmother) that we all shared when I broke the news that I received my doctorate.

Arguably, the most important family member is my mother. You have, without a doubt, been influential to my life in more ways than I can document. You have always supported my dreams and challenged me to reach my goals. Thank you for supporting my thirst for knowledge and reading with the many trips to local libraries and bookstores. Thank you for nurturing my inquisitive nature and for tolerating my "unique" personality. You have been there for me through the lowest and highest points of my life, and I am honored that you continue to believe in me even when I do not believe in myself. I also want to thank you for your service in the U.S. Navy. As a child, I really struggled with how your various deployments impacted my life. Each time your ship departed and returned, I worked to process how and why the military and nation did not understand the impact your military service had on your children. I now realize that the families I study give me the chance to process our familial experiences, and I am appreciative. Your life experiences have been critical in helping me explore key topics for this project. I love you, and I hope I do you proud.

My collegiate journey was neither easy nor clearly defined. But one thing I highly valued was being blessed with professors that invested time in helping me—graduate. Valencia College was critical in helping me figure out that I not only belonged in college but that I could excel. I have nothing but praise to heap on my professors there. I am honored to have graduated from and been an adjunct professor at the University of Central Florida. Numerous professors in the Department of History saw something in me that I did not even realize. Words cannot do justice to the influence that Barbara Gannon, Richard Crepeau, John Sacher, and others have had on my life. The fact that my bonds continued over a decade after graduating illustrates that these individuals truly are invested in my long-term success.

I am forever appreciative of the Department of History at the University of Iowa for giving me the privilege of studying in their graduate program. I had no idea how that decision would lead me to rethink how I see the world, my family, and myself when I began studying there. Learning from Leslie Schwalm, Shelton Stromquist, Tom Midtrød, Michael Moore, and others profoundly reframed me. I not only became a well-rounded scholar, but I also became a person who could more deeply discuss the complexity of life and why it matters. Studying under these scholars has meant the world to me. Thank you all for supporting my scholarly interests and pushing me to reconsider things I thought I knew.

The University of Iowa, unbeknownst to me at the time, would introduce me to some lifelong friends. Sylvea Hollis and Naoquia Callahan are not only amazing scholars but they are amazing friends. I sincerely love when we get together for our various Blackademic conversations to laugh, uplift, and catch up. They keep me grounded and empower me as a scholar. I always look forward to hearing about their new projects and life updates.

Words cannot express how much I owe to the Department of History at the University of Alabama for awarding me a postdoctoral fellowship, during which I wrote the majority of this book. At the same time, I workshopped many ideas and drafts of the project with my colleagues (including, but not limited to, Lesley Gordon, Joshua Rothman, Erik Peterson, Sharony Green, and Julia Brock). Feedback was immensely helpful to me. And thank you to John Beeler for the rides to work and conversations in your office, where we talked extensively about my project. Your critiques are, without a doubt, critical to this book.

Working at the University of Alabama also allowed me to learn from scholars in the Department of Gender and Race Studies. More specifically, I want to thank Hilary Green, Sara-Maria Sorrentino, and Utz McKnight. Their advice and knowledge had me thinking deeper about my work in ways I did not initially envision. My many forays into theoretical concepts are due to their insight. Additionally, they (along with the Writing Group) pushed me to write more concisely and clearly. Their wisdom and guidance helped me publish three articles and write most of this book. They were heavily influential in molding me to become more efficient with my time. I will always value the skills they taught me.

I would like to thank the various institutions and organizations that supported my work. I've had the opportunity to present pieces of this project with the Society for Civil War Historians, *Muster*, *Black Perspectives*, the African American Intellectual History Society, the Association for the Study of African American Life and History, British American Nineteenth Century Historians, the Smithsonian Institution, the National Park Service, the Organization of American Historians, the Nau Center, the Virginia Center for Civil War Studies, the University of Lynchburg, and others. I am also indebted to the staffs of various archives for helping me during fellowships and finding primary sources. More specifically, I am grateful to the Historical Society of Pennsylvania, the Library Company of Philadelphia, the National Archives and Records Administration, and the New-York Historical Society. I would also like to thank the Furman University Humanities Center for helping to fund this project.

There are so many scholars that I must thank, to acknowledge their mentorship and input in this project. They include (in no particular order), Andy Slap, Douglas Egerton, Caroline Janney, Kelly Mezurek, Judith Geisburg, Brooks Simpson, Andrew Frank, Lisa Tendrich Frank, Sally Hadden, Jane Dabel, David Silkenat, John Hayes, Ruth

McClelland-Nugent, William Link, J. Matthew Gallman, Kevin Levin, Keith Harris, Kenny Whitman, and my former students at the University of Alabama and Augusta University. The latter allowed me to workshop pieces of this project with them.

I must thank Hilary Green, Barbara Gannon, and Adam Domby for their influence, guidance, and insight. Having them as friends has meant the world to my family, even beyond the scholarship. I will always be thankful that you uplifted me when I have been down. And my sincerest apologies to anyone that I have forgotten; it is not intentional.

Words cannot express how joyful I am to work with the UnCivil War Series of the University of Georgia Press. The entire staff has been nothing but wonderful to me throughout the process. I always love talking about the Arsenal and Chelsea rivalry with Mick Gusinde-Duffy. Learning and getting feedback from Amy Murrell Taylor and Stephen Berry is something that I treasure. Both have made me a better scholar, writer, and teacher. I am truly honored to be working with Amy, who I consider a mentor, colleague, and friend. It still boggles my mind that you have been one of my biggest advocates, especially when it began with a random email I sent after reading an essay of yours. Every conversation leaves me inspired—and laughing at some arbitrary point we discussed.

Finally, to my amazing wife Teresa. You are my best friend, and the woman I prayed for as a youth. I still remember telling my mom and Dan, after a date, that I was going to marry you. Life with you (and our fur babies) is a joy. Seeing your passion for life, faith, people, and animals is truly inspiring. There is no limit to what you can achieve, and I am grateful that you have joined me on the journey of life. Thank you for supporting, challenging, and loving me.

The War after the War

INTRODUCTION

On April 8, 1884, Mary Williamson, the widow of Benjamin Davis, a deceased soldier in the Sixth United States Colored Infantry (USCI), arrived at a Bureau of Pensions local office in Philadelphia, Pennsylvania. Williamson provided testimony to a special examiner regarding the validity of a minor's pension case for her now adult son, Jerome. During a deposition two years earlier, the presiding pension agent questioned the legitimacy of Williamson's common-law marriage to Benjamin and connection to the child that the marriage produced. Perhaps tired of having to explain herself to yet another federal government representative, she emphasized how the Civil War forever changed their family.

> "I kept him [Jerome Davis] until he was seven or eight months old, when I took him to his grandfather[']s at his father[']s request, and he [Jerome's grandfather] has brought him up, and took him ever since [1864.]"
>
> "What is the reason you did not keep him or care for him?"
>
> "Because I had to go to service, and they were willing to care for him. They [the U.S. Army] drafted men, and left me no means of support to work ourselves."[1]

Williamson's statement illustrates the harsh reality that she, and countless other working-poor African American Philadelphians, experienced during and after the Civil War. Unfortunately, many of these families would continue to experience financial hardships while dealing with invasive (and often racist) oversight from federal officials for decades to come.

Scholarship on United States Colored Troops (USCT) regiments has long emphasized certain aspects of military service, such as wartime mobilization, combat, and racism in the military. Some of this literature explores how soldiers used their service as a direct pathway to African American male suffrage.[2] Other works reveal how men served in order to have their manhood recognized by white society.[3] Many of these studies focus on southern African Americans to investigate the transition from slavery to freedom in the lives of enslaved men who enlisted, as well as their kin. The lived experiences of working-poor northern USCT soldiers' families, however, have been largely overlooked.[4]

Williamson's testimony sheds light on how the war tore African American Philadelphian husbands from wives, fathers from children, children from parents, and friends from friends. The USCT was pivotal in carrying out U.S. military objectives. Yet the mobilization of hundreds of thousands of able-bodied African American men into service devastated many African American families. Some families were left to grieve and struggle economically after their male kin died in service. Other families tended to the disabilities—physical, emotional, and psychological—of surviving veterans while also fighting to survive financially.[5]

Northern USCT soldiers' families had already fought to make ends meet before the war. Systematic racial discrimination, orchestrated by whites, ruptured many northern African American families' household economies throughout the mid-nineteenth and early twentieth centuries. Whites created barriers that often denied African American families the ability to establish financial stability. Relying on social welfare programs, accepting charity, or needing other household members to work meant, in many cases, that men, especially African Americans, were not living up to an idealized notion of masculinity that many middle-class white men promoted and demanded.[6] In all likelihood, working-poor African Americans worried more about their families' material realities than white notions of manhood.

The enlistment of able-bodied males only made the situations for many African American Philadelphian families worse. Due to soldiers' deaths or various disabilities obtained in the war, USCT veterans' families toiled for generations after 1865. Families struggled to subsist economically as the deterioration of veterans' minds and bodies made it extremely difficult for them to return to civilian life as employed workers. As a result, the war's toll drained the economic resources that the men's families pooled together. Some of the soldiers' kin sought monetary assistance from the federal government. However, the complicated Civil War pension application process, coupled with white pension agents who often harbored racist views, limited the economic stability of numerous working-poor African Americans nationwide.[7] Only by examining their experiences can we comprehend the full impact of the war on African Americans.[8]

This book explores how freeborn African American Philadelphians strived to create and maintain families while continuously fighting against various forms of racial discrimination from 1850 to the 1920s. Despite its association with the advancement of rights and citizenship for African American men, soldiering had the potential, due to racial discrimination, to make African American families' already dire circumstances even worse. Many USCT soldiers either died or became permanently disabled, consequently threatening the security of their household's finances, sometimes across multiple generations, as their families experienced various forms of racial discrimination in most aspects of living.

Unfortunately for the families examined here, racial discrimination shaped African Americans' experiences, including, but not limited to, occupations, housing, education, and interactions with the Bureau of Pensions. This book sheds light on the often understudied experiences of freeborn northern African Americans by examining how such basic necessities of life were impacted by racism. This collective of African Americans dealt with their own hardships of racial discrimination in ways that were unique compared to their formerly enslaved southern brethren. At least seventy-nine thousand African Americans served in northern USCT regiments—and their service affected the lives of tens of thousands more family members.[9] Many of them, including most of the USCT veterans examined here, remained in the North and comprised a sizeable population of racial minorities living outside the former Confederacy.

Discovering the Families of USCT Soldiers

The Families' Civil War investigates native-born African American Philadelphian men who served in one of Pennsylvania's first three USCT regiments—the Third USCI, the Sixth USCI, and the Eighth USCI. Although Pennsylvania raised a total of eleven USCT regiments, this book focuses on the earliest regiments because of the prominent wartime attention they received both locally and nationally.[10] Their exploits and struggles received extensive coverage in the African American press, and they persevered in the face of relentless racial discrimination.

As a result, this project examines a subgroup of 185 USCT soldiers who served in these three regiments and the 771 multigenerational family members connected to them.[11] (The average household size for these multigenerational families was 4.2). Therefore, this study investigates the lived experiences of hundreds of African Americans over seventy years. The soldiers themselves are neither the beginning nor the end of the analysis. Instead, they serve as a focal point to locate and trace more extensive familial histories. By exploring the lived experiences of this specific group of African American Philadelphians who created families despite racial oppression, economic crises, and attacks on their familial structure, one can better understand the perseverance of racial minorities in American history.

As appendix 1 notes, the 185 USCT soldiers were chosen from a careful examination of primary sources—regimental books, Compiled Military Service Records, the U.S. Census, and Civil War pension records. To qualify for this study, the records had to indicate that the soldiers were born in Philadelphia. If there was contradictory data on a soldier's birthplace, I did not count them in the study's data set. No such parameters were set for their kin, as I examine all the individuals connected to the soldiers to uncover how military service, in varied and unintended ways, impacted their lives.

To locate and examine these historically marginalized people, this study uses a collection of primary sources, including recruitment documents, city directories, public speeches made by prominent individuals, and newspapers (white and African American). Many of these primary sources presented African Americans' lives through a filtered white lens and voice. Even with their limitations, however, these materials collectively shed light, holistically, on African Americans who are frequently set in the background of scholarly studies. Reexamining these readily available sources illustrates that it is feasible to place African Americans at the forefront of a scholarly analysis.

Living in the City of Brotherly Love

For numerous reasons Philadelphia serves as the ideal location for an expansive examination of African Americans. From the eighteenth to the early twentieth centuries, Philadelphia was an important northern city that demonstrates how systems of race, class, and gender were constructed and perpetuated for local residents and national citizens.[12] During the Civil War, the United States depended heavily on Philadelphia's wartime mobilization, whether it was providing war materials from its factories or functioning as a transportation hub.[13] For instance, in 1863 there were twenty-three railroad companies and twenty-seven iron or coal companies operating in the city.[14] In addition to industry, Philadelphia was a densely populated urban area with, according to the 1860 U.S. Census, the nation's largest population of free African Americans, at 22,185 people (or 4 percent of the city's total population). Compared to other northern cities, Philadelphia also had the largest population of free African American males between the ages of fifteen and fifty years old (5,273, or 3 percent of its total population).[15] This specific subgroup of the population was the War Department's target for USCT mobilization beginning in 1863.

Philadelphia became an important location for Pennsylvanian USCT regiments. Recruitment, enlistment, and training all occurred in the city. For instance, potential officers and enlistees traveled to 1216 Chestnut Street for recruitment.[16] City streets flowed with thousands of prospective USCT enlistees from surrounding counties and states. The interactions prompted by these hubs may have influenced some local African Americans to agitate further for equality.

Philadelphia was an epicenter for national and state politics and a hotbed of partisanship that shaped the northern abolition movement. Due in part to Quakers' long-established antislavery stance, Philadelphia had an extensive abolitionist network that fought for African Americans' rights. It also had a long history of racial violence.[17] The violence experienced by some African American Philadelphians throughout the antebellum era likely influenced some men's decisions to enlist and fight back. It may also have influenced how some USCT veterans came to understand their military service years later. Lastly, the city had long served as a focal point for northern African American culture and a beacon for the region. Both popular consciousness and scholarly analysis have focused on Philadelphia for its political, religious, social, and cultural movements, such as the city's participation in the Underground Railroad, role in the creation of the African Methodist Episcopal Church, and experience of multiple instances of antiabolitionist violence.[18] Furthermore, Philadelphia, especially in the nineteenth century, is a city that scholars continually investigate to examine how economic racial discrimination negatively impacted African American families.[19] Through their writings and actions, many local African Americans made Americans of all races notice the importance of Philadelphian African Americans. Thus, this book examines how the Civil War left lasting scars on this center of African American culture over multiple generations.

Seeking Inclusion in the Scholarship

Historians of slavery recognize that enslaved families did not conform to white middle-class models. In most cases the hardships of the enslaved experience, which included forced separations of family members, required many African Americans to structure their families in response to their chaotic lives. Such adaptations also reflected a cultural inheritance from West Africa, where families were often large, clan-based networks that pulled together people bound neither by law or blood.[20] In freedom, African Americans continued to struggle in ways that forced modified living situations for survival. Racism, economic struggle, religious connections, protection, and other motivations led African Americans to establish complex living situations. Like the families examined here, northern freeborn families adjusted their family structures out of necessity as well—they needed to survive.

Many of the households featured in this book included people who were not bound together by law or blood but shared living spaces and pooled their resources to support one another. I argue that they are better understood as "fictive kin," a term other scholars use when referring to families who consider or treat an individual (or individuals) as "family" or "kin," even if they had no adoptive, biological, or marital ties.[21] Applying this term allows me to be more sensitive to the complex family forms created by African Americans.

Documented sources, like the U.S. Census, are not always explicit in describing the relationships among the people who lived together. However, many African Africans repeatedly opened their homes to non-blood-related individuals, which suggests they were likely more than mere boarders. Their willingness to take in "fictive kin" shows that northern African American families continually adapted their families in order to survive—and were genuinely concerned with assisting others in fighting racial discrimination and creating stability.

The Families' Civil War provides a holistic analysis of the lives of USCT soldiers and their entire families while arguing that the Civil War was one battle in a long war for racial justice. The national conflict provided African American Philadelphians with the ability to expand the theater of war beyond their metropolitan and racially oppressive city and into the South to defeat the Confederates and end slavery as armed combatants. That war may have come to an end in 1865—but the war waged against them by white northerners back home never ended. Serving in USCT regiments was *not* the first time Philadelphian-born USCT soldiers engaged in battles, nor did it mark the end of their fight. Every day of their lives was a campaign against systemic racism.[22]

Keeping this battle at the center of our view helps us remember that Civil War soldiers came into the war from very diverse places and with very different points of view. Historians, reenactors, military enthusiasts, public demonstrators, private organizations, and heritage groups have kept discussions on the meaning of the war alive. In all this academic and public work on the Civil War, soldiers often get lumped together as men experiencing roughly the same thing in their service. However, this study acknowledges that race and class differentiated men's experiences, too, and thus takes an intersectional approach—examining the intersections of gender, race, class, and region—to fully illuminate the experiences of freeborn northern USCT soldiers and their kin.[23]

Historians tend to focus on particular phases in USCT soldiers' lives to illustrate the various hardships they and their kin endured. Studies of the war years denote how racial discrimination made service as USCT enlisted men dramatically different from the service of other soldiers.[24] Other scholars explore how USCT veterans and their families attempted to use military service to redefine their status in a reconstructed American society in the immediate postwar years.[25] These studies provide valuable perspectives on particular periods in USCT soldiers' lives, but it leaves their history fragmented. Rarely are the experiences of soldiers' families before, during, and generations after the Civil War pulled together and placed at the center of the scholarship.

A historical study that fully and properly situates African American families' role into the historical narrative, rather than segmenting soldiers' experiences or limiting them to portions of a monograph, is long overdue. Historian Richard M. Reid wisely recognized that African Americans' military service stretched far beyond the contributions of enlisted men. He writes, "The bloody war, and the role played by black troops in it, had an enormous impact not only on the soldiers' lives during and after the war but also on the lives of their families and friends."[26] Other scholars have made similar assertions about the importance of understanding how the Civil War affected the lives of USCT soldiers' families. Historians Ira Berlin and Leslie S. Rowland argue that joining the military was never solely a man's decision. "Enlistment was a family decision," Berlin and Rowland assert, "since it entailed profound consequences for those who remained at home as well as for those who marched off to war."[27] Yet, even with these moments of academic acknowledgment of the importance of the role African American families had in the lives of USCT soldiers, few historians have made these families the primary focus of a monograph. To date, only James G. Mendez has given northern USCT families such focus. Mendez states, "Until now, the full story of these African-American families has not been truly told because the focus has been on the men who went to war."[28]

Even with the wealth of USCT scholarship, one might forget that their historical importance went unnoticed by many white scholars until the 1950s. Frederick M. Binder and Dudley Taylor Cornish published studies in that decade that provided overviews of the USCT regiments.[29] In 1965 James McPherson followed suit, examining the processes of wartime mobilization and immediate postwar issues relating to African Americans.[30] Collectively, these studies sought to illuminate a forgotten past. "The history of the Negro soldier in the Union Army has remained an obscure chapter in American history," Cornish explained.[31] This statement was perhaps correct for white nonacademics and scholars, but numerous African Americans have always known otherwise.

White scholarly amnesia to studies on USCT soldiers actively ignored the fact that many African American scholars published work two years after the Civil War ended and continued producing work well into the early twentieth century. One African American civilian, William Wells Brown, composed his monograph, *The Negro in the American Rebellion: His Heroism and His Fidelity*, in 1867 after noticing that white historians either downplayed or ignored the historical significance of USCT regiments. "I waited patiently, before beginning this work, with the hope that some one more competent would take the subject in hand; but, up to the present," Brown lamented, "it has not been done, although many books have been written upon the Rebellion."[32] The literature of William J. Simmons, George Washington Williams, Joseph T. Wilson, Alexander Heritage Newton, and Isaac J. Hill all investigated their wartime sacrifices as soldiers.[33] Meanwhile, some USCT veterans made it their mission to inform civilians such as Carter G. Woodson about their wartime exploits.[34] Susie King Taylor, a formerly enslaved woman, published her experiences as a laundress and nurse for the Thirty-Third USCI and the postwar struggles that her family experienced.[35] Thus, African Americans and their allies have fought for decades for inclusion in the historical memory of the Civil War—but the impact of their efforts did not materialize until the modern civil rights movement got underway.[36]

Five of the historians previously mentioned served in northern African American regiments.[37] Afterward, these veterans-turned-historians confronted whites—scholars and nonacademics—and some African Americans who ignored the historical significance of USCT soldiers.[38] Simmons, for instance, lamented in 1887 the fact that his students (most likely at Simmons College in Kentucky) knew little about USCT soldiers. "I have noticed in my long experience as a teacher, that some of my students were wo[e]fully ignorant of the work of our great colored men—even ignorant of their names," Simmons states.[39] Ultimately, *The Families' Civil War* builds on the efforts that began more than 130 years ago to uncover the personal histories of USCT soldiers and their extended families in a manner that will bring their names and experiences to the forefront.

At least for Simmons, his monograph's dedication allowed him to honor the prominent role African American women had in shaping all African Americans' lives. "This volume is respectfully dedicated to the women of our race," he wrote, "and especially to the devoted, self-sacrificing mothers who moulded the lives of the subjects of the sketches, laboring and praying for their success."[40] Simmons understood the invaluable contributions that African American families, especially women, made in USCT soldiers' lives. But rather than limit a discussion of kin to a small portion of a book, like the dedication, USCT soldiers' families deserve a turn at the center of historical analysis. Doing so reveals how northern African American families continuously fought against racially discriminatory barriers imposed by whites, even those who fought alongside them as allies in the war. The Civil War was neither just a conflict between two armies nor was it solely about political disputes that spanned regions and races. It was a war that provided African Americans with the opportunity to demand equality in American society. Even so, lasting problems materialized for the USCT soldiers and their families as a result of their participation in the war.

The Families' Civil War is more than a Civil War history. It is also a contribution to scholarship on northern urban African Americans. Studying the lived experiences of Philadelphian-born USCT veterans and their kin over multiple generations provides new avenues of scholarly analysis. Moreover, this holistic approach shows readers how these important but understudied historical figures fought and persevered against racism. Thus, it is time to acknowledge that USCT soldiers' lives and their families' lives did not stop or start with a specific historical moment. Rather, they existed over an extended period that transcends our conventional periods of historical inquiry.

The Deeper Meanings of African American Family

Historically, American citizenship has rested on a determination of who was and was not deserving of inclusion. A major dilemma for Americans before 1866 was that the definitions of citizenship varied among individuals, states, and the federal government.[41] Throughout the early and mid-nineteenth century, whites kept many free African Americans from acquiring voting rights or enjoying protection of their civil rights outside of bondage. Many people understood that citizenship comprised various duties, rights, and privileges that evolved.[42] In short, there was no single or concrete classification for citizenship across the entire United States.

Cultural citizenship (which refers to an individual's pursuit of belonging) provided marginalized people, including African Americans, with the ability to reframe their relationship between themselves and the national community.[43] As the families examined here demonstrated, African Americans used Civil War military service and the pension system to petition for inclusion in American society. Northern African Americans already believed that they belonged to the United States. But it would take military service for northern whites, at least momentarily, to recognize that African Americans were also members of the larger national community. However, white acceptance was not universal or lasting.

The Civil War pension system provides one of the best avenues to investigate the contested battle between African Americans and whites over cultural citizenship, particularly during the war and generations after. As later sections will explore, the pension application process was highly complex and bureaucratic for pension-eligible veterans and their dependents—legal widows, progeny, biological parents, and possibly siblings. Honorably discharged veterans, before 1890, needed to provide documentation of their war-related ailments in the hopes of receiving a pension. Dependents of deceased veterans were pension eligible after documenting their relationship to the deceased. Pensions gave needed financial injections to awardees. At the same time, each application reveals African Americans' desire to become part of the Civil War's national remembrance in a lasting and meaningful way. Maybe their continuing battle for recognition disappointed some of the men and their families who felt that serving in a USCT regiment already demonstrated their commitment and connection to the nation. Unfortunately, they learned that Civil War pensions created yet another battleground in the fight for recognition of African Americans' cultural citizenship from a white society that continually denigrated racial minorities.

Previous scholarship has done an exceptional job examining the hardships that African Americans experienced as they navigated the Civil War pension process.[44] Furthering their efforts, this book expands the importance of pensions for the federal government and northern African American families by acknowledging that these historical records (even in rejected cases) illustrate how both parties recognized the wartime sacrifices of numerous African American families and their potential impact on future generations. African American pension claims should also be understood as comprising a political movement among various applicants who did not necessarily know each other or apply together. Even so, their cumulative effort to seek recompense demonstrates a unified effort by a subordinate group to seek financial compensation and have their cultural citizenship recognized via a pension.[45] This sort of politics—what some scholars have called "infrapolitics"—allowed this marginalized group of veterans and their families to push for change despite possessing little formal power and influence over the federal government.[46] Through the pension system, northern African American families demanded that the federal government recognize their definitions of a family structure in an attempt to be part of an imagined community—in this case, the nation.[47]

Rather than acting in isolation, these African American families resided in communities that developed a shared knowledge of the pension process, which historian Brandi Clay Brimmer calls the "grassroots pension network."[48] Philadelphian USCT veterans and their kin benefitted from the African American press and U.S. organizations such as the Grand Army of the Republic (GAR).[49] Both the GAR and African American press were influential in publicizing information about the pension process, including highlighting lobbying efforts for expanding the eligibility of pension applicants, that many African Americans might have found helpful. Therefore, the broader pro–United States and African American community became invested in protecting and maintaining USCT veterans' families.

The following chapters trace the various developments that African American Philadelphians experienced over many generations. These northern African American families fought daily to remain intact while navigating racial discrimination during pivotal moments in American history. During the antebellum era, the Civil War, the Reconstruction era, the Gilded Age, and the Jim Crow era, these African American families experienced racially discriminatory policies, legal and informal, used by whites to maintain societal dominance. The stories and experiences of family members, such as Mary Williamson, are just as fascinating and important as the USCT soldiers connected to them. Keeping the focus on Philadelphian USCT soldiers and their kin reveals both the specific ways that the Civil War compounded this racial oppression as well as how northern African American families persevered in their lifelong battle against racism.

CHAPTER ONE

The African American Family in the Free North

Before the Civil War, many African American Philadelphians fought against racial discrimination that pervaded northern society. Systemic racism did not discriminate between African Americans' age, gender, occupation, and socioeconomic standing. As children, future USCT soldiers discovered these truths by witnessing the hardships that plagued their families and communities. Others learned that school attendance was not always an option for working-poor families. Moreover, if a child did attend school, there was no assurance that he or she would remain in class. For instance, Francis Hawkins was forced to leave school to bolster his household income because his grandmother did not earn enough as a washerwoman, an occupation performed by many African American women. "I stopped to go to work several times and then went back to school again," Hawkins stated.[1] While Hawkins's case is not representative of every African American Philadelphian, he does illustrate the myriad ways in which racism limited opportunities for entire families.

Workforce Racism in Philadelphia

In the antebellum era, racial discrimination in the northern workforce crippled household finances for many African Americans; it placed them in unskilled jobs that were physically demanding and hazardous, paid low wages, and regarded them as easily replaceable.[2] The lack of employment opportunities for African American men in various manufacturing industries, including textiles, clothing, lumber, iron, and steel, in the 1850s came when white Philadelphian workers in the industrial sector produced 6 percent of the nation's products.[3] Yet, there seemed to be little to no opportunities for northern African American men.[4] In 1848, for instance, a significant number of African American Philadelphian men worked as laborers.[5] Racially exclusionary practices, which were endemic to other northern cities, did not go unnoticed by northern African Americans. On October 19, 1855, *Frederick Douglass' Paper* criticized how widespread and unending racially discriminatory practices hindered most northern African Americans' employment opportunities. "Whilst the free Negro continues as he is now, rising no higher than the ready waiter or the adept barber, whist the depths of the degradation to which the great mass of his fellows sink, especially in Northern cities," the paper lamented, "has apparently no limit to its downward progress, there can be no mitigation of the popular aversion to his color."[6] During labor strikes, white men used violence against African Americans working in the place of white laborers.[7] Ultimately, the racialized assault on the economic stability of northern African American families was oppressive.[8]

Even with systematic barriers imposed on African Americans, most fathers of future soldiers found employment in 1850. The majority of fathers in this study worked as laborers. Their work experiences as laborers paralleled those of many African American men locally and in Weeksville, New York.[9] In Philadelphia, it was not uncommon for recently arrived European immigrants to use violence to keep semiskilled and skilled African Americans from plying their trades.[10] In other instances local white employers used racially prejudicial hiring practices, such as refusing to hire African Americans, to make laboring professions seem like the "appropriate" occupation for African American men.[11] Even with these formal and informal structures of racism, some fathers of future USCT soldiers found employment beyond labor work. Some of the fathers in this study worked in semiskilled occupations, including that of oysterman, farmer, gardener, waiter, sexton, carter, and porter. Others worked in skilled professions, including those of barber, shingle weaver, and shoemaker.[12] It is clear that racial discrimination effectively limited work opportunities in skilled occupations for many of the fathers examined here. Still, not all men succumbed to white supremacy or the economic distress that occupational racism attempted to impose. Therefore, each case of a man avoiding work as a laborer in 1850 was a victory in the racialized workplace battle.

The numbers of wage-earning fathers who successfully maintained steady work in various occupations held relatively steady from 1850 to 1860. Some fathers continued working as laborers. Others worked semiskilled occupations, including those of waiter and coachman. Meanwhile, some fathers worked in skilled trades, including those of stone cutter and master barber.[13] The ability to find employment in either semiskilled or skilled occupations in 1860 was a testament to the fathers' continued successes against racial discrimination. Every one of these cases of semiskilled and skilled occupations was unique since, as historian Theodore Hershberg notes, "eight out of every ten working men were unskilled laborers."[14]

White Victorian middle-class idealizations of gender roles asserted that it was a father's sole responsibility, as the "breadwinner," to earn enough money to keep his household economically stable.[15] Still, some African American men hoped to demonstrate that this gendered ideal, in many cases, was unattainable. However, many fathers, especially those who were either unemployed, underemployed, or laborers, rarely made enough to provide for their entire family.[16]

Once white and African American women reached childbearing age, society dictated that women enter motherhood. Elite African Americans, primarily concerned with avoiding persecution from whites who denigrated African Americans' actions, championed women raising their children "properly," especially girls. In the opinion of a *Christian Recorder* article, a mother's sole responsibility was to teach their daughters about their future domestic duties and prepare them for adult responsibilities within the home. The anonymous author wrote, "I think before she is out of her teens, upon which she has not yet entered, that she will have some idea how to cook. . . . It seems to be a good arrangement, and a most useful part of their education."[17] The *Christian Recorder* championed the politics of respectability—the notion that African Americans conform to aspects of white middle-class life, such as demonstrating "manners" and "civility," to (potentially) nullify negative racial stereotypes—for African Americans.[18] Regardless of their economic standing, the anonymous author made it clear that women had an essential responsibility to their households.[19]

Like the author of the previously mentioned *Christian Recorder* article, some elite African Americans believed African American women should stay at home and prepare young women to replicate a fantasized version of a woman's household role for future generations. Some abolitionists, including African Americans, argued that a defining aspect of "respectable" motherhood was protecting children from labor, which assumed that the women remain in the home and focus on child-rearing.[20] Therefore, the full-time work of a woman was her family. If the 1850 census enumerators are to be believed, then none of the mothers in this study worked full-time, wage-earning occupations while USCT soldiers were children, which, in theory, allowed the women to fulfill their familial responsibilities.[21] However, data collected by mid-nineteenth-century census enumerators failed to recognize the varied and important contributions of women who did not participate in the market economy on a full-time basis.[22]

Like many other African American women, mothers were essential and valuable participants in their family economies. The U.S. Census only occurred once every decade, and enumerators would try to assess what "value" these mothers added to their families. Often, census enumerators left the "occupation" column blank for women. In reality, women's unpaid daily contributions—cleaning, cooking, raising children, tending to the "needs" of her husband, and other household tasks—were undocumented but still critical.[23] Therefore, their lived experiences provide a counternarrative to census enumerators' portrayals.

Some working-poor northern African American women were key contributors to their households' income, earning wages on a temporary or seasonal basis, which census enumerators did not denote.[24] Mothers contributed to the economic stability of their families by performing work such as weeding, sewing, cleaning neighbors' homes, watching neighbors' children, or gathering and cleaning clothes.[25] Some women bartered and traded for raw goods and materials to produce various products, such as handkerchiefs, in urban markets.[26] Such women's work did not occur regularly and was glossed over in census enumerators' quick assessments of their contributions.

The 1860 census saw a slight but significant change for the mothers of future USCT soldiers, as some mothers found full-time wage-earning positions. These mothers worked semiskilled occupations to bolster their family's income. For example, John Thompson and Joseph Hooper had mothers who were washerwomen. William Henry's mother, Mary, was a waiter.[27] There was a clear difference in the occupational experiences between these types of work. Washerwomen worked at home, often near their children.[28] Meanwhile, Mary Henry's job removed her from her home. It is plausible that these mothers found their employment through extended female networks common in northern cities.[29] For middle-class men, the employment of women, even those performing wage-earning duties in the home, created a disquieting home environment that challenged male authority.[30] Conversely, these three mothers demonstrate that becoming breadwinners forced them to assume supposed male responsibilities to keep their households stable.

The employment that Mary Henry, the mother of future USCT soldier William Henry, had outside of the home was not a unique experience for many working-poor women in the early and mid-nineteenth century. In rural and urban areas, women of all races often performed work beyond the confines of their domiciles, which was essential to keeping their families from living in abject poverty. Working-poor women (due to necessity) became second breadwinners for their families.[31] Sometimes these women worked alongside their spouses and children.[32]

As young children, future USCT soldiers also resided with male and female fictive kin who were valuable contributors, in various ways, to their residences. While providing money was not always a requirement to become fictive kin in Philadelphian households, any wages earned benefitted the families that opened their homes to these individuals. From 1850 to 1860, fifteen of the forty-five future soldiers that could be examined in the prewar period had a total of thirty-two fictive kin—people who were not related to the family by blood, marriage, or law—living with them.[33] Most adult men had jobs in unskilled or skilled work, including as laborers, barbers, farmers, and cabinet makers. At the same time, twenty-three adults did not have full-time wage-earning employment.[34] Some of these adults may have cared for children while the parents worked. However, it is also possible that African American Philadelphians simply made conscious, emotional decisions to open their homes to help others.

Blood-related extended adult kin were also present in the homes in 1850. John Thompson's family had William and Susan Parker (his uncle and aunt) and Hannibal Thompson (another uncle) residing with them.[35] Both of John's uncles, similar to his father, James, worked as laborers. It is feasible that all three men worked together and collectively pooled their wages to support their sizeable household. Census enumerators did not catalog Susan as having a full-time wage-earning job, but she most likely did the family's laundry while living with them. Meanwhile, Thomas Williams had Samuel Williams (his uncle) cohabitating with him. Samuel was a unique addition to Williams's household because he was a brickmaker while Thomas's father, Charles, was a laborer. The Williams men's combined wages possibly facilitated the household decision to send all school-age children to school.

Individuals were not always required to earn a wage to earn their keep.[36] Perhaps these individuals had seasonal or temporary employment. It is also plausible that some adults contributed through their unpaid labor, such as by raising children. Some may have provided emotional support to other members of the household. Perhaps USCT soldiers learned, as children, that they could include extended kin and fictive kin in their residences.

Prewar Familial Creation

Familial constructions for many Americans contracted and expanded as individuals used biological, economic, emotional, marital, conjugal, occupational, political, and even spiritual dynamics to navigate their ever-changing life crises. Blood relation was never the sole defining characteristic that determined familial relationships.[37] Wealthy and poor whites, in addition to African Americans, for differing reasons, created and modified their familial dynamics by sometimes including fictive kin, which allowed these families to navigate American society. For instance, 20 percent of household occupants in all New York state residences had non-blood-related inhabitants in 1850.[38] This sect includes cases of northern white families who were providing shelter for recently arrived European newcomers.[39] Still, for African American families, financial need was not always the determining factor when welcoming fictive kin into the family's home. In many cases it was an attempt to cope with the never-ending onslaught of racial discrimination that destabilized African American families.

As young children, many future soldiers lived with biological parents, a common experience among most working-poor African American Philadelphians. In 1850, formerly enslaved African American families had both biological parents residing in the home 80 percent of the time, while 77 percent of freeborn homes had two parents rearing children.[40] For context, 41 percent of the parents to future USCT soldiers examined here came from states where slavery existed when the Civil War began.[41] After arriving in Philadelphia, they successfully removed their shackles and created new lives as free people in Pennsylvania, including as the parents of future USCT soldiers. As children, 93 percent of the future soldiers who could be examined lived with both biological parents in 1850, while only 22 percent did so in 1860.[42] The significant decline most likely occurred as the children grew up and began living independently as young men.

There were also instances where soon-to-be soldiers either lived in a single-parent home or without any biological parents. In 1850, John Brown and James Gray lived with single parents. John, his sister, Mary, and his mother, Mary, all became fictive kin to Rosana Hamilton. Meanwhile, James Gray lived with his widower father, Henderson. A decade later, Joseph Woodson and Charles Tobias were children living with single mothers. For instance, Woodson resided with his mother, Margaret, and two siblings.[43] Single mothers challenged white upper-class gender notions that assumed women needed husbands to keep their families stable. But single women raising children was not exclusive to African American women as a group. Many Irish American women also raised their children without a husband, whether it was due to desertion, domestic violence, or death.[44]

Rather than relying on a husband to fulfill their supposed role as sole breadwinner, single mothers adapted for economic survival. For instance, by 1860, Charles Tobias and his family experienced a dramatic restructuring after his father, Zeholar, was, for unknown reasons, no longer living in the residence. Ten years prior, Zeholar was the family's sole wage earner as a bookmaker.[45] Caroline, Charles's mother, did not let Zeholar's absence create economic peril for her family; she became a successful dressmaker, amassing $500 in real estate and $100 in personal estate. For Caroline and the few other landed African Americans, real estate may have given them a sense of personal pride during a period when African Americans had few opportunities to amass wealth.[46] While not widespread in Philadelphia, property-owning African American women were rather common in places like Hartford, Connecticut, where nearly one-third of its African American population were homeowners by 1860.[47] Real estate ownership was an invaluable investment, as it allowed individuals to avoid steep rent payments, which were usually twice that of white occupants and undermined economic stability.[48]

The Tobias family also welcomed fictive kin, including the Scott family and Amelia Walker. Rachell Scott, a single mother, and her daughter, Madeline, worked as dressmakers, feasibly with Caroline Tobias, while Theodore Scott was a seaman and Walker was a domestic servant.[49] In the Tobias household, economic subsistence mattered more than replicating middle-class notions of gender respectability where only adult men worked. Ultimately, the Tobias household illustrates how single mothers could establish economic stability even when society derided wage-earning women.[50]

Meanwhile, Joseph Woodson's mother, Margaret, was a single woman working full-time as a laundress during his childhood. She had the heavy responsibility of supporting her family as the only adult wage earner. Fortunately, she was not the only wage earner in their family. Joseph's older sister, fifteen-year-old Josephine, also worked as a laundress.[51] Therefore, Joseph Woodson lived with two women who were pivotal to the family's economic stability. Woodson's experience likely gave him an understanding of gender roles wherein it was acceptable and normal for women to be wage earners for a household.

Some future soldiers became fictive kin themselves. Charles Penn is an example of a child who lived without biological parents. After his mother and father died in 1852, he lived in the House of Refuge for Colored Children (HRCC), an African American orphanage. For children like Penn, residence at the HRCC exposed them to a prison-like environment that included corporal punishment for disobeying the stringently regimental routines. Additionally, African American children experienced overcrowding and even deaths at the white-run institution. To combat overcrowding, HRCC administrators instructed African American children to become "morally industrious youths" who lived outside the facility.[52] Part of the orphans' "moral training" was the apprenticeship into trades that they could continue working as adults. As a result, Charles worked as a farm laborer for John L. Burrows.[53] Since the organization focused more on "moral training" and job apprenticeship rather than scholarship, it shows that the white-run organization felt their noblesse oblige *was to* "help" make African American children, including Penn, competent workers; intellectual growth was secondary. Still, the HRCC's questionable practices eventually led Penn to a home with John L. Burrows.

In 1860, Isaac D. Henderson and his four sisters (Frances, Sophia, Anna, and Florence) lived with Rachel Gray, an eighty-nine-year-old formerly enslaved woman from Virginia. Rachel may have permitted the Henderson children to live with her because of physical limitations due to advanced age and a weary body ravaged by slavery; it would have been nearly impossible for her to work full-time.[54] Frances worked as a tailoress, and Sophia was a dressmaker. Meanwhile, Isaac was school age, but he did not attend school. Perhaps Isaac was responsible for providing care to his twelve-year-old sister Anna, who was mentally ill, his two-year-old sister Florence, and Rachel.[55] If that were true, then Isaac performed the supposed feminine responsibilities of nurturing his kin, while his older sisters assumed masculine roles as wage earners. In the end, their household made choices demonstrating that aid and care for dependents was what mattered.

Miles Parker's childhood experience was stark by contrast. In 1850 Parker resided with the Claytons, a wealthy white Philadelphian family.[56] The Clayton family had ten members living together, but only Jacob, the male head of household, worked full-time as a farmer. It is possible that Hannah, Jacob's wife, and their two children, Susanna and Elizabeth, helped Jacob with his work or found other ways to add to the family's income. The remaining six children, including Parker, all attended school.[57] The Clayton's willingness to provide Parker with an education denotes that at least one white family nurtured the intellect of an African American child and treated him like their own children.[58] Perhaps the Claytons made Parker their fictive son to fill the void of having no biological ones.[59] Regardless of the specific reasons, their familial construction disputed claims that peaceful interracial cohabitation was impossible.[60] Parker's example was unique, as his wealthy white family, who lived in a city with a history of racial violence, discounted such issues to provide a nurturing space for an African American boy.

Residing with nonbiological family members was a reality for other future USCT soldiers during their childhoods. From 1850 to 1880 some future soldiers, as children, resided with fictive kin. It is important to recognize that there was no universal experience for these children. For instance, Richard Duffy lived with the Moore family—William, Ann, and Sarah—who also took in Jesse Johnson. Neither Richard nor Jesse attended school. Instead, they worked as chimney sweeps. William Moore was a musician, while Ann and Sarah contributed through their paid and unpaid labor.[61] Richard and Jesse's fiduciary additions were invaluable to their family, but their earned wages came with a price, as the boys worked a dangerous occupation. Laboring as chimney sweeps not only caused long-term skin damage but also made them susceptible to skin cancer.[62]

Familial Decisions Concerning Children's Education

From 1850 to 1863, twenty-eight of the fifty boys whose educational status could be confirmed went to school, while the rest did not.[63] School attendance in childhood was not a universal experience for African American Philadelphians in the mid-nineteenth century. Less than 60 percent of four thousand reported school-age African American children in the city went to school in 1856.[64] Perhaps some of these future soldiers were students at the Institute for Colored Youth (ICY). Others might have studied at institutions affiliated with local African American churches.

Educating children was an important issue for many African Americans. Northern newspapers, such as the *National Era*, emphasized that intellectual growth might improve future generations' social, political, and economic standing.[65] Jacob C. White Jr., a Philadelphian student and future supporter of USCT regiments, championed the importance of scholastic endeavors during a May 24, 1855, visit by Pennsylvania Governor James Pollack.[66] White professed that African American students needed resources equal to whites to succeed. Then he informed the governor that imposing racial segregation in public schools denied children equal opportunities. "For you see us, sir," White stated, "a little family by ourselves, set off from other youth in this great Commonwealth, and in common brotherhood."[67] His criticism came one year after the Pennsylvania legislature passed a law stating that public schools with over twenty African American pupils must segregate.[68] White wanted Governor Pollack to understand that ending racial segregation in public schools would show others intellectual equality among all children.

White claimed that public schools were the ideal training ground for defining African American citizenship for men. He argued, "We are nevertheless preparing ourselves usefully for a future day, when citizenship in our country will be based on manhood and not on color."[69] For White, preparation for citizenship began long before adulthood, and his gendered beliefs privileged men and ignored women. Pollack remained silent on both issues, indicating that his visit focused more on public relations and less on actual African Americans and their citizenship aspirations.[70]

Adult African Americans openly complained about racially discriminatory policies that put their children in public schools that were inferior to white schools.[71] Northern clergy members, parents, and community members lamented how African American schools continually dealt with overcrowding, underfunding, dilapidated buildings, and a high turnover of faculty and administration.[72] Even with these problems, some African Americans still believed that public schools served a larger purpose for youths' intellectual elevation.[73] In an 1863 article, the *Christian Recorder* espoused that an African American public school was better at intellectually developing pupils, even with fewer resources than white schools. "The High School for colored youth is 717 Lombard St., a very bad location," the article noted, "with very limited accommodations. Its curriculum will compare well with any High School in this city. We invite comparison!"[74]

Finding quality Philadelphian teachers remained on the minds of northern African American newspapers throughout the mid-nineteenth century. In Jane Porter's eulogy, the *Douglass' Monthly* praised the white teacher's passionate work educating African American children in an openly racist and violent city.[75] Porter's death depressed local African Americans who understood that they had few local allies. "Her death is deeply lamented by many families outside of those of her immediate relations," the article stated.[76] Sadly for African American students, other white teachers were not as caring. A Miss Donnelly of the Colored Public School on Sixth Street received sharp criticism from the *Christian Recorder* for her offensive tone with students, and the paper advocated for her removal. The anonymous author noted that Miss Donnelly showed "hatred and prejudice against us" that raised concern within the local community.[77] The author stated that if Miss Donnelly continued to teach, then African American families would "break the school up by preventing our children from going; and we will do it rather than have our children taught by such teachers."[78] Perhaps Miss Donnelly took the job to accomplish a self-appointed role as a "savior" to African American children. It is also plausible that her primary concern was earning money. Regardless, both examples reveal that African American Philadelphian children interacted with an assortment of educators, which possibly influenced their parents' decision whether or not to send them to school.

The ICY, meanwhile, allowed local children to receive a different scholastic experience.[79] The school's curriculum included foreign languages and mathematics taught by male and female faculty. Teacher advertisements made it clear that African Americans were the ideal candidates. "We hope one will be found, as there are those among 'our people' [who are] amply qualified," the *Frederick Douglass' Paper* noted.[80] Students attending the ICY had the privilege of learning from influential abolitionists, including Sarah Mapps Douglass and Octavius Catto. Therefore, African American children had differing educational experiences depending on which institution they attended.[81] African American abolitionists worked in racially segregated public schools as well. For instance, Junius C. Morel was a principal at Colored School Number 2 in Weeksville, New York.[82] In summation, African American children conceivably learned from or at least interacted with abolitionists while acquiring education in public and private northern schools.

The ICY sought to provide practical vocational training and prepare pupils to work in professions beyond labor. The school prided itself on training and graduating five new teachers in 1861, whom the school believed should begin working at the Sixth Street Colored School.[83] Therefore, becoming an ICY student could provide upward socioeconomic mobility for a new generation of African Americans while simultaneously fighting racism through their employment.

Sending African American children to school was a significant decision for every family, especially for the working poor, who relied on every household member's contributions to their household finances. Willingly removing potential child wage earners from employment opportunities to supplement their homes was a hard choice, as kin weighed their immediate needs against the possible long-term benefits of intellectual growth and racial betterment. Many African American abolitionists believed that this lasting growth and progress mattered more than familial finances. Ultimately, mothers often decided whether school-age children found work or went to school.[84]

At least two future soldiers split their time between being students and finding regular wage-earning employment. George M. Shorter and Francis Hawkins not only went to school but still found time for work. In Hawkins's case, he intermittently left school to supplement his household economy, possibly as a laborer, since his grandmother's income as a whitewasher was not enough for their family.[85] While the Hawkins family's material realities necessitated Francis's removal from school, they never ended his aspirations for receiving an education, as he continued to attend school intermittently. George M. Shorter and his brother, John, also went to school but worked as engine firemen with the African Fire Association (AFA), a group of racially segregated local fire companies that focused their efforts on protecting African Americans.[86] The formation and continuance of the AFA occasionally led to moments of racial violence by local white firemen. Racist whites desired to establish a monopoly and deter competition, which they perceived as a devaluation of their worth as white men. Therefore, the Shorters' employment may have given their family economic stability, but it simultaneously threatened their safety as they balanced their academic endeavors.

As children, five of the fifty-five school-age future soldiers worked as either a servant, errand boy, farm laborer, waiter, or cabinet maker. This collection of jobs illustrates that these adolescent African American boys found semiskilled and skilled occupations when many African American adult men did not. Circumstances for employment differed greatly for each child. For instance, Richard Carter resided with the Edsons, a white family. The Edson family's home had nine individuals. Nathan Edson, a wealthy cabinet marker, had five of his apprentices, including Carter, living with his family.[87] Carter's employment was rare since he worked a skilled trade, and his cohabitation provided another instance of an interracial household amid an era in Philadelphia when racial violence was commonplace.[88]

Fifty-eight children, including the siblings and fictive kin of future USCT soldiers, attended school between 1850 to 1863. Their attendance was split nearly evenly among boys and girls. Deciding to have girls attend school illustrates a historical moment of transition when many Americans began embracing girls' education, even as some people remained tied to older beliefs. The *Christian Recorder* published an article arguing that young women must place more value on their domestic duties than schooling. "A knowledge of books is certainly important, but that your daughter should receive proper home training is more important to her future well-being," the article asserted.[89] In the anonymous author's opinion, learning how to cook, clean, repair clothes, and practice fiduciary frugality encompassed the "necessary" life training that girls needed to find a potential mate. Being a learned woman was not seen as a universally appealing trait.

Boys, on the other hand, were told to focus themselves on academic pursuits.[90] Thus, there was a clear gendered dynamic to the value of education in the northern antebellum African American press. And yet, some of these working-poor African American Philadelphian families prioritized their children's scholastic endeavors in the hopes of improving their futures.

Young Adulthood and Family Creation

As the future soldiers reached adulthood, some of the men chose to find spouses. Men of all races had advice literature, prominent individuals (such as clergymen), and even family members that advanced the ideal of family creation as an essential component of manhood.[91] The *Christian Recorder* asserted that marriage was the best deterrent from a life of crime. The article claimed, "Marriage renders man virtuous and more wise."[92] Conforming to a nuclear family structure was imperative, in the opinion of African American elites, to proving that free African American men were similar to white men, by subjugating their dependents and situating themselves as protectors and providers.

Perhaps working-poor African American men sought to adhere to this rhetoric as they began courting potential mates. Others may not have cared to listen to such opinions as they preferred to choose their partners using their inclinations and desires. The specific circumstances for the creation of intimate relationships for the future soldiers examined here remain unknown. Still, each couple's formation created important bonds that could assist both individuals as they navigated a racially and politically divided urban city. In the end, all of the marriage advocacy failed to convince numerous young men to marry. Only twenty-five of the 185 men (whose marital status is known) married between 1850 and 1863 (before enlisting in the U.S. Army).

The decision to marry brought another layer of complexity to African American life as they had to select between having a common-law or legal union. Legal marriages provided couples with rights and privileges, including legal protections over property ownership, making such marriages appealing.[93] Historian Donald R. Shaffer asserts that many northern free African Americans preferred to wed, even as countless southern enslaved people could not do so legally.[94] Some formerly enslaved people saw a legal marriage as a demonstration of their newly acquired freedom.[95] Furthermore, their act provided them with a formalized union and a legal document (between a couple and the state) that legitimized that intimate bond to white society.[96] Maybe some northern African American men chose a legal marriage to demonstrate their manhood because they had the freedom to decide on a spouse.[97]

However, the prewar unions of Philadelphian-born African American men also provide a counternarrative to the notion that free African Americans flocked to marry legally. Of the men whose marital status is known, only nine forthcoming soldiers and their partners decided to wed legally between 1850 to 1863. Seven of these marriages took place in various northeastern Christian churches of either Methodist or Episcopalian denominations. The couples' wedding sites did not necessarily entail that they were congregants of the churches in which they wed. Affirming a legal marriage at a church perhaps appealed to the couples seeking to have the ceremony within their community and officiated by an African American clergyman.[98]

Two couples wed outside of the church. Richard Black and Anna Lamberson had E. Kelly oversee their wedding on September 24, 1860.[99] Meanwhile, George Glascow and Margaret Clark had the justice of the peace of Indiana County, Pennsylvania, perform their wedding ceremony on December 26, 1852.[100] Neither couple offered any explanation for having their marriages outside of the church. Regardless of the couples' preferences for who officiated their marriage, all of these unions were legitimate in the eyes of the state and federal government. Even though all the couples could not know it, their legal unions would make the newly formed families potentially eligible for economic aid from the federal government once the husbands enlisted.

Sixteen future soldiers and their partners, meanwhile, chose a common-law union. In the opinion of legal marriage advocates, none of these bonds were respectable. The significant number of common-law marriages during this period meant that societal pressures, both inside and outside the local African American community, ultimately failed to influence these couples' private lives. Some couples might have chosen a common-law marriage due to the expensive cost of a formal marriage. In other cases, couples, including formerly enslaved people, already considered themselves married and saw little need to legalize their union. Because family members and friends acknowledged their marital status, such couples may have considered a legal marriage pointless.

Forgoing a legal union, however, offered African American women select advantages. By choosing a common-law marriage, African American women maintained their legal identity as feme sole, a term used for women living without husbands. By keeping their feme sole status, women could keep the money they earned for themselves. Another benefit to avoiding legal marriage was the couple's ability to dissolve their relationship, for any reason, without divorce fees.[101] And, yet, even with these benefits, the couple's decision would eventually have an impact on whether the women and children of USCT soldiers would be pension eligible.

In 1858 Benjamin Davis and Mary Leighton (later Williamson) were an example of an African American couple who began cohabitating without legally marrying. Within their local community, the two were a legitimate couple. Elizabeth Bond remembered Benjamin publicly declaring his marriage to Mary: "I heard Benjamin say that he was married to her, and went as man and wife. She was called by all the neighbors [as] Mrs. Davis," Bond testified.[102] Ann Tunnel recalled the Davises slightly differently but still noted that the couple had the respect of African Americans in their neighborhood. She stated, "He was living with a woman[, Mary], that everybody supposed was his wife."[103] The Davis union highlights the point that communities such as theirs did not shun couples for not marrying legally.

Wilson Day, meanwhile, provides a complicated case for understanding how a common-law union could materialize and disintegrate. Day began an intimate relationship on an unknown date with Kate (maiden name unknown). Their relationship eventually ended, and they split up.[104] Following their separation, Day began telling some of his friends that it was Kate's fault. Michael R. Frederick, a friend, stated that Day dissolved the relationship with "his former wife because she threw a 'spell over him that offended his brains.'"[105] His decision to leave Kate required no financial compensation for lawyers or governmental officials, which feasibly made it easier for Day to leave. "He just left her," Frederick said.[106] Day's termination of his marriage paralleled the actions of white husbands who, for whatever reasons, deserted their wives.[107]

Children were present in both legal and common-law unions. Between the two, common-law marriages had a higher rate of children per marriage.[108] Every child increased the potential financial drain on its family. In homes where children did not work, they used precious resources and did not replenish them. James Ellsbury and Catherine Harrison, for example, informally wed on May 6, 1857, and three years later the couple was raising two children—William Ellsbury and eight-year-old Emma Costa. The Ellsburys decided not only to allow Emma to live with them but also to put her in school, even though she could have financially contributed to the household through wage-earning work.[109] Perhaps Emma was an orphan; alternatively, she might have been the child of a friend and was living with the Ellsburys because her parents wanted her to attend school. In the latter scenario, they would have paid for her to live with another family, which some African American parents did.[110]

Nearly all married (legal and common-law) future soldiers were the only full-time wage earners in their households, putting most of the economic responsibilities on them. Some of these men worked either in semiskilled occupations, such as that of salesman, waiter, servant, canal worker, apprentice, and farmer; other married men had skilled jobs, including that of engineer or blacksmith.[111] Each of these men successfully avoided various racial barriers that sought to keep African American men from finding such work, and the money they earned offset the economic challenges experienced by many other African Americans.

A quick examination of all Pennsylvanians' annual wages in 1859 shows that skilled workers could earn sizeable incomes. Engineers, such as Samuel Brown, could feasibly collect over $424 annually, whereas blacksmiths, including Solomon Hoff, might earn $540 per year.[112] For comparison, the average laborer earned $300 annually.[113] Therefore, African American men, such as Brown and Hoff, could acquire significant annual salaries. However, such large incomes was never a guarantee for most African American Philadelphians, who usually received lower wages—typically three to four dollars less per month—than their white counterparts due to racism.[114] Perhaps the complex and dynamic work gave them a sense of pride in their masculinity anyway, even if their wages were not always comparable with the wages of their white counterparts.

On the flipside of the employment spectrum were the married men who worked as unskilled laborers.[115] The ensuing financial hardships that these men and their families experienced put African Americans in a subjugated status to whites; their financial instability limited accessibility to resources, food, and even housing. Therefore, the assertion of white dominance, in terms of social status and economics, had a significant effect on African American families' fiduciary sustainability. Richard and Isabella Duffy, for example, were a couple in which both husband and wife were wage earners: Richard was a laborer, and Isabella was a whitewasher.[116] The money that they earned was vital to providing for their three children, Charlotte, Pauline, and Charles. Adherents to middle-class gender ideology castigated women such as Isabella for failing to perform domestic duties and chastised men like Richard for not making enough money to support his entire household. The Duffy's situation is an example of a working-poor African American family whose material realities ran counter to a gender ideology championed by middle-class adherants.

In two cases, couples made conscious decisions to further challenge their economic stability by adding fictive kin (who were children) to their households. William Glasgow lived with James and Hannah White.[117] Meanwhile, Anna White stayed with Joseph and Elizabeth Perkins.[118] In both cases the children were school age. Only Anna attended school. The Perkinses' willingness to take Anna in and put her in school implies that the couple valued access to education even though it drained resources. On the other hand, the Whites' inclusion of William in their home highlights one working-poor African American family that sacrificed their limited resources to assure a safe space for a child, even though traditional schooling did not take place.

Bachelorhood and Familial Responsibilities

Reaching young adulthood did not necessarily mean that men created new families. A significant number of men, for various reasons, avoided getting married before the war. Perhaps they had intimate relationships with a sundry of partners that never progressed beyond the initial stage of courtship. Alternatively, the relationships may have ended, either amicably or otherwise, before a couple married. Other men may have enjoyed their independence and engaging in various forms of vice. For example, Charles Howard enjoyed his freedom of movement and finance.[119] Upon investigation into his personal life to determine his pension application's validity (later determined illegitimate), the special examiner commented on Howard's bachelorhood: "He just ran around New York [City]," the special examiner stated, "and lived with different women until his money ran out."[120] A desire to make independent decisions about how to spend money and perhaps explore carnal desires transcended racial lines for young, single men, though various social figures critiqued such bachelors for not practicing sexual purity, showing a lack of self-restraint, and failing to recognize their perceived responsibility to others.[121]

Some single men experienced difficulties acquiring regular employment. For example, Richard Bryant and Henry Richardson remained economically dependent on their family members even as adult men. Bryant, his mother, and three siblings relied on the collective wages of his father Jacob, a shopkeeper, and his two brothers, both waiters.[122] Perhaps Bryant had intermittent employment working with his father. It is also likely that Bryant found temporary work to supplement his household finances. On the other hand, Henry Richardson and his younger sister were wholly dependent on the wages that his single mother, Margaret, made through her work as a washerwoman.[123] Margaret provided a living counterargument to the belief that only men could (or should) be the sole wage earner for a family.

Some bachelors, meanwhile, found work as laborers. Their employment in unskilled occupations was normative for most African American men throughout the mid-nineteenth century.[124] Work as an unskilled laborer was physically demanding and paid low wages, yet these future soldiers, including Joseph Perkins, remained critical fiduciary contributors to their families.[125] Perhaps some of these young male soldiers could perform either semiskilled or highly skilled work, but whites imposed racial barriers on their employment, hindering African American men from working profitable occupations.[126]

Being a laborer and a bachelor created opportunities for some school-age youths to receive an education. In 1850 William Cooper and his father were the only employed workers in their household, which consisted of seven family members. Twelve-year-old Ann Eliza and ten-year-old Sarah both went to school because of the men's collective efforts.[127] Cooper's familial dynamic had some similarities with other working-poor African Americans. In 1860 Josiah Allen and Richard Black were laborers who, along with their fathers, were the primary wage earners for their families. Their unified wages made it possible for two children in each family to attend school.[128] For many Americans, sustained bachelorhood was a sign of a young man forgoing his responsibility to become independent. As a result, bachelors garnered condemnation for their supposedly selfish actions.[129] However, William Cooper, Josiah Allen, and Richard Black illustrate that remaining bachelors did not prevent them from assuming important familial responsibilities by contributing wages and making it possible for their siblings to attend school. Furthermore, through their contributions they assumed the duties of fathers by providing for young dependents, even though their fathers were also in the home and working.

Some nonlaborers took on similar responsibilities to their unskilled counterparts by becoming vital wage earners for their families. Numerous future soldiers worked semiskilled or skilled occupations while they were single adults. Thomas Johnson worked as a cabinet maker, while his brother was a porter whose wages helped their mother and four sisters survive.[130] Edward Purnell Jr. was a porter, and his sister worked as a maid; they both contributed financially to take care of their aging parents, who no longer worked.[131] These dual-earning cases illustrate that African American children were essential to some families' survival. Their nonlaborer occupations meant they were not critically destitute, and they could circumvent the worst of racial discrimination, which would have African Americans live in abject poverty. These advantages, however, still did not translate to affluent circumstances for their families.[132]

The sudden death of a father forced at least two young men, Alexander Robinson and George Henderson, to become breadwinners for their families. Robinson's father died in December 1861, whereas Henderson's father died in 1863 (but stopped working in 1861).[133] Afterward, Robinson found work as a wagon driver; he earned eight dollars per week, which he regularly sent to his mother. Theresa Thomas and Horace Potter both testified, "This money he regularly gave to his mother for her support. That she appropriated it to the purchase of food, fuel, . . . and the necessities of life and toward the payment of the rent."[134] Meanwhile, Henderson worked as a porter, earning six dollars per week before his enlistment.[135] Similar to countless white bachelors, both men became the breadwinners for their mothers. However, their experiences were different from most young white men because racism was an inescapable burden that jeopardized finances, civil rights, and humanity every day.

A laboring stepfather's disabling hernia and rheumatism forced Andrew White to become the family's breadwinner once he found work as a farm laborer. At one point, White's mother, Sarah, confided in her friend Francis Hayes about their household's economic restructuring due to her husband James Reeves's ailments. Hayes testified, "She stated to me [that] she had to depend on him[, White,] for support."[136] Hayes expounded her point by noting that Reeves's disability rendered him "unable to support [Sarah] on account of [his] rheumatism."[137] White's wages were vital to his mother and his stepfather, sister, and three brothers. Community members knew that White financially supported his family. Henry Hopkins remembered: "As he[, Andrew,] earned money[,] he gave his mother nearly all of it for her support. He was a good industrious young man and done all he could for his mother."[138]

White's and Reeves's decisions reveal a complicated gender dynamic as the son assumed the stepfather's idealized household role. The main catalyst in creating their change was occupational racial discrimination, which forced men, like Reeves, to perform physically grueling work that often led to bodily ailments. For some Victorian-era whites, Reeves failed in his supposed masculine role as the primary wage earner, yet such thinking routinely ignored or downplayed societal racism that kept Reeves from living up to an unattainable masculine ideal.

Before serving in USCT regiments, numerous African American Philadelphians fought to keep their families together and households financially stable. Northern whites used various tactics to enforce racial supremacy and subjugate African Americans. Nevertheless, future soldiers and their kin were not submissive. Instead, African American families demonstrated their resiliency by working diverse occupations, educating children, and embracing fictive kin, whether to protect them or bolster finances. And they would continue fighting for their families as the nation descended into war.

CHAPTER TWO

The United States Needs African American Men

As the Civil War erupted, African American Philadelphians discovered that their fight for equality would evolve to include serving in the U.S. Army, ending slavery, creating a pathway for citizenship, and having African American manhood recognized by white society. Supporters of USCT regiments, such as Frederick Douglass, repeatedly touted soldiering as a way to fundamentally change American society to become more inclusive. "To fight for the Government in this tremendous war is, then, to fight for nationality and for a place with all other classes of our fellow citizens. The great to be done first of all is," Douglass proclaimed, "to get an eagle on your button and a musket on your shoulder."[1] Unfortunately, such calls to mobilize would have an immediate, and in many cases lasting, impact on families already in precarious living situations due to racism.

A Whites-Only War

African American Philadelphians fought every day for their survival as the events of the Civil War transformed their lives. When Confederate forces overtook the U.S. military installation Fort Sumter, loyal white Unionists began calling for a direct and violent response.[2] In Philadelphia, deeply entrenched political divisions, economic ties to southern industries, and varied opinions on slavery led to violence. Pro-U.S. Philadelphians made it clear to dissonant locals that spreading pro-Confederate rhetoric or images, including flags, would not stand.[3] A collective of U.S. supporters physically assaulted a young male Confederate sympathizer, using "a dozen or so boots [that] left imprints upon his body."[4] This example highlights the history of violence in Philadelphia.[5] Before the outbreak of the Civil War, Philadelphia had already established a history of large-scale violence that stemmed from either racial, ethnic, class, or religious tensions.[6] The Civil War, however, opened a new era in an already volatile urban city.

But in the minds of state and federal government officials, Philadelphia's tumultuous dynamic was not as important as mobilizing for the war. President Abraham Lincoln promptly called on seventy-five thousand men to respond to the Confederate attack on Fort Sumter (a U.S. military installation). White men sought to demonstrate their collective patriotism and manhood in military service.[7] Andrew Curtin, Pennsylvania's governor and one of Lincoln's confidants, began organizing recruitment campaigns to convince able-bodied white men to serve.[8] With its sizeable male population, extensive transportation networks, shipping ports, wealthy Republican supporters, and industrialized factories, Philadelphia was important to accomplishing Lincoln's war aims.

Whites refused to call upon African American men to participate in the national conflict. Northern whites, especially Democrats, rejected African American men in uniform because they feared that military service would entail citizenship and voting rights. Additionally, many white men viewed military service as solely their domain—a way to display their manhood in uniform and with weapons as they fulfilled an obligation of citizenship.[9] U.S. Army and state militias both mandated that only white men could serve. In doing so, white men defined national citizenship as an exclusive domain for them alone.[10] Meanwhile, as some African American men clamored to serve, whites denied them the opportunity to have their cultural citizenship acknowledged.

Some white men made it clear in the early stages of the Civil War that their ranks should never include African Americans.[11] A white Ohioan derided African American men for aspiring to become U.S. Army soldiers. "We want you d——d niggers to keep out of this; this is a white man's war," he stated.[12] This racist sentiment led the U.S. Army to implement policies barring African American men from taking part in the war as soldiers. At least eighteen thousand African American men and eleven African American women served in the U.S. Navy, some long before the mobilization of USCT regiments.[13]

Meanwhile, European immigrant men, such as Germans and Irishmen, viewed military service as a way to prove their national loyalty and create a pathway for their citizenship. Their hope of acquiring citizenship rights came only after willingly sacrificing their lives for the "greater good" of the nation. In Philadelphia, German immigrants eagerly joined six different regiments with hopes of gaining recognition as American citizens.[14] Numerous Irishmen enlisted in U.S. Army regiments, partly to refute stereotypes promulgated by xenophobic native whites.[15] As a result of the initial success in recruiting white able-bodied men, the U.S. Army avoided recruiting African American soldiers.

Barring African American Men from Service

Even before the Civil War, local home guards were an organization in which men drilled to defend their communities and demonstrate their honor.[16] Sidney George Fisher, a white man and prominent local Republican supporter, believed home guards could be invaluable for quelling local discontent. Fisher noted, "It may be needed to preserve order at home."[17] However, these groups rarely, if ever, allowed African Americans to participate, which may have fostered resentment among those excluded.

In response, some northern African Americans tried to create their own home guards. African American Philadelphians were unsuccessful in forming a home guard after local officials (all white men) had the group immediately disband.[18] Local officials contended that only whites were capable of being protectors. Still, African American Philadelphian professor Alfred M. Green felt proud that local African American men sought to demonstrate their manhood as soldiers. "They will make Herculean defenders," Green claimed.[19] Green remained persistent in urging African Americans to seize upon the war to transform American society.[20] He understood that convincing African Americans to enlist would not be a simple task. However, he prioritized enrollment and a focus on the future. "It is a foolish idea for us to still be nursing our past grievances to our own detriment," Green said.[21] Becoming soldiers, in Green's opinion, would allow African Americans to demonstrate their patriotism. Additionally, they could help end slavery and hopefully reap postwar benefits.

Responses to Green's call were swift and critical. Various authors composed newspaper editorials for the *Weekly Anglo-African* questioning his call to serve. An article stated, "I am satisfied that recruiting, drilling or fighting will never break this innate prejudice, imbedded in the hearts of this nation."[22] Meanwhile, a New Jersian felt that mental and moral training was more important than wasteful military drilling since they had been excluded from the war.[23] Isaiah C. Wears, a prominent figure within the African Methodist Episcopal (AME) Church disagreed with Green's urgency to provide military service.[24] Wears asserted, "Colored men could not be spared at such a time, and in such a cause."[25] Northern African Americans could not agree on whether to support soldiers. Even so, these important discussions failed to consider how the lives of African American families would forever change, not necessarily for the better, if men joined the military.

Call To Arms!

With the passage of the Militia Act of 1862, which permitted freedmen to serve as laborers for the U.S. Army; the Enrollment Act of 1863, which established a federal draft that would conscript men into the U.S. Army regardless of race; and the Emancipation Proclamation, which authorized the U.S. Army to enlist African American men as soldiers, the U.S. Army finally included African Americans.[26] Plus, northern whites began claiming that African American men must now "prove" themselves as soldiers. After two years of "seeing the elephant," some U.S. whites were seeking reinforcements.[27] Sidney George Fisher reflected on the fact that Philadelphia's combative fervor eroded after two years. "War was a novelty then; it is an old story now," Fisher wrote.[28]

Other northern white men found the idea of African American soldiers appealing once the Enrollment Act mandated that each state supply an allotted number of volunteer enlistees or face a draft.[29] An unnamed Illinois veteran gladly welcomed potential African American soldiers—to benefit white men who did not want to serve. The veteran proclaimed, "I think if a negro could save their lives by sacrificing theirs[, then,] they would be willing' to accept blacks."[30] Seeking to bolster white support, even among racists, a white Illinoisan civilian made a similar claim about saving white lives: "'Let the negro-hater remember that every black [man] who enlists in Illinois, counts ONE and take[s] the place of *a white man*, perhaps himself.'"[31] Meanwhile, some white men already serving desperately sought to end their time as soldiers by deserting if necessary. Others tried to avoid reenlisting by endorsing the mobilization of African American regiments.[32]

George Templeton Strong, a member of the Union League Club of New York, approved of African American soldiering because it spared white men. He stated, "Nigger recruiting prospers. Rumors of a *Corps d'Afrique* to be raised here. Why not?"[33] Strong asserted that whites must take advantage of a population eager to serve. "Let us accept, with contrition and humiliation, the service of this despised and rejected race," Strong professed, "and be thankful that it is willing to enlist in the cause of a nation from which it has received only contumely and persecution."[34] His comments show that even when supporting African Americans and opening up military service, racism persisted.

Like Strong, some white men were finally willing to accept African American men's cultural citizenship, but only because of African American persistence and white weariness to the seemingly unending war.[35] Missing from these endorsements was the acknowledgment that some white men's disdain for service stemmed from an aversion to performing a duty of citizenship. Furthermore, some white men no longer viewed military service as a requirement for manhood or citizenship and avoided service.

The mobilization of Pennsylvanian USCT regiments greatly benefitted from African Americans' collective support of the war effort. It is important to recognize that the African American community, not white men and their organizations, had the most sway over their potential recruits. Many African Americans worked diligently to encourage potential recruits to become soldiers. For instance, local churches became unofficial recruitment stations as pastors exercised influential spiritual leadership over some enlistment decisions.[36]

Northern African American newspapers eventually became staunch supporters of the military, frequently writing about soldiering's potential benefits. African American newspapers would receive submissions from prominent African American abolitionists who attempted to galvanize their community. Frederick Douglass emphasized how potential enlistees' decisions could impact future generations. "To hold back is to invite infamy upon ourselves and upon our child," Douglass professed.[37] Then, he informed his audience that white society might finally recognize new aspects of African American manhood due to military service. "To fight for the Government in this tremendous war is, then, to fight for nationality," he argued, "and for a place with all other classes of our fellow citizens."[38] Douglass's statement did not acknowledge that military service never assured universal male suffrage. Moreover, if it did, then it would only come at the cost of African American men's lives.

While published articles focused on reaching the literate northern African American population, enlistment advocates sought to reach a larger base of potential enlistees through public speaking engagements. African American men, such as army recruiter John Mercer Langston and Philadelphia teacher and abolitionist Octavius Catto, scoured northern cities and rural towns for potential soldiers, hoping that each event would culminate with invigorated men flocking to recruiting stations.[39] African American women also worked individually to bolster northern U.S. Army recruitment efforts. For instance, Mary Ann Shadd Cary became a paid recruiting agent for the U.S. Army as she tried to convince northern African American men to enlist.[40] Collectively, all of these people were important in reconfiguring national politics to recognize and include African American men.[41]

If USCT recruitment was ever going to succeed in Pennsylvania, then it would require the money and political influence of wealthy white men loyal to the United States. The Union League of Philadelphia (ULP) comprised elite Republicans and Democrats that supported African American soldiering, especially in a city with a sizeable male population. Even though white politicians slowly moved toward accepting the idea of African American soldiers, the ULP used their connections with prominent government officials, such as Secretary of War Edwin Stanton, to begin raising Pennsylvania USCT regiments in the fall of 1863.[42] After receiving approval, the ULP was responsible for conducting an extensive recruitment campaign, organizing a subcommittee (the Supervisory Committee for Recruiting Colored Regiments), financing the state's multiple USCT regiments themselves, and aiding in the construction of Camp William Penn.[43] In the end, the ULP's energies resulted in the mobilization of multiple Pennsylvanian USCT regiments.

The ULP soon realized that their endeavors hinged on whether African American men actually enrolled. This realization led the organization to assemble members' resources to spread the word, emphasizing the patriotism of African Americans. The ULP raised $35,000 to create a publication committee that distributed numerous pamphlets and handbills between April and October 1863.[44] ULP member George H. Boker composed a pamphlet recognizing the military sacrifices made by African Americans in previous national wars. By emphasizing the earlier soldiering of African American men, Boker's plea was similar to African American enlistment advocates' rhetoric.[45] He then chastised his white compatriots for their continued trepidation about USCT regiments. Boker wrote, "If our fathers in 1812, and our grandfathers in 1776, did not hesitate to put muskets in the hands of Negros as soldiers, why should we?"[46] His defiant tone implies that he, and by extension the ULP, believed that African Americans were already part of the nation due to their sacrifices in past wars.

Various supporters of Pennsylvanian USCT recruitment feared the loss of potential recruits to other states. Their concerns was that native-born Pennsylvanian African American men would decide to enlist in other states. And indeed, recruiters from the First Kansas Colored Infantry trekked eastward as far as Pennsylvania in 1862.[47] For various reasons, 294 African American Pennsylvanian men traveled to serve in the Bay State's African American regiments, including the Fifty-Fourth Massachusetts.[48] For instance, once recruiting began in Massachusetts, Benjamin Davis's desire to enlist spurred him on a 310-mile trip to enroll. Left behind was Davis's wife, Mary Leighton (later Williamson), who gave birth to Jerome not long after Benjamin went to demonstrate his manhood in the military. During his journey Benjamin incurred a staph infection that kept him from enlisting.[49] Regardless of race, by choosing the U.S. Army, men had to decide what mattered more, remaining the protector and provider of their families or becoming a defender of the nation.[50] Perhaps African American Pennsylvanian men, like Davis, were upset with their home state for moving too slowly in organizing its regiments. Alternatively, perhaps becoming part of an imagined community—the nation—was more important to Davis than remaining home with his wife and newborn son. Maybe African American men like Davis wanted to fight for the liberation of enslaved African Americans. Either way, Benjamin left Philadelphia when USCT soldiering elsewhere became a reality. Many other men would make the same choice.[51]

Filling the Ranks

After all the various obstacles for African American soldiering in Pennsylvania disappeared, the state and the nation needed able-bodied men. Droves of men eventually came to Philadelphia seeking to serve in a Pennsylvanian USCT regiment. In the end, 185 Philadelphian-

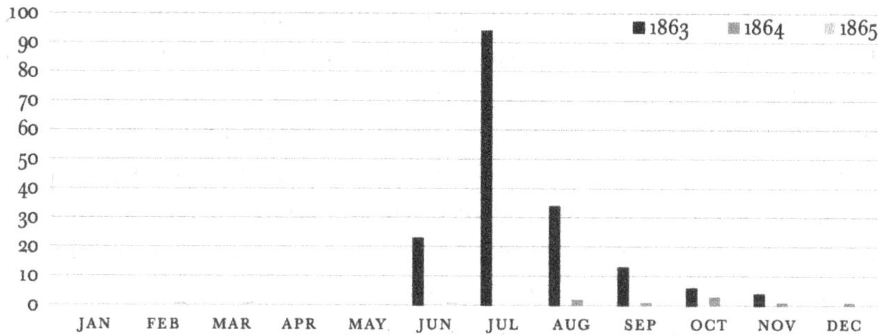

FIGURE 2.1 Enlistment data for Philadelphian-native men

born men enlisted in either the Third United States Colored Infantry (USCI), the Sixth USCI, or the Eighth USCI. And their decision to do so forever changed the lives of their families.

As figure 2.1 shows, most of the men in all three Pennsylvanian regiments (nearly 83 percent) enlisted in the summer of 1863, between June and August. Enrollment declined significantly after October and November 1863, primarily because the units had already been organized and filled; there was never more than one enrollee in a month, if at all.[52] The quick enrollment of all three regiments illustrates the effectiveness of various recruiters.

Women undoubtedly had a role in convincing African Americans to enlist. Some whites and many African American northerners recognized that the United States' hopes for fully manned USCT regiments would not succeed without African American women. The *Weekly Anglo-African* beseeched young African American women to use their femininity and intimate relationships to encourage enlistment. One author wrote, "Let our maidens vie with each other in urging the young men forward to their duties."[53] James Henry Gooding of the Fifty-Fourth Massachusetts made a similar statement about the pivotal role African American women had in militarizing African American men. "Let the young women drive all these young loungers off to the war," Gooding stated.[54] During a July 6, 1863, USCT recruitment event, Pennsylvanian Congressman William D. Kelley issued a direct plea for African American women's action. Kelley first informed single women of the potential "dangers" of engaging in a relationship with a man avoiding military service. He advised women to avoid the advances of a "spruce dandy" and "let him know that you would rather marry the wooden leg and empty sleeve jacket of a war-worn hero than a man who might require you to tuck him in during every thunderstorm."[55] He then informed African American mothers that they did not suffer through childbirth to have a man who was a coward, in Kelley's opinion. "Mothers . . . gather . . . your sons around you," Kelley proclaimed, "and spurn him who will not prove that when you suffered the pangs of maternity it was to give birth to a *man*."[56] African American women, in many ways, performed the same actions that garnered white women praise for their soldiering support.[57]

For some men, enlistment was a family decision. There were even examples in both armies of blood relatives who chose to become soldiers together.[58] Brothers William H. and Robert G. Parker, and their cousin, John Thompson, exemplify how one African American Philadelphian family sacrificed three young men.[59] Whether out of nationalist zeal or a desire to protect each other, some families and community members chose to serve together.

U.S. Army advocates repeatedly urged African Americans to support the war effort by encouraging men to leave their families. Enlistment rhetoric was positive and rarely recognized the possibility that military service could fundamentally restructure African American families, especially the working poor.[60] Jacob G. Jackson's decision to enlist on October 5, 1863, meant, for example, that he would miss his wife, Martha Ann, giving birth to their daughter Victoria on December 9.[61] Records do not state if he ever saw his wife and child before departing for the frontline. Tragically, Jacob would die in service from a fatal wound at Olustee, Florida.[62]

Enlistment prompted some African Americans to create or legitimize, in the federal government's opinion, their families even as they trained for the war. Like many soldiers in other conflicts, some USCT recruits married their sweethearts just before heading off to war. On October 18, 1863, four months after his enrollment in the Third USCI, Solomon Hoff wed Anna Elizabeth, and the following day their son, George, was born.[63] Charles Deets provides a different story: he married Hannah on September 10, 1863, and then enlisted in the Sixth USCI on the same day.[64] The Deetses already had a child together, Ella Irene, who was nearly a year old.[65] Perhaps Deets and Hoff chose to legally wed their partners to provide financial protection for their dependents, especially in the event of their deaths. In 1862 the federal government had modified its pension law, making an honorably discharged soldier's dependents pension eligible. The policy made no racial designation, meaning it may have influenced some couples to wed legally.[66] It also meant that couples who did not legally marry jeopardized their finances by not conforming to white societal norms.

The war forced men to choose whether they should offer their lives to support the United States' objectives. The decisions these men made reverberated within their families. The militarization of able-bodied men ultimately fractured the financial stability of numerous northern families of all races. Because recruitment rhetoric was inescapable, potential enlistees were constantly asked to weigh the value of their lives and their families against national patriotism.[67] Like other urban northern African Americans, African American Philadelphian families experienced the United States' call to arms differently from their white counterparts.[68] Racial discrimination was interwoven into every aspect of Philadelphian society. These systemic conditions meant that removing a family member, especially a wage-earning adult man, had the potential to devastate the family's economy.

The Difficulties Financing USCT Soldiering

Calling African American Philadelphian men to the military did not mean that the federal government concerned itself with the financial well-being of recruits' kin. Many African American families scrambled to make ends meet as African American men enlisted. They had to hope that the government—local, state, or federal—would provide aid, in the form of enlistment bounties, to perhaps cover the absence of the men's earned wages. Various bounties were not the only possible forms of financial compensation, as enlisted men did receive monthly wages. Some scholars deride bounties "as an irritant or a stigma that enervated the recruiting effort."[69] In reality, bounties were pivotal to families of all races seeking to survive on the home front during and after the war. Bounties, in short, were immediate, one-time cash injections that could benefit enlistees and possibly their kin after enlistment. In many cases enlistees exchanged their individuality and potentially their lives for such payments, which some desperately needed. In the end, bounties were crucial for economically destitute families.

While USCT enlistees did not receive federal bounties in 1863, white recruits had been receiving them since 1861.[70] Perhaps the federal government believed patriotism should be the primary motivator for African American enlistees. Yet again, skin complexion benefitted white men, who had access to money from the federal government.[71]

But some white supporters of USCT regiments publicly recognized, in 1863, that racism kept African Americans from receiving enlistment bounties.[72] The *New York Times* recognized that money was not forthcoming to African American enlistees. "You are offered no bounty by the Government," the editor complained.[73] Meanwhile, during the Sixth USCI's regimental flag presentation in the fall of 1863, U.S. Army lieutenant colonel Louis F. Wagner commended the soldiers who "had left friends, kindred and home, and volunteered when the bounties and pay of whites were denied."[74] These examples demonstrate that at least some whites were aware of the racial discrimination behind the denial of federal bounties.

Many soldiers worried about their family's perseverance in the battle for financial survival.[75] African American men, unlike white men, suffered more due to racial barriers imposed by the federal government.[76] The majority of the men studied here, similar to the families of enlisted men in the First South Carolina Volunteer Infantry Regiment (Colored), Second South Carolina Volunteer Infantry Regiment (Colored), and multiple North Carolina USCT regiments, received no enlistment bounties.[77] Northern African Americans lived on the economic fringes compared to whites, which meant that enlisting most assuredly impacted the families of USCT enrollees.[78] Thus, the federal government endangered the finances of many African American families.

Once military policies were modified early in 1864, four men—Malachi Bird, William Griffin, William Tallman, and Edward Davis—received an enlistment bounty from the federal government when they enrolled. Griffin earned thirty-three dollars and three cents upon enlisting on September 13, 1864.[79] Meanwhile, the remaining three men received $100 upon their enlistments, which occurred after December 30, 1864.[80] The difference in payment was due to the Army Appropriation Bill of 1864, a federal policy regulating bounty payments for USCT enlistees.[81] The families of these soldiers were fortunate to receive money; many others did not.

Part of the federal government's rationale was its fear that some men would not honor their military contracts and abscond from military service if they received bounty payments upon enlisting. And some did exactly that, deserting immediately after enlisting, making bounty jumping a potentially profitable venture.[82] By consciously defrauding the federal government and fleeing after registering as soldiers, bounty jumpers actively avoided their contractual obligations to the U.S. Army. The patriotism of such men was questioned, and some viewed the bounty jumpers as cowards.[83] Desertions of this type led families to languish without economic aid due in part to the federal government's concerns over individual financial profiteers.

In the absence of federal bounties, various local bounties—privately funded by a town, city, county, or state—provided the best or, in many cases, the only avenue for immediate financial assistance for African American recruits and their families. Payments differed greatly throughout the war, ranging from $10 to $1,000, which worked to the advantage of African Americans on occasion.[84] New Bedford, Massachusetts, provided African American recruits with a twenty-five-dollar bounty.[85] A military committee in Athens County, Ohio, offered African Americans, similar to white recruits, $100 bounties "as a way to help the families left behind, not as an encouragement for enlistment."[86] The Commonwealth of Pennsylvania paid African American recruits fifty dollars.[87] In Philadelphia, the ULP began paying $250 bounties after December 1863 to stimulate recruitment into Pennsylvania USCT regiments, an effort to curb declining zeal for enrollment.[88] Even if the ULP bounty payments were not intended for families, it is feasible to assume that some of the USCT soldiers used the money for their dependents.

Some men even collected multiple bounties upon enlistment. For instance, Peter Vandermark, a soldier with the Twentieth USCI, got a $500 bounty from Kingston, New York, and a $300 bounty from Ulster County, New York.[89] Therefore, men could acquire a laborer's annual wage of $300, or possibly exceed it, depending on the financial inducements geared toward African American men.[90] Perhaps local bounties directly influenced northern African American men to join a USCT regiment. By doing so, USCT enlistees could provide a sizeable cash injection for African American families. Notably, soldiers drawn to this sudden influx of monies may have been focused on short-term economic gain and not potential, long-term issues that could materialize if the men came home with a disability or did not come home at all. African Americans who enlisted without a bounty demonstrate that motivation to join was not always tied to money.

Local governments, military recruiters, and draft-eligible whites fully understood that potential USCT enlistees had multiple options on where they could join and how much profit they could earn in the process. Money became a driving force in northern USCT recruitment, which led to tension and unofficial competitions to offer the most appealing financial incentive to African American men.[91] The *Weekly Anglo-African* informed potential New York recruits that they should consider enrolling in Rhode Island, especially regarding financial compensation. "She gives, in addition to the best treatment, three hundred dollars bounty," the editor advised, "and will probably add State aid to families. This is the offer that colored men should avail themselves of, and not wait for New York to move."[92]

Meanwhile, the *New York Times* noted that Pennsylvania's mobilization was ineffective in convincing its native-born men to forgo joining an African American Massachusetts regiment. The paper reasoned that Pennsylvania should take similar actions to Massachusetts and seek out men from neighboring states. "Our [recruitment] field, therefore, should not be limited by the narrow boundaries of our own State," the editor professed.[93] Indeed, northern states had legitimate concerns and a vested interest in convincing African American men from across the nation to join locally.[94]

Even with the extensive recruitment campaign urging African American Philadelphian men to join one of Pennsylvania's first three USCT regiments, only 185 men enlisted. For comparison, Philadelphia had a sizeable free African American male population between fifteen to fifty years old (5,273 or 3 percent of the city's population), but many did not enlist in these regiments.[95] Some men in Pennsylvania's USCT regiments came from inside Pennsylvania, including Lancaster, Harrisburg, Pittsburgh, Berks County, Montgomery County, and Chester County. Men from Delaware, Maryland, North Carolina, Virginia, Florida, New York, and New Jersey also enrolled. Men born in other countries, including Canada and Jamaica, also enlisted.[96] The Third USCI, the Sixth USCI, and the Eighth USCI successfully brought together men from inside and outside of America to represent Pennsylvania during the war. Thus, enrollment in Pennsylvania's USCT regiments, similar to other USCT regiments, represented a greater population than that of its home state.[97] It also shows that the regiments failed to attract a bevy of Philadelphian men to their ranks.

One might interpret the low number of Philadelphian-born recruits as illustrative of Philadelphia's ineffectiveness in recruiting locals. However, simply viewing mobilization efforts as flawed ignores African Americans' agency as they debated and, in many cases, refused military service. There was no singular rationale for why some men chose to remain civilians. The denial of full citizenship rights and the refusal to recognize all African Americans' humanity were frequent complaints.[98] These grievances were valid arguments made by African Americans who criticized the idealistic rhetoric emphasized by USCT supporters.

Another pressing concern for African American men was making ends meet for their families in their absence. For some African American men, continued support of their families through their civilian wages was more appealing than receiving a USCT soldier's reduced monthly payments with no federal bounty. For comparison, men working as laborers could earn $300 annually, while a USCT soldier (without federal bounties) would receive $156 for the year.[99] Anxiety over material realities was something that whites also struggled with during the war.[100] Unfortunately for USCT soldiers or potential enrollees, they would earn three dollars less per month than white men of the same rank. These payment issues forced African American men to choose whether their civilian wages or nationalism was more important. African American Philadelphian men who avoided USCT service for economic reasons and self-preservation may have aligned with Junius C. Morel, an African American abolitionist, who questioned the purported merits of military service. "Men in the North will not leave their homes and families, their avocations, at wages of $25 and $30 per month, to be sent to South Carolina, or Georgia, to fight rebel white men," Morel proclaimed, "with the prospect of [a] dog's death by the minions of Jeff Davis should they be captured, all for $10 per month, without bounty at that."[101]

Training for the Nation

Convincing African American men to become soldiers was only the first step in militarizing the United States' sable arm. The next, and arguably the hardest, step was training the men to be U.S. Army soldiers. Even with the inundation of USCT recruitment campaigns, advocates of enlistment rarely, if ever, spent time detailing what military training would look like. Henry S. Harmon of the Third USCI commented on the harsh reality of military service. He stated, "Men overflowing with the spirit of patriots did not stop to consider the hardships attending camp life."[102] The veracities of becoming a soldier overwhelmed many men, including USCT soldiers.

Numerous USCT advocates avoided informing prospective soldiers about how emotionally, psychologically, and physically challenging military training would be. Maybe African American men, similar to white men, did not want to hear that becoming a "good"—or at least serviceable—soldier meant giving up one's sense of individuality.[103] For the U.S. Army to achieve its goals, it subjected African American men (like all men) to intensely regimented training.[104] USCT soldiers had to learn to submit to a military command structure headed and controlled by white men.[105] By doing so, USCT soldiers would become part of an imagined community—the United States—through their willingness to sacrifice their lives and perform ritualistic training.[106]

Adapting to military life was not easy for many USCT soldiers—and there were many reasons for this. Some men found it hard to submit to the authority of white USCT officers, who were sometimes openly racist toward their subordinates.[107] Some USCT officers meted out draconian forms of punishment to African American soldiers for infractions, both minor and major, while white soldiers rarely experienced such treatment.[108] Other USCT soldiers became angry over commands to perform physical labor and wanted to know when they would engage in armed combat against Confederates. For other men, resentment stirred regarding inequality in pay compared to their white counterparts. The interconnection between these and other issues meant that African American men continually felt that their sense of manhood was under attack and disrespected.[109] USCT soldiers challenged the military's rigid structures with various forms of resistance. More specifically, soldiers who demonstrated various forms of military disobedience, including desertion and disobedience of direct orders, refused to submit to authoritative figures and asserted their own definition of cultural citizenship.[110]

Unfortunately, even with the 1862 Militia Act prescribing that USCT soldiers earn ten dollars per month, many enlisted men earned just seven dollars monthly after the military deducted three dollars for clothing.[111] Meanwhile, white enlisted men collected thirteen dollars monthly. Thus, the U.S. Army cheapened African American soldiers' contributions with inequitable compensation for their service. Some African American men focused their vitriol on U.S. Army paymasters.

Joseph H. Walker of the Fifty-Fifth Massachusetts resented the fact that African American soldiers like himself performed their work but "get no money to send to our wives, children, and mothers, who are now suffering."[112] Perchance Walker's anger stemmed from the fact that he had $4.25 of his monthly pay docked for losing military equipment. Toward the end of his service his rank was reduced from sergeant, possibly over issues regarding pay.[113] Still, paymasters had the unenviable task of demonstrating to African American soldiers that the federal government valued African American soldiers less than white soldiers.[114]

By late 1863, Edwin Stanton, the U.S. secretary of war, openly called for pay equalization for white and African American soldiers, which prompted U.S. Congressman Thaddeus Stevens to offer a bill to remedy the issue. After months of contentious debates, the U.S. Congress eventually passed the Army Appropriations Bill on June 15, 1864, which equalized pay for all African American regiments. Furthermore, the soldiers retroactively received back pay from their enlistment date. The bill did state that African American soldiers were only eligible if they were free by April 19, 1861.[115] None of the soldiers examined here ever referenced this policy. However, it undoubtedly had a significant impact on their families back home.

Over a month before the Army Appropriations Bill passed, Lieutenant Colonel Louis F. Wagner commented that a paymaster designated to Camp William Penn, where all three Pennsylvanian USCT regiments trained, refused to pay USCT soldiers equalized payments. "The Paymaster of this department refuses to pay more than seven dollars ($7.00) per month," Wagner reported.[116] Perhaps the paymaster refused to pay more because the Army Appropriations Bill was not yet enacted. At the same time, Wagner's complaint demonstrates that he desired pay equality sooner than the U.S. Congress did.

Even with the eventual regulation of pay, the federal government remained unable to establish an organized pay distribution process. The primary problem stemmed from inefficient methods of getting money directly into the hands of soldiers of all races in a timely and organized manner.[117] As a result, both soldiers and their families suffered without money.[118] Perhaps African Americans assumed that the military would operate as a well-functioning organization that paid its men in a timely fashion and provided efficient, streamlined communication networks for maintaining soldiers' contact with their kin. Unfortunately, soldiers and families learned that this was not the case. Of the Sixth USCI, Andrew White complained to his mother that a lack of cash limited his ability to communicate with his family regularly. White wrote, "Dear Mother[,] I hope you will not think hard of me for not [w]rite you any sooner [because] paper is very hard to get here without money."[119] White's inability to exchange letters with his mother led to frustrations that many soldiers and their kin experienced.[120]

Meanwhile, friends of Sixth USCI soldier Alexander Robinson knew that he struggled to send money home to his financially destitute mother. They testified, "After he went in the army he never received any. But he wrote her that [soon] as he received his pay[,] he would send it."[121] Both men are examples of bachelors who desired to remain close to their families and keep their households financially stable. Their concerns were similar to those of all USCT men who had to fight against racism among their U.S. military comrades as well as their Confederate enemies.[122]

Like bachelors, married African American soldiers worried about their families remaining economically steady as they simultaneously dealt with military service hardships. Married men served amid continual fear about whether their families could survive as the war persisted.[123] Some men complained about how delayed payments of soldiers' wages made it difficult to forward money back home to their families.[124] USCT soldiers' desperation to send money home was more than a desire to demonstrate their manhood; their desperation formed over concerns about keeping their families fed and housed. In Third USCI soldier Tillman Valentine's letters to his wife, Annie Elizabeth Valentine, he discussed his hopes to provide financially for his kin while on the frontlines. Valentine asked his wife on April 25, 1864, "whether you have anything or no the little ones is looking up in your face asking for bre[a]d and you got none to give them."[125] His family's inability to feed itself perchance weighed greatly on Valentine's mind and psyche as he fretted over his oft delayed military payments. Maybe Valentine's concerns intensified because he had not received an enlistment bounty, and from July 30, 1863, to February 29, 1864, he only received seven dollars per month.[126] Valentine was not alone in experiencing inner turmoil as he continued soldiering. Other soldiers' letters show that agony over starving families was felt by white and African American soldiers alike; the war placed a heavy burden on the home front.[127]

On occasion USCT soldiers turned to other military men to assist in transferring money back home.[128] Maybe some enlisted men preferred to use this method when soldiers of the same regiment received furloughs. Perhaps some of the men examined here used similar methods in moments where they could not afford or acquire postage. Not every attempt to dispatch valuables to families was successful. For instance, Liza Francis notified her husband, Edward Francis, of the 114th USCI, that a ring he previously sent her, maybe to sell or to keep as a memento, may have been stolen during shipment. "When I got your letter, it had been opened and it was nearly worn out," she wrote.[129] Unfortunate circumstances sometimes led to the loss of sizeable amounts of enlisted men's money. Several men of the Twenty-Seventh USCI trusted their captain, Alfred W. Pinney, with $350 to send to the soldiers' families. Unfortunately, Pinney's death at the Battle of the Crater meant his subordinates' families never saw the money, as it was possibly stolen from his belongings.[130] These cases reveal an unintended barrier to receiving money and valuables that caused African American families additional suffering.

By 1863, the U.S. Army was successfully calling droves of African American men into service. Their process of becoming soldiers was arduous for both soldiers and their families. Enlisted men discovered that recruitment rhetoric often did not reflect the day-to-day experiences of being a soldier. Meanwhile, their families were left without a key wage earner when a member of their households enlisted for the "greater good" of the United States. The hard realities of military service would only continue to become apparent.

CHAPTER THREE

The Idealism versus the Realism of Military Service

Like countless other U.S. Army recruits, many African American Philadelphian men discovered that soldiering was a grueling experience for their minds, bodies, and emotions. Furthermore, tensions surrounding competing notions of gender and racial ideologies made the soldiering experience even harder for African American men. Due to these and other factors, life as USCT soldiers put them in a battle against Confederates and also with their own military. On the home front, families of deceased USCT soldiers began petitioning the Bureau of Pensions in the hopes of acquiring recognition and financial compensation for their familial wartime sacrifices. In short, USCT military service forced many African American Philadelphians to experience the war in differing and important ways.

The Hardships of Service

Clothed in the U.S. Army's prestigious blue uniform, adorned with the eagle-imprinted button, and armed with military equipment, African American men, in the opinion of USCT supporters, publicly proved their manhood to white society.[1] Service in USCT regiments became gendered and racial battlegrounds as U.S. Army men, white and African American, competed over the definition of African American manhood.[2] For differing reasons, including ethnic, religious, and class divisions, white enlisted men quarreled among themselves and with military officers, sometimes violently, over their divergent understanding of white manhood.[3] The clear difference between white and African American enlisted men was that the latter lived with the inescapable stigma of their race that hindered every aspect of their lives, while the former could acculturate into society or hide their (ethnic, religious, and class) identities from xenophobic natives.

While differing views of African American manhood were not the sole reason for insubordination, it was frequently an underlying and occasionally an explicit factor for USCT soldiers who disobeyed orders. Out of the 185 soldiers examined here, twenty-seven men were charged for various forms of military disobedience, including drunkenness, disrespect toward commanding officers, absence without leave (AWOL), and desertion. Benjamin Davis, Henry Richardson, and Charles W. Sewell are examples of USCT soldiers who ran afoul by not personally submitting to white officers. Each man received a court-martial and was sentenced for their defiance, resulting in a combined six months in jail between the three men.[4]

Time, location, date, weather, and even money were all important variables that resulted in USCT enlisted men receiving disciplinary charges. Cases involving theft were not common, as only two instances occurred among the men in this sample. One involved John Brown of the Sixth USCI, who stole a rifle from one of his tent mates. Brown never revealed his motive for the theft, but it is possible he mistook his comrade's weapon as his own.[5] Meanwhile, William B. Johnston of the Third USCI was found guilty of embezzling twenty dollars from a fellow USCT soldier.[6] Perhaps Johnston took the money out of desperation when his payment was late. Maybe Johnston's debt of $6.73 to the military for lost equipment, including canteen, cartridge box, and bayonet, influenced his actions.[7] Alternatively, his theft might have been an act of greed.

Desertion was a common problem in both armies throughout the war.[8] Several of the men studied here committed the infraction. Seventeen of the 185 soldiers examined in this study deserted from service a total of eighteen times. One of the seventeen soldiers was charged with being AWOL instead of receiving the more severe desertion charge.[9] Military officials, who often struggled to delineate the difference between the two charges, usually categorized a soldier as AWOL if he voluntarily returned after some time.[10] Men who left with no intention of rejoining the ranks were classified as deserters. While this book's numbers pale compared to the recorded 12,437 USCT desertions, each was a case of an African American man questioning why he should remain in service.[11]

The U.S Army learned that forcibly reinstating deserters to their service roles did not always result in the men's compliance.[12] For instance, John Mason of the Third USCI left his regiment during a march in the field. After his arrest and eventual reintegration into the ranks, Mason deserted for a second time, and he succeeded in evading capture.[13]

There were few similarities in the circumstances that led each man to remove himself from the U.S. Army. Some men deserted when the harsh realities of training began to overwhelm them. A total of 127 Pennsylvanian USCT soldiers training at Camp William Penn deserted from service before the Third USCI, the Sixth USCI, and the Eighth USCI departed. For comparison, only ten soldiers deserted from New York's three USCT regiments while they trained at Rikers Island, which illustrates that Pennsylvanian USCT soldiers deserted at a higher rate than their northern counterparts.[14] It is possible that New York's lower desertion number was because the East River separated Rikers Island from the mainland.

Some soldiers resorted to extreme measures to end their military service. William Thomas of the Eighth USCI went to jail after feigning insanity to obtain a medical discharge.[15] Of the Forty-Third USCI, Joneses Nelson tried to end his service with a perilous attempt to slice his throat with a razor. While his military struggles remain undocumented, Nelson's action illustrates the desperation felt by some USCT soldiers.[16] Self-mutilation and attempted suicides were a problem for Confederate enlisted men as well. For instance, Thomas Stringham, a Confederate soldier, also tried to cut his throat to avoid military service.[17] Suicide became a problem in the greater U.S. Army too.[18] During the war, some whites took a more sympathetic tone toward suicidal men, at least soldiers, who struggled to cope with military service.[19] Meanwhile, after the Emancipation Proclamation, African American views of suicide were more often negative because of the belief that African Americans had a duty to their community and race to survive.[20] Therefore, some African Americans may have viewed Nelson's attempted suicide harshly. Still, self-inflicted violence indicates that some men struggled with the expectation that they demonstrate an idealized notion of manhood as soldiers.

Most African American soldiers viewed the U.S. Army as dishonorable for failing to pay soldiers. As a result, some men chose to leave the military, even without authorization. Many of the First Kansas Colored Infantry's soldiers deserted after failing to receive payment for their service; the presumed explanation was that the men felt that the federal government did not honor their military contracts.[21] Elsewhere, two Fifty-Fourth Massachusetts soldiers attempted to flee after the enlistment bounty promised by recruiters was not received.[22] Financial concerns weighed heavily on soldiers' minds, forcing them to decide whether to continue serving or return to civilian life.

Maybe the deserters examined here missed their families on the home front. U.S. Army officers and doctors recognized that soldiers became "nostalgic" for civilian life.[23] Such language, however, obscured the tragic circumstances that the war created for soldiers and their families. The proximity of warring armies, wide-scale devastation to localities, and continual threats to the safety of their kin led many men to desert.[24]

The choice to desert had tragic consequences for the men who were eventually caught and charged.[25] Some USCT soldiers found guilty of desertion by U.S. Army court-martials avoided execution with punishments of lost pay, jail time, and hard labor.[26] But such rulings were dependent on commanding officers' leniency, which was not always forthcoming. Sixth USCI colonel John A. Ames absolved desertion charges levied against Charles W. Taylor after Ames took pity on Taylor's ignorance of the penalties for leaving camp.[27] Simultaneously, executions of USCT soldiers occurred throughout the war as some officers hoped to reassert control over their insubordinate men. It was usually the responsibility of fellow USCT soldiers to witness and kill the offender(s), and these events were terrifying.[28] James Henry Gooding recalled the awkward interaction between spectators and a soldier on his death march after receiving a guilty verdict for desertion. "He seemed to look each man in the vast assembly in the eye with a vague and melancholy appeal for sympathy," Gooding reflected.[29] These events unquestionably scarred the psyches of the USCT soldiers who bore witness to them.

Military infractions also brought about economic consequences for the offender. George White, for undisclosed reasons, had his pay halved for a month while he was in jail.[30] Five enlisted men lost a combined thirty-one months of their pay for charges including embezzlement, disobedience of orders, and disrespect toward commanding officers. Most of the men lost six months' worth of wages for their infractions.[31] Hiram Waters received the lengthiest docking of pay—an entire year's earnings—along with a dishonorable discharge once his yearlong jail sentence ended for sleeping at his post.[32] In contrast, Samuel Derry was confined at the guardhouse for an undisclosed amount of time when he was found sleeping at his post.[33] One might speculate that the charges of violent acts and disrespect toward commanding officers might carry more severe penalties than falling asleep during sentry duty. However, U.S. Army officers viewed sleeping guards as an egregious and selfish act that jeopardized military operations and endangered the lives of the soldiers in camp. Ninety U.S. Army soldiers were sentenced to execution for sleeping at their posts. Waters and Derry were fortunate to be spared an order of execution for falling asleep.[34]

Perhaps these varied forms of military disobedience enacted by northern USCT soldiers represented another space for African American men to demonstrate their individuality while the U.S. Army attempted to enforce conformity. Simultaneously, collective forms of military disobedience by northern USCT soldiers complicated their hopes of becoming part of an imagined community, as they sought inclusion in the United States on their own terms.[35]

A War on Bodies and Minds

As African American men acculturated themselves to military life, they may have believed that their training with various weapons and hand-to-hand combat would lead to military engagements against Confederates.[36] However, USCT soldiers soon learned that their main purpose was to perform fatigue duty on the frontlines. The War Department and U.S. Army acted on racial stereotypes that cast African American men as inherently strong physically and therefore most suitable for digging ditches, building roads, burying dead bodies, erecting fortifications—thus saving white soldiers for frontline battles against the enemy. Some whites also claimed that if Confederate soldiers witnessed USCT regiments engaged in combat, many of the unspoken and informal courtesies of war, such as prisoner exchanges, would end.[37]

Nevertheless, some USCT soldiers felt that working as laborers with little chance to fight against the Confederate Army was demeaning and denied USCT men combat experience. Twentieth USCI soldier Nimrod Rawley expressed his frustrations to President Lincoln when he lamented, "Instead of the musket[,] It is the spad[e] and the Whe[e]l-barrow and the Axe[.]"[38] Rawley's unsolicited correspondence went unanswered, and there was no shift in military policy. In a letter to his mother, Andrew White informed her of his eagerness to fight. "I have not binn [*sic*] in a fight yet But [I] have binn [*sic*] on some hard Marches for a fight but the rebel was afraid to stand up," White wrote.[39] His proud tone reveals that he surmised his regiment's manhood was on full display while Confederates, in his opinion, demonstrated an unmanly evasion of armed combat. Maybe his family took pride in Andrew's self-defined bravery, but it also meant that their breadwinner desired to put his life at risk in service to his nation.

To many USCT soldiers, working solely as physical laborers and not as combatants was an affront to their manhood.[40] And they vocalized their displeasure. James Henry Gooding defiantly questioned his purpose as a soldier in a letter to President Lincoln. "Are we *Soldiers*, or are we LABOURERS," Gooding wondered.[41] Nimrod Rawley also informed President Lincoln that USCT regiments were eager and ready to fight. "Remember we are men standing in Readiness to face thous [*sic*] vile traitors an[d] Rebels who are trying to Bring your Peaceable homes to Destruction," Rawley stated.[42]

Other USCT soldiers offered a differing opinion that framed their assigned fatigue duty in a positive light. In an article submitted to the *Christian Recorder*, John C. Brock of the Forty-Third USCI argued that working as a laborer was an essential component of defending the country. "The boys shoulder their shovels and picks nearly every day, and out front to the trenches," Brock professed, "ready and willing to do everything in their power that will lead to the capture and overthrow of the rebel stronghold."[43] Brock's statement highlights that he believed some USCT soldiers found dignity in the performance of fatigue duty.

Most USCT soldiers labored for hours in harsh conditions that could be extremely dangerous.[44] The circumstances that led to men's injuries differed greatly, but the overall result was broadly debilitating, and their bodies were never the same. During construction of one military road, for example, a log snapped and struck James Burk (an Eighth USCI soldier), hitting him directly in the pelvis and causing a hernia.[45] Burk's duty may have helped the military's logistical plans, but the accident left him hobbled. Samuel Derry a Third USCI soldier, developed a rupture in his side and back while pulling a heavy cannon at Morris Island, South Carolina. The injury occurred after he was "struck either by a rope or stick that was used in pulling heavy ordnance up the beach[,] sticks were placed at intervals along the rope for men to take hold of to pull and one of the ropes broke."[46] Trench digging was another potentially treacherous task for soldiers. John Short a Sixth USCI soldier, suffered from sight issues while digging at Dutch Gap, Virginia, after the sun's reflection on white sand and red clay hit his eyes. Short's fellow soldiers scoffed at his complaints about his vision. Some men even referred to Short as "Red Eyed Ox."[47] John Burton recalled that the "majority of the men laughed at him and thought he was a fool."[48] Burton, however, took sympathy on Short and helped him as the regiment marched toward Deep Bottom, Virginia, but they separated when enemy fire broke out. Both men survived the conflict, but Short's eyes continued to fail him.

Laboring for the U.S Army led some soldiers to work with animals that transported men and materials, and even became food for starving men. Being alongside animals, such as horses and mules, created dangerous working conditions for both soldier and animal. Animals were sometimes cantankerous or spooked by sounds, which created life-threatening situations for enlisted men.[49] Jacob Purnell a Third USCI soldier, received a serious head injury when a mule kicked him on the right side of his cranium. Purnell survived the powerful, potentially fatal blow. Still, the accident left Purnell paralyzed on the entire left side of his body.[50]

Human error was at fault in the death of Joseph Perkins of the Third USCI. Friendly gunfire occurred throughout the war and claimed the lives of men in both armies. However, Perkins's death was the result of a gunpowder explosion while he was resting in camp. Fellow soldier John Cooper stated, "A spark from his camp, accidentally fell on powder from an ammunition cartridge which was stored in the house and the key exploded."[51]

Many soldiers wanted their courage and honor tested in battle rather than labor on fortifications and grave digging. Men visualized and sometimes fantasized that their military service would include battles.[52] Soldiers who desired to fight thought that having witnesses to their combat performances might illicit public validation of bravery. Men who were eager for such adulation affirm arguments previously made by historians that public perception among a man's peers was a crucial component to defining one's manhood, especially in the context of war.[53]

Eventually, some USCT soldiers were granted their long-awaited wish to harden themselves under fire. The Third USCI did so by participating in the sieges at Forts Wagner and Gregg in South Carolina, beginning in August 1863. By December 1863 the Sixth USCI joined in South Mills and Camden Court House in North Carolina. Meanwhile, the Eighth USCI waited until February 1864 to participate in an expedition that ended in Jacksonville, Florida. Throughout the war, the regiments examined here took part in at least nineteen officially recognized military confrontations against the Confederate Army.[54] Only eleven men (or nearly 6 percent) examined in this study died in combat.[55] For comparison, 2,751 of the 179,000 USCT soldiers (or 1.5 percent) died from combat wounds.[56] Thus, the combat-related deaths among men examined here were nearly four times higher than that of USCT regiments altogether. Even so, maybe some Americans interpreted these soldiers' deaths positively as a sacrifice for a higher cause.

USCT advocates praised the sacrifices of men who died for the nation's protection—and argued that their masculine heroism made them deserving of inclusion in the national community.[57] Death in military service took on a unique meaning throughout the war. Americans often told soldiers that they were serving, and potentially dying, for a higher purpose—gendered, religious, nationalist, even racial. For instance, the families of slain Indiana veterans viewed it as an honor to willingly risk their kin for the war.[58] Even if that were true, it still does not account for the long-term emotional and economic losses experienced by families who lost kin in the war. Some African Americans argued that dead USCT soldiers transformed the men into citizens because they gave their lives.[59] Literary scholar Allison M. Johnson asserts that for deceased USCT soldiers, "his symbolic death is integral to reconceiving the place of African Americans in the United States."[60] Her point aligns with the views of USCT supporters and Thomas B. Webster of the Forty-Third USCI, who thought that dead USCT soldiers were responsible for "a new dawn of equality" that soldiers paid for with their lives.[61] But idealizing the deaths of USCT soldiers ignored the fact that the men themselves did not reap the benefits of their sacrifices as their bodies lay sprawled across battlefields. As subsequent chapters will show, USCT families found little solace in these discussions of honor and equality.

Many Philadelphian USCT soldiers received wounds that left them with physical disabilities. Their injuries occurred primarily in Florida and Virginia, with the majority of the men incurring wounds at the Battle of Olustee and the Battle of Chaffin's Farm. When the Battle of

Olustee took place on February 20, 1864, U.S. forces of 5,500 soldiers experienced a 37 percent casualty rate in a conflict won by the Confederates.[62] The Battle of Olustee was one of the bloodiest military battles for USCT regiments.[63] Some of the men examined here received gunshot wounds that left damaging marks, sometimes severe. Ephraim Maloney of the Sixth USCI had two bullets pass through his right leg during an engagement at Church Hill, Virginia, on September 29, 1864. Regimental doctors feared Maloney's pierced tissue would become infected with bacteria, as the "left knee contract[ed] & great liability to ulceration."[64] Henry Thompson, an Eighth USCI soldier, fully recovered from an injury sustained at the Battle of Olustee.[65] Joseph Anderson, a Third USCI soldier, began experiencing hearing issues after heavy cannonading while stationed in Florida.[66] George Henderson of the Third USCI received a wound during the siege on Fort Wagner.[67] Two men of the Sixth USCI—Charles Brant and Hezekiah Wilson—both sustained significant injuries to their hands. A projectile tore off Brant's little finger while rendering his middle and ring fingers useless. Wilson lost his ring finger.[68]

Bullets could also disfigure one's face. Third USCI soldier Crawford Hardy lost partial sight in his right eye when a bullet fragment struck him.[69] George Roland of the Sixth USCI had a particularly horrific experience during the Battle of Chaffin's Farm after a bullet tore through his lower jaw and destroyed most of his teeth. Medical records stated that Roland had a significant physical deformity since the right side of his face was now smaller than the left.[70] The modernization of Civil War weaponry, in this case, the minié ball, caused an alarming amount of damage to bodies.[71] Men injured during the war were left with permanent and, in many cases, painful reminders of their time as soldiers, as the same war that bolstered their manhood also altered their bodies in unimaginable ways.

Heavy artillery shells tore through the flesh of five of the men examined here, scarring them forever. Shrapnel pierced and seared the bodies of men. Some of the cannon injuries were due to direct attacks from the enemy. Third USCI soldier George H. Buck had a shell fragment strike his brain at Fort Wagner's siege. Surgeons were unable to remove the foreign object, which remained lodged in Buck's head for the rest of his life.[72] The thunderous sounds from cannon explosions blasted the eardrums of soldiers. Cannon shells detonated at close range during an attack left Lorenzo George completely deaf in his left ear and partially deaf in his right ear. But George remained in service despite his hearing loss.[73] Fellow soldiers would relay information and orders to George by yelling into his "good" ear.[74] It must have been difficult for George to hide his hearing loss from his commanding officers. Perhaps his fellow soldiers chose to aid George because they wanted to help him continue to demonstrate his manhood as a soldier, even if it had potentially disastrous results for himself and others. Not all cannon-related injuries were due to an enemy attack, however. Of the Third USCI, James Hogan went completely deaf, ultimately leading to his military discharge, when an explosion occurred near him.[75] These and other men's lives were never the same as they traversed postwar life with physical and auditory disabilities.

When receiving medical attention, soldiers' lives were often predicated on the compassion and quality of care given by nurses and doctors.[76] Both doctors and nurses witnessed the horrific aftermath of military engagements. For instance, Susie King Taylor, a nurse in the Thirty-Third USCI, recalled injured soldiers writhing in agony "with their legs off, arm gone, foot off, and wounds of all kinds imaginable."[77] Military doctors and surgeons were not held in high regard by soldiers of any race due to their lack of sympathy and empathy toward their patients.[78] Doctors, such as E. W. B. Beck, often performed multiple surgeries in one day. Sometimes they had only minutes to decide whether to operate.[79] When surgeons decided to amputate a soldier's body part, they often used the "guillotine method." By implementing this sawing motion, they hoped to quicken the process and stave off any potential flesh-rotting infections.[80] The U.S. Army had a 26.33 percent mortality rate for its thirty thousand amputations.[81] None of the soldiers examined here died on the surgeon's table. Surviving the battlefield and the surgeon's tent presented wounded soldiers with a new reality and arguably complicated their claims to masculinity.

Only five of the soldiers investigated here had body parts removed, which usually led to a medical discharge.[82] Attempting to delineate which amputations were worse than others would be unfair. Every soldier who had an excision left the operation wondering how their physical reductions would affect their self-image. Jacob Thornton of the Third USCI had a leg amputation.[83] The remaining four amputations occurred in the Sixth USCI. William Butler had his right thighbone removed.[84] Though surgeries on the lower extremities had a fatality rate of 40.2 percent, Butler's surgeon and nurses skillfully performed the medical procedure, and he survived.[85] John Turner and George M. Shorter had upper-body surgeries. Turner's right finger was cut off, and surgeons amputated Shorter's entire left hand.[86]

Maybe it was a mistrust of surgeons that led Robert Johnson of the Sixth USCI to defiantly oppose the amputation of his right calf bone after the Battle of Fort Fisher in North Carolina. The regimental surgeon implored Johnson to allow the operation to proceed. Johnson refused outright.[87] One might also wonder if Johnson's reticence was from the fear that he would lose his manhood along with his amputated body part. If that were the case, then Johnson chose to have his body wholly intact and hobbled with pain rather than see himself as fragmented.

The removal of limbs, while lifesaving, forced soldiers to confront their idealized notions of manhood.[88] Some U.S. Army soldiers with amputations struggled over their role in the military as disabled men. After all, in many cases they entered service physically fit and left forever scarred from combat wounds and the resulting amputations. Meanwhile, it was not uncommon for newspapers and periodicals, such as *Harper's Weekly*, to publish illustrations conveying a soldiers' amputation as a sacrifice that "embodies his commitment to the Union cause."[89] Competing notions of manhood undoubtedly left men confused about how they and others saw themselves inside and outside of service.

Even though so many USCT soldiers spent time away from direct battle against Confederates, they were not assured of their safety from physical, psychological, or emotional harm. Furthermore, sometimes these injuries endured for the remainder of their lives. Thirty-one soldiers studied here incurred noncombat injuries during their service. Civil War pensions and military service records did not always detail the circumstances that led USCT soldiers to seek medical attention. More specifically, for many injuries in the records it cannot be determined whether they were combat or noncombat related. This lack of detail could jeopardize a soldier's eligibility for a pension.

While combat occupied a fraction of the average soldier's time in service, hard and lengthy marches were much more common. Every soldier and regiment suffered the same fate of sore muscles, bruised feet, and tired bodies.[90] William Brown, a Sixth USCI soldier, regularly grumbled to John Marshall about their lengthy movements. "He would often complain of marching and pain in his left side," Marshall recalled.[91] Perhaps the grueling demands of marching were to blame for some soldiers' crippling rheumatic pain throughout their lower extremities.[92] Suffering from rheumatic pain, which was incurable, became a common ailment, as doctors cataloged 287,000 cases by the war's end.[93]

During the war, many USCT soldiers became seriously ill. Bacterial infections and viruses spread across USCT regiments, causing numerous men to become sick and extracting them from the ranks. Military camps were breeding grounds for communicable diseases.[94] In the summer of 1865, William B. Johnston reported that fever had spread across nearly half of the regiment's soldiers in Jacksonville, Florida.[95] Bug infestations disseminated diseases that caused spikes in body temperature, skin irritations, and other physical maladies among soldiers.[96] Thomas C. King Sr. of the Third USCI developed a severe fever and ague during his time in Fort Clinch, Florida, where mosquitoes were prevalent.[97] Malnutrition, brought on by improper diets, may have been the one problem the U.S. Army could have remedied. However, an inadequate supply of nutritionally balanced meals for USCT soldiers, especially those stationed in Texas, led to vitamin deficiencies.[98]

Water contamination from blood, dirt, animal and human waste, and possibly dead bodies also caused internal problems. For some doctors, the primary concern was providing soldiers with accessible water, even if it was unclean, regardless of how it might damage soldiers' bodies.[99] Lorenzo George, already dealing with partial deafness, contracted diarrhea and piles (or hemorrhoids), most likely from drinking impure water. His illness was so severe that his compatriots recalled the bloody bowel movements that caused George great pain.[100] Samuel Derry, who previously suffered from a rupture of the side and back, later contracted piles at Morris Island, South Carolina.[101] John Thompson of the Third USCI also developed piles on top of his existing rheumatic pain.[102] Meanwhile, nearly half of the ten thousand soldiers stationed in Brazos, Texas, did not receive clean water.[103] Stacey Hemenway, a surgeon of the Forty-First USCI, estimated that 60 percent to 80 percent of the regiment suffered from scurvy in 1865 while stationed in Texas.[104]

Unclean drinking water became one of the most dangerous hazards for the men examined here. Unclean water slowly wrecked USCT soldiers' bodies from within in excruciatingly painful ways. Typhoid fever, dysentery, chronic diarrhea, and cholera morbus killed eight of the USCT soldiers examined here.[105] These illnesses left each dying soldier to writhe in agony, possibly leaving them to contemplate whether their sacrifices were worth the hellacious pain.

Many USCT soldiers battled the elements as they fought to survive.[106] Harsh weather did not racially discriminate. Previous scholarship asserts that USCT soldiers from northern cities, including Philadelphia, like their white counterparts, had weakened immune systems, making military service harder to bear as their bodies broke down.[107] Extended exposure to extreme hot and cold temperatures, dry and humid climates could cause permanent harm to men's bodies. Edward Brown contracted catarrh due to exposure to the southeast's dramatic weather changes. He lamented that the culprit was a "change of climates as we much exposed while we were moving as we were in several states in less than two months."[108]

All soldiers risked dying in service. Many men probably imagined that it might occur in a fight against Confederate enemies. The First Kansas Colored Infantry lost 6 percent of its soldiers in combat. The Forty-Third USCI had three officers and forty-eight enlisted men killed and mortally wounded in combat, while 188 enlisted men in the same regiment died from disease. Collectively, all USCT regiments lost only 1 percent of their men while fighting Confederates.[109] As previously noted, eleven soldiers examined here died in combat. Meanwhile, in this study sample, seventeen soldiers died from circumstances not related to combat while serving in the military.

Disease was the greatest killer of U.S. Army soldiers.[110] Dying from a camp disease was a prominent fear of Fifty-Fourth Massachusetts soldiers. James Henry Gooding wrote, "Daily we hear the muffled drum, accompanied by the shrill, shrieking tones of the fife, which tell us that the 'fell destroyer, Death,' is near."[111] The Sixtieth USCI lost 262 soldiers to various diseases.[112] And the Sixty-Second USCI, the Sixty-Fifth USCI, and the Sixty-Seventh USCI had 44 percent of their combined regiments die from different diseases throughout the war.[113] While records do not disclose information on the Third USCI's casualty rates, 264 soldiers from the Sixth USCI and the Eighth USCI died from disease.[114] USCT soldiers, unfortunately, learned that their demise was more likely to come from nonhuman causes than their southern enemy.

Airborne pathogens were responsible for killing Third USCI soldiers Joseph Watkins and Moses Schneck. Watkins succumbed to consumption, while Schneck died from chronic pleurisy.[115] Both were pulmonary diseases that filled the lungs with fluid, leading the sick to experience severe difficulty breathing.[116] Before the war, pulmonary disease was a relatively common medical issue in northern urban cities.[117] Perhaps hailing from Philadelphia was a factor in both Watkins's and Schneck's illnesses.

Prison deaths loomed dangerously for captured USCT soldiers and were classified as noncombatant deaths. More than 35 percent of African American prisoners died during their time in Confederate prisons.[118] Before USCT mobilization, both armies, on July 22, 1862, agreed to establish the Dix-Hill Cartel, a plan to release prisoners before ten days expired and encouraged the men not to fight until a fair exchange occurred. Unfortunately, once USCT regiments became a reality, the Confederacy refused to abide by the previous agreement, partly because Confederates viewed USCT soldiers as inferior to white soldiers.[119] Meanwhile, some white U.S. prisoners of war (POW) took the Confederate oath of allegiance and donned the enemy's uniform. Sometimes white U.S. POWs joined the Confederacy out of resentment that the U.S.'s war aim changed from reunification to emancipation.[120] Some Confederate POWs also would take an oath to the United States, sometimes to end their service and return to their families or start new ones after their imprisonment ended.[121] For other white POWs, some changed sides in the hopes of escaping or even out of a sense of resentment toward the northern home front, as some men believed civilians and the army forgot about them during their imprisonment.

However, prisoner exchanges were a white soldier's privilege.[122] The belief, North and South, that POWs might influence other inmates to swear allegiance and possibly fight for the enemy highlights another white privilege because African American prisoners did not have the same opportunity.[123] African American soldiers had no hope of ever being exchanged because the Confederate Army preferred to end the Dix-Hill Cartel rather than treat USCT and white prisoners equally. Initially, each side displayed mercy to surrendered or captured soldiers.[124] But once Abraham Lincoln's final Emancipation Proclamation was set to take effect, Confederate States of America president Jefferson Davis issued an 1862 policy instructing units to execute captured African American combatants for attempting to incite a rebellion among enslaved people.[125] Additionally, James Seddon, the Confederate secretary of war, made it clear that USCT soldiers who were freeborn were not, in his opinion, considered POWs. "They should not be treated as prisoners of war," Seddon stated, "but dealt with so as 'to mark our stern reprobation of the barbarous employment of such inciters to insurrection.'"[126] The Confederacy nullified the prisoner exchange policy after the organization of USCT regiments because, theoretically, it meant that USCT and white prisoners were equal.[127]

The actual treatment of African American POWs differed greatly—from civil to barbaric.[128] Forty freeborn men in the Fifty-Fourth Massachusetts eventually earned their freedom from jail in Charleston, South Carolina, after Confederate officials, including Jefferson Davis, debated internally about what to do with the soldiers.[129] After the Fort Pillow Massacre it became less likely that USCT soldiers would even become POWs.[130] Confederates executed three hundred USCT soldiers who were attempting to surrender there.

The atrocity at Fort Pillow highlights the fact that the Confederate Army refused to honor the Lieber Code, which was established to protect the rights, humanity, health, and safety of prisoners. Instead, some Confederates chose to use the "black flag" policy in which some Confederate soldiers refused to accept the surrender of African American soldiers.[131] John R. Eakin, the editor of the *Washington Telegraph* (an Arkansas newspaper), stated that treating captured USCT soldiers as POWs was not an option for Confederates. "It follows irresistibly that we cannot treat negroes taken in arms as prisoners of war," Eakin wrote, "without a destruction of the social system for which we contend."[132] Furthermore, he asserted that "we must be firm, uncompromising, and unfaltering. We must claim the full control of all negroes who may fall into our hands, to punish with death, or any other penalty, or remand to their owners."[133] Even so, James Robinson of the Eighth USCI survived his imprisonment, earned his release, and returned home safely to Philadelphia.[134]

Many prisoners were not so lucky and endured horrendous experiences that ultimately led to their deaths. At Andersonville, at least one hundred USCT detainees starved; died at the hands of fellow prisoners or their captors; or experienced physical, emotional, and psychological torment that left them scarred.[135] William Edwards, an Eighth USCI soldier, died at Andersonville from diarrhea; the most likely culprit of his demise was impure water.[136] Edwards was one of the thirteen thousand POWs to die at the infamous prison. Even though the U.S. Army enforced racial segregation in its regiments, dying at Andersonville led African American and white soldiers to be buried together.[137]

As a prisoner, Benjamin Davis's manhood was directly challenged by his captors. Confederates captured him after their engagement at Deep Bottom, Virginia, and decided to keep Davis and other USCT prisoners alive as laborers rather than kill them. Davis refused to perform the work. Maybe he felt that being forced to perform physical labor for the Confederacy was an affront to his manhood as a free man: he simply could not obey orders to do what enslaved people did for the Confederacy. Perhaps believing he would die anyway, Davis chose to demonstrate his manhood through an act of defiance. In the end, Confederates killed Davis as his fellow prisoners watched.[138]

The Pension System and African Americans

Civil War pensions became another space in which thousands of USCT veterans, their dependents, and their local community members publicly pushed for their inclusion in the nation. Moreover, the federal pensions gave them an official platform for demanding recognition for African American families as part of the American polity. The battles for inclusion were an assertion that not only were African American veterans heroes but their entire families deserved recognition for their sacrifices too.[139]

Military service–related federal pensions have a long history in the United States. Following an 1817 address that President James Monroe gave to Congress, the federal government began recognizing the economic problems soldiering created for formerly able-bodied men and their families, as many soldiers could no longer earn wages. In President Monroe's opinion, the nation had a financial obligation to provide for national heroes. He believed that disabled and destitute veterans deserved a pension.[140] In 1818 the Revolutionary War Pension Act became an official federal government policy, which essentially established a social welfare program for a specific subset of Revolutionary War veterans.[141] Even though the U.S. Congress intended the pension system to exist only for a short time and limited accessibility, the program continued long after and was expanded dramatically over time, well beyond its originators' intentions and an initial projected budget of $155,000.[142]

Once the Civil War began, the U.S. Congress wisely recognized that the war would create economic crises for a select group of men in the military. In 1861 the federal government awarded pensions for men if their physical disability occurred in the line of service. However, the

1861 pension law only made soldiers who enlisted before July 22, 1861, pension eligible.[143] The pension law also recognized that widows and children would suffer if their nuclear family member died in service. It stipulated legal widows and minor children could get a payment of $100 and a one-time disbursement of any outstanding money owed to the soldier.[144] With the passage of the 1861 policy, the federal government acknowledged that it would provide some economic restitution for veterans and their nuclear dependents if the physical ailment occurred in the military. By extending pension eligibility to legal widows and minors, the federal government sought to assume some responsibility for a financial provider's role in the absence of the men. But by permitting only legal spouses and minors to collect pensions, the federal government refused to acknowledge some Americans' preference for common-law unions. As the number of disabilities incurred in the U.S. Army increased, the federal government recognized that some soldiers were now incapable of resuming their pre-service employment as civilians.

In 1862 the federal government passed a new pension law that dramatically changed the pension system and potential accessibility to the pension rolls. For "invalids," the 1862 Pension Act made any man eligible who suffered a service-related physical disability, including both wounds and diseases, that impacted their wage-earning abilities as civilians. The U.S. Congress differentiated the payouts depending on the disability grading and rank of the injured. For instance, an officer could get thirty dollars per month for his disability, while enlisted men would earn eight dollars monthly.[145] The hierarchical payments for physical disabilities showed that the federal government valued officers more than enlisted men. By doing so, the federal government disregarded the fact that enlisted men performed the necessary and often dangerous work of war. Thus, there was little uniformity within the Civil War pension system.

Meanwhile, the 1862 law was greatly beneficial for some dependents of deceased U.S. military servicemen, provided that their deaths occurred during their time in the service. Legal widows and minor children qualified for a monthly pension with some conditions. Widows had to provide documentation substantiating their claim and would void their right to a pension should they ever remarry. Legal minors only received pensions until their sixteenth birthday. In the absence of a legal widow and minor, a biological mother or a sister under the age of sixteen could receive a monthly pension if they previously were financially dependent on the deceased soldier.[146] Similar to the 1861 policy, the 1862 law privileged nuclear dependents in legal unions. But unlike the 1861 pension law, the new one demonstrated the federal government's understanding of the financial loss suffered by mothers and sisters after a soldier's death. The expansion further encoded the idealized notion of masculinity as the men were assumed to be the breadwinners supporting the children and adult women connected to them.

Previous scholarship states that there was little public fanfare over passage of the act at the time.[147] This is plausible since attention was mostly on the war itself. However, even if people did not initially celebrate the policy, it would yield great benefits for the dependents of deceased veterans. For many families, the knowledge that the federal government enacted legislation geared toward subsidizing the lost wages of their deceased male kin undoubtedly had a profound impact. By placing dependents on the pension rolls, the federal government acknowledged the citizenship of those grieving the loss of men who died while performing a duty of citizenship.

Importantly for African Americans later, the 1862 law never made any race-based stipulations.[148] This allowed numerous Civil War veterans to have their service not only commemorated but acknowledged in national policy and memory.[149] Thus, even though USCT soldiers regularly experienced racism in service, the pension system, at least on paper, instituted a racially egalitarian policy.[150] Nevertheless, the pension system's expansion was not without its critics, however, as some civilians resented veterans who received these payments.[151]

An unnamed author lamented in the *Vincennes Weekly Western Sun* that less than two years after the war ended, some white northerners quickly forgot the sacrifices of U.S. veterans, especially the physically disabled. "Now that 'they have come to plague' these loyal, hypocritical rascals, the latter are very slow to make good [on] their professions of love. The soldier," the author stated, "is an elephant that they are terribly troubled what to do with."[152] While these feelings of apathy toward U.S. Army veterans were not universal, they highlight a wavering of support for soldiers, particularly after the war. Criticizing military service pensions traced back to the post–Revolutionary War era. In the early nineteenth century, some Americans openly derided the nation's first pension system because it, in their opinion, denigrated the virtue of service. In essence, early critics of the pension system felt that providing economic aid to physically disabled veterans made it seem as if men soldiered in the hopes of obtaining long-term social welfare afterward.[153] Therefore, pension system detractors refused to acknowledge the lingering hardships of soldiering while idolizing the idea of serving in the military.

Because civilians believed that some, or perhaps many, veterans made fraudulent claims, the Bureau of Pensions required an individual to provide extensive documentation to prove eligibility.[154] Invalid applicants had to provide honorable discharge papers and submit evidence to corroborate a veteran's claims that their disability was legitimate. Additionally, applicants needed claim agents and lawyers to gather information, record witness statements, and communicate with the Bureau of Pensions on behalf of their clients.[155] Assuming that a disabled applicant made it through the hurdles—they also had to get a medical examination administered by the Surgeon General's office (until 1889) to confirm the claimant's disabilities;[156] a final reviewer would inspect the application before approval.[157]

Sadly, many African American applicants experienced racial discrimination throughout the pension process. Pension agents, who were all white men, served as local representatives of the Bureau of Pensions. Their important position gave them the authority to assess applications and either recommend them for approval or rejection. Although the Bureau of Pensions had no official policy on a claimant's race, pension agents often considered African Americans, especially freedpeople, to be untrustworthy and inferior.[158] Similar issues arose for other pension applicants.[159]

Before 1866, eight veterans studied here applied for an invalid pension due to physical disabilities incurred during service. The potential pensioners submitted honorable discharge papers, acquired various witnesses to (possibly) corroborate claims, provided medical documentation, underwent a medical examination, and had their applications analyzed by reviewers. In 1865 all but one (Hezekiah Wilson) were approved for pensions due to various physical disabilities, including a facial deformity, an amputation, vision problems, and various gunshot wounds.[160] Due to unanticipated delays during the medical examination, Wilson did not receive official approval until 1866. The high percentage of invalid application approvals in this subset may have been due to their highly visible physical ailments and their location once discharged from the military.

Their approvals were part of the 35,880 pensions approved in 1865 for invalid former soldiers. While this number is impressive, it comprised only about 2 percent of the 1,830,000 living U.S. veterans.[161] The success of these men in securing a pension is not representative of the experiences of most other USCT veterans who learned that potential reviewer scrutiny made difficult their quest for economic aid and public recognition for their physical, psychological, emotional, and financial troubles.

By 1866 the monthly pay disbursements for the eight pensioners examined here varied from one to fifteen dollars. Henry Thompson got one dollar per month; James Crippen collected two dollars per month; Hezekiah Wilson, George Roland, Nathaniel Logan Sr., and Ephraim Maloney all received four dollars monthly; Six dollars per month went to John Short. Meanwhile, William Butler collected eight dollars per month in 1865, but it increased to fifteen dollars per month the following year. The apparent difference in pay disbursements varied due to U.S. Congressional pension laws, first in 1862 and then in 1864, which graded pensions for invalids due to the applicant's rank and the medical examiner's rating of the severity of the ailment(s). The 1862 pension law stated that "totally disabled" veterans, who were incapable of working manual labor jobs, would receive eight dollars per month. By 1864 the pay rate increased to twenty dollars each month.[162]

Butler's higher pension payouts suggest that his medical examiner believed that his right thighbone amputation—while retaining the rest of his leg—prevented him from performing any manual labor. He later became a domestic servant, in 1870, meaning Butler's disability may have been less than total.[163] How Butler could demonstrate a near "total disability" to a medical examiner and later work a physically demanding job remains unknown. Nevertheless, he accomplished both. A gunshot wound created a severe facial deformity for George Roland, leading to his military discharge. He could neither perform manual labor nor properly masticate for the remainder of his life.[164] Despite this life-long disability, his pension payout never equaled Butler's full wage-earning capacity. Ultimately, Butler's and Roland's pension experiences suggest that officials viewed leg amputation more severely than a deformed jaw.

While Butler's pension was the highest of the first wave of invalid pensions, it did not mean that he amassed a sizeable amount of money. After 1866 Butler had an annual pension of $180. If Butler had returned to work as a teamster (his pre-service occupation), then he would have potentially earned three times that amount by 1870.[165] To be clear, pensions, from the federal government's perspective, were meant to supplement a pensioner's income.[166] However, such a rationale seemed to ignore the reality of those who were "totally disabled" and therefore most likely had no other means of acquiring money. Regardless of their inadequacy, all disabled veterans and their dependents considered pensions essential—and they were even more critical for economically disadvantaged racial minorities.

With William Butler's high pension for a right leg amputation, one might assume that fellow veterans, Robert Johnson and Jacob Thornton, who also had right leg amputations, would be granted the same pension rate as Butler. However, neither veteran did, and there is no apparent reason for the difference. Former officer George A. Armes, testifying about Thornton's qualities as a soldier before his injury, perhaps influenced pension agents, helping Thornton receive a high pension payment. Armes lamented that in "parting with him[,] I los[t] the best man in my command."[167] Armes later added that even after Thornton received a severe leg injury that later led to his amputation, he was calm and collected in combat. In Armes's opinion, Thornton displayed "bravery, cool behavior and prompt action [he] was a good and encouraging example to his comrades."[168] Even if Armes's character appraisal was not a factor, it is evident that the reviewers had some latitude, which did not bode well for some applicants.

In the end, USCT soldiers discovered that the idealism of soldiering often did not match the reality. Enlisted men went months without receiving money, struggled with lengthy separations from family, loathed performing fatigue duty, incurred various wounds, and sometimes died in service. Thus, "seeing the elephant" was more grueling and life threatening than perhaps some men envisioned. Moreover, this is only the view from the battlefield. Life on the home front proved no less difficult for the families they left behind.

CHAPTER FOUR

Familial Hardships during the Civil War

Northern African American families continued struggling to make ends meet while fighting against various forms of racial discrimination. The soldiers' military service had lasting, and in some cases permanent, damaging effects on their family members' lives. Even so, some family members, especially African American women, made their way to military camps, supporting the war while attempting to remain physically and emotionally close to their male relatives. As the regiments trained and later headed to the frontlines, African American Philadelphian families witnessed the war pull families apart, sometimes in dramatic ways.

African American Communities and Military Camps

The departures of recruits to the war immediately created emotional and financial problems for families. The men may have enlisted to demonstrate aspects of African American manhood, emancipate enslaved people, and prove that African American men were capable of acquiring full and equal citizenship rights. Nevertheless, their departure left their families to adjust to new living situations in the absence of the men who had contributed financially and had provided various forms of support against racial discrimination.

Some of the women in these families responded by visiting their men at Camp William Penn whenever possible. Curious women living near Camp William Penn toured the encampments out of a desire to tangibly connect with the war. Other African American women, such as Mary Craig, began working for the U.S. Army as washerwomen for enlisted men after arriving in a camp.[1] Many African American women who traveled to USCT camps were not merely gawkers; they were either women in relationships with or related to USCT soldiers.[2]

Camp William Penn often had numerous African American women on its grounds to see their loved ones in training. Due to the high frequency of camp visitations, Lieutenant Colonel Louis F. Wagner barred civilians "between the hours 10:30 and 11:30 a.m. and 3:30 and 4 p.m."[3] Perhaps Wagner chose those specific times because regiments at Camp William Penn often had guards mounting in the morning and the drill battalion where the soldiers focused on training.[4] The mothers of Sixth USCI soldiers Peter Marsh and John Dilton came to the grounds to reconnect with and support their sons. Rachel Dilton was eager to spend time with her son before his regiment's departure.[5] Lydia Marsh moved into a hotel near the military grounds to be near Peter.[6]

U.S. Army wives of all races made themselves visible on military grounds.[7] Some undoubtedly wanted to remind their husbands that they loved them. Others may have come seeking to find ways to keep their families together as the men trained for war.[8]

Visits to military camps also extended African American women's long-standing fight against racial discrimination in northern society. By continually visiting Camp William Penn, African American women positioned their bodies in public spaces in ways that reshaped their sense of self and how they were perceived by others. Before USCT mobilization, many white Americans championed white women who sacrificed their families by sending their sons to war.[9] With USCT regiments organizing, African American women illustrated that they, too, sacrificed their sons for the nation. Therefore, visiting military camps empowered African American women to show that concern for loved ones was something that transcended race.

Nevertheless, whites refused to acknowledge northern African American women's attempts to demonstrate their womanhood positively. Thomas B. Webster, the head of the Supervisory Committee, imagined that most African American women at Camp William Penn were "'harlots' whose behavior was 'blasphemous and obscene.'"[10] It was true that prostitutes were visible in both armies during the war.[11] However, Webster's broad and derogatory categorization of African American Philadelphian women meant that only white women, including the wives of white USCT officers, were deemed capable of respectability and patriotism through their prominence at military camps.[12]

Getting to and from military camp was no easy task for northern African Americans. Many of them relied on public transportation, which then became a battle site with whites over race, gender, civil rights, and humanity. Some northern whites saw free African Americans as threats to white domination when they exercised freedom of mobility in white spaces. The confinement within public physical spaces heightened insecurities among whites who feared they might—and occasionally they did—have intimate experiences, even "illicit glances," that threatened the racialized and gendered status quo.[13] Long before the Civil War, various northern public transit outfits implemented racially discriminatory policies against African Americans. In 1838 Boston established the first form of Jim Crow segregation on a railcar.[14] By the mid-1850s Philadelphian and New York City passenger cars could legally deny transit to African Americans. In 1861 a Philadelphian judge stated that it was legal for local transit companies to discriminate against African Americans because they were, in his opinion, racially inferior. Racially discriminatory policies toward African Americans, unfortunately, persisted even after USCT mobilization.[15]

However, northern public transportation also provided African Americans with new ways of challenging this social oppression. Public transit became "moving theaters" where battles over race, gender, and class prejudices played out every day.[16] In some instances, northern African Americans fought back against racism on various forms of public transportation.

The open defiance shown by northern African Americans had consequences for their safety. Physical assaults occurred in numerous northern cities.[17] White conductors and passengers exercised their legalized racism, often using physical violence and verbal intimidation, against African Americans well after northern USCT regiments trained. Nevertheless, African American women continued using public transportation to travel to military camps to be near their male kin.[18] Doing so placed countless African Americans, especially women, into potentially violent encounters with angry whites. Still, African American women consciously used their bodies on public transportation to challenge established racial and gendered hierarchies as USCT regiments trained.[19] As a result, they enacted civil rights demonstrations, in this case sit-ins, to demand racial equality.[20] In Philadelphia, African American women filed multiple lawsuits against local streetcar companies for their discriminatory policies and sought racial egalitarianism in public transit.

Even though none of the mothers, wives, and other women connected to the soldiers examined here brought civil suits, they defied the denigration of their humanity, race, and gender every time they used public transportation.

U.S Army enlistment was not always a joyous occasion for a family. Before enlisting in the Sixth USCI, Benjamin Davis left his pregnant common-law wife, Mary Leighton (later Williamson), to enroll in the Fifty-Fourth Massachusetts. But he incurred a staph infection on his journey and did not join. When the Sixth USCI began mustering in recruits, Davis enlisted. Leighton recalled that Davis wanted her to give up guardianship of their newborn son, Jerome, to the child's grandparents in town.[21] As an adult, Jerome later testified that he heard a rumor that his father believed his mother was unfit to raise their son. "I have heard the folks say," Jerome testified, "that my father thought my mother was too young to bring me up, or that she might not bring me up right."[22] Nevertheless, his wife's actions later helped their son secure a dependent's pension. Not long after traveling to Camp William Penn, she gave up her son to her in-laws. The mother and son never interacted again. Jerome lamented, "My mother has had nothing to do with me, as far back as I can remember, and she says she never has since she left me with my grandparents."[23] Perhaps Mary chose to stay away due to either personal shame or resentment toward others for not providing for Jerome monetarily.[24] It is also possible that she had a complicated relationship with her in-laws that made maintaining a bond with her son difficult. In the end, the Sixth USCI had Benjamin Davis in its ranks. Meanwhile, the Davis family broke apart. While the Davis family is only one case, they illustrate how the fragmentation of an African American family could be worsened by USCT mobilization.

Leaving Home for the United States

Once the mobilization of USCT regiments occurred in Philadelphia, numerous African American families adjusted to their new reality as military families and the constant fear over each other's safety that entailed.[25] Until the soldiers returned, families struggled daily to survive.

From the moment that U.S. Army recruiters came to northern cities and towns, families had plenty to dread. The Brown family learned that Lee Othello Brown made the decision for himself, but it did not make the news any easier for his kin. In May 1864 he ran away from his home in Baltimore, Maryland. He then changed his name to Solomon Wilson and joined the Thirty-First USCI in New York. Wilson's father, three sisters, and brother were wholly dependent on his civilian wages as a farmer. After his enlistment, they received no money from their male kin. Nearly four months after joining, Wilson died in Petersburg, Virginia, about 170 miles away from his family.[26] Maybe Wilson left his family to demonstrate his manhood and establish his independence. If that were the case, one might surmise that the nation and soldiering were more important to Wilson than his family's economic survival.[27]

Unexpectedly, military service presented families with a universal experience of grieving.[28] Emilie Davis recalled her aunt Mary being concerned that her uncle Alfred was a possible draftee. "Mary is quite worried. I hope he will not have to go," Davis wrote.[29] Meanwhile, Benjamin Davis visited his aunt, Amelia Jannis, once his enlistment became official. "He came to my house . . . and bid me good bye," Jannis remembered, "and said he was going out to the camp at Chelton Hill."[30] Maybe Davis sought out his aunt because he believed death was possible and wanted a final moment with her.

Suffering was not entirely a woman's domain, however.[31] Children also agonized over the separation from their fathers, USCT soldiers' fathers eagerly waited for their son's (hopefully) safe return, and extended kin and members of the soldier's local community clamored for news of the departed soldiers.[32] USCT soldiers had many individuals desperately waiting for news about their return home.[33]

Familial Wartime Struggles

After Confederate general Robert E. Lee's surrender, on April 9, 1865, American civilians began celebrating as news broke that many white U.S. regiments were done serving. Unfortunately, many African American families learned that their male kin were not leaving the U.S. Army.[34] Delayed demobilization of many USCT regiments only exacerbated an already difficult situation for enlisted men and their families. Some U.S. Army officials rationalized the expedited demobilization of white soldiers because they had fulfilled their national obligation after a lengthy service, which possibly began in 1861 or 1862.[35] U.S Army general Philip Henry Sheridan claimed that few USCT soldiers wanted to leave the military because they enjoyed more rights as soldiers than they would as civilians.[36] Such logic, however, failed to acknowledge that some USCT soldiers desperately wanted to resume their civilian lives.[37]

As white U.S. Army regiments demobilized, Confederate POWs began to be released. No longer held by their U.S. Army captors, Confederate POWs began reconnecting with family and friends and returning to civilian life.[38] By granting these now ex-Confederates their freedom, the U.S. Army demonstrated its new focus on reconstructing the South by showing mercy to the Confederate soldiers who fought to destroy the United States. Ironically, many USCT regiments were not permitted to leave the military and return home.[39]

The reasons many USCT soldiers called for an end to their military service differed. Formerly enslaved USCT soldiers worried about the safety of their families living in locations where the protection of their freedom was often dependent on U.S. Army soldiers and the federal government stopping ex-Confederates from attempting to reassert authority.[40] Others questioned whether the U.S. Army would protect their families now residing in refugee camps built by the military, sometimes hastily and with limited resources, in order to give freedpeople a space to live outside of bondage.[41] Some soldiers found serving as the occupying force in the former Confederacy extremely difficult because former rebels refused to follow USCT soldiers' orders. While stationed in Olustee, Florida, in June 1865, William B. Johnston of the Third USCI lamented: "The rebs here seem to die very hard at the idea of having black troops to guard them."[42] USCT soldiers also had to contend with often tragic news of their families in financial trouble at home.[43] In short, because of racially discriminatory military policies, many USCT soldiers were unable to reunite with their families, both freed and freeborn, and offer them support and protection in their unending fight against racial discrimination.

African American families did not sit idly by waiting for their men to return. Instead, they used letters to express their discontent with being separated and their eagerness for the men to return. Etta Waters wrote a letter to her unnamed husband, a soldier in a New York USCT regiment, informing him that his sick son missed his father. "Oh Husey I have sad news for you[,]" Waters wrote, "little Fay is vary sick[.] . . . [He has a] feaver and vometed and bowel complaint. . . . Oh how I wish you could be hear Fay wants you to get a fourloug[h] and come home."[44] Correspondences from African American women also reached prominent political figures. Lucy Bailey pleaded with Secretary of War Edwin Stanton on May 11, 1865, for information about whether her husband, John Bailey of the 100th USCI, was alive. If he was, then she wanted him to be with her. Bailey wrote, "I wish you please grant him afourlough [*sic*] to come home[.] He was promised one when he went away and he has been gone over ayear [*sic*] and I do wish you would be so kind as to let him come home if he is alive."[45] Little did she know, John deserted from his regiment on July 18, 1864.[46] Collectively, these women, similar to many others, used letters to demonstrate their refusal to conform to assigned gender roles where women were expected to patiently support men and resist the temptation to disrupt military morale or question the U.S. Army.[47]

In both armies and among all races, furloughs appealed to soldiers and their families by offering a reprieve from extended separations.[48] Acquiring time off, however, was not easy. Furloughs were usually granted at the discretion of the soldier's commanding officer.[49] Throughout the war, soldiers learned that furloughs went to a select group of men.[50] Some soldiers left the frontlines due to injuries and illnesses.[51] Some of these detached members became part of the Invalid Corps, which allowed them to heal among other reserves. Unfortunately, the Invalid Corps did not permit injured USCT soldiers into their ranks.[52] Marital status was also a determining factor in whether some men could obtain a furlough.

The majority of the men examined here were not granted permission to return home. In total, only nine men in this study sample obtained a furlough. Three of those men were married. For some commanding officers, military necessities outweighed familial concerns, thereby limiting the number of furloughs awarded. By witholding furloughs, U.S. Army officers kept soldiers from visiting home, even if only briefly, to resume their gendered responsibilities to their dependents in person.

All three married men who received furloughs—John W. Jackson, James Ellsbury, and William Brown—were Sixth USCI soldiers. Garnering the admiration of their commanding officer helped these men obtain leave. Regimental Adjutant William R. Hammond wrote on behalf of the three men as he sought to provide them with a respite from their service. In his letter, written after Robert E. Lee's surrender, Hammond stated that family reunions and honorably performing their military duties made the men, in his view, eligible for a furlough. On May 8, 1865, Hammond penned, "I have the honor to request a furlough for (30) days be granted to Sergeant Major John W. Jackson . . . to visit his home and family in Philadelphia, Pennsylvania."[53] Then, on June 20, 1865, Hammond desired to have Brown "visit his family in [the] State of Pennsylvania."[54] On the same day, Ellsbury received approval for his absence after Hammond expressed, "In my opinion[,] he well merits the furlough applied for."[55] Even though Hammond never explicitly mentioned Ellsbury's family, his wife, Catherine, most likely welcomed his homecoming to assist in comforting her, since nearly one year prior their two-year-old son had died.[56]

Hammond's sympathy toward some of the men's families highlights how one officer took pity on enlisted men and the military's hardships endured by the soldiers and their kin. Perhaps Hammond used his authority to temporarily free some USCT soldiers from their restrictive military experiences. Still, many soldiers discovered that the U.S. Army was simply indifferent to their familial struggles back home.[57] As a result, many African American men could not reconnect with their families immediately after the war.

The Emotions and Finances of Grieving

News of a male relative's death only compounded the hardship and fear that northern African Americans experienced throughout the war.[58] Families dealt with the war's adversities, especially when they received an update about a deceased male relative. As a result, the war changed the makeup of northern African American households.

Throughout wartime mobilization, families had been told that they must convince men to answer the nation's call to arms. When advocates of enlistment acknowledged death as a possibility, it was generally to emphasize the men's heroism and sacrifice. For some northern USCT regiments, prominent white men directly told soldiers that their deaths would forever change how white northerners viewed African American manhood. During the Sixth USCI's flag presentation in September 1863, Lieutenant Colonel Louis F. Wagner informed onlookers, white and African American, that the regiment's flag was a symbol of state and national inclusion and the elevation of African American manhood. Wagner proclaimed, "The soldiers to whom this flag is committed will be found true as they were true. They will follow it to victory, or, falling, they will fall only when the flag falls with them."[59] Meanwhile, Union League Club of New York president John Jay took a slightly different view during the Twenty-Sixth USCI parade in March 1864. Jay claimed that dead USCT soldiers would become honored champions of the U.S. cause. He stated, "If you fall, as fall you may, your memories will be fondly cherished with those of the noble-hearted, who have died for their country."[60] While these words would have been undeniably powerful for USCT soldiers to hear, they provided minimal comfort for African American families when death in the war became a reality.

After the departure of USCT regiments, African American men attempted, in private correspondence and public letters to northern newspapers, to assure their readers that dying would serve a greater purpose—and that USCT soldiers were prepared for death. Thomas Morris Chester, a correspondent for the *Philadelphia Press*, asserted this view after learning that Confederates would kill USCT soldiers rather than continue prisoner exchanges.[61] "The colored troops have cheerfully accepted the conditions of the Confederate Government, that between no quarter is to be shown," he wrote.[62] Chester's assertion most likely gave minimal relief to the families of slain prisoners. For Third USCI soldier Henry S. Harmon, dying allowed African American men to demonstrate how grief was a racially egalitarian experience on the home front. "When you hear of a white family that has lost father, husband or brother[,]" he stated, "you can say of the colored man[,] we too have born our share of the burden."[63] Isiah H. Welch of the Fifty-Fifth Massachusetts advised northern African American families that their willingness to shoulder the war's sorrows would benefit all African Americans hoping to be recognized as part of the national community. "I would say for the encouragement of wives, mothers, and beloved ones to grieve not if you hear of the fall of those whom you cherish; bear in mind they fall not in cause disgraced, but honorable and just," Welch stated.[64] Furthermore, he informed parents, "if it takes you your favorite son, let him go and fight and die, if need be, for his race and country."[65]

News confirming soldiers' deaths was universally troubling for Americans. Newspapers became the most common forum for disseminating information about dead soldiers to wide audiences. Wartime correspondents reported on soldiers dying beyond the battlefield, in military camps and regimental hospitals.[66] Families and communities feared seeing their loved ones' names listed among the casualties and missing. For others, notifications to USCT soldiers' families came by telegraph lines, thanks to technological advances.[67] Word of mouth about deceased soldiers sometimes came from other soldiers upon their return.

For those on the home front, hearing the tragic news was like being hit by "invisible bullets" as they processed the reality of losing a loved one.[68] Some individuals never recovered from their unseen "wounds."[69]

Letters became another, and usually more personal, way to inform a family of the heartbreaking news. When John Dilton of the Sixth USCI wrote his mother, Rachel, he told her that two Sixth USCI soldiers—John Bryant and Benjamin Davis—had died. Rachel then relayed John's communication to the kin of the deceased men.[70] Rachel's decision to update the other mothers shows that these three families were in relationship, making it permissible and perhaps imperative for her to disclose the sad news. It also meant that that mourning, at least in cases such as these, became a communal affair for some USCT families.

On occasion, fellow soldiers assumed the responsibility of writing directly to families about a comrade's death. For instance, Third USCI soldier Alfred Rothwell relayed his final words through fellow serviceman Thomas R. Rockhold to Elizabeth Rothwell. Rockhold, writing on behalf of the now-deceased Rothwell, notified Elizabeth that Alfred had said, "Goodbye dear wife. Please don't grieve for me, I died in a good cause."[71] Perchance Elizabeth took comfort in the fact that Alfred saw his death as necessary to reshape American society. Either way, she was now a war widow raising three children by herself.[72]

Alfred Rothwell's final words, through Rockhold, reinforce the notion of the "good death" for a dying soldier (excluding those executed for desertion) as a way for a grieving family to find comfort or even a deeper understanding of the soldier's passing. The term "good death" refers to an unofficial script that, for the family, details the particulars of a soldier's death, including the last words, in order to provide kin with some solace upon hearing the tragic news.[73] Whether it was on the battlefield, in military camps, hospitals, or Confederate prisons, each soldier's final departure could earn him praise on the home front.[74] Therefore, good deaths privileged a select group of soldiers during the war.

Correspondence detailing a "good death" usually followed an unofficial script that sought relief for bereaved family members desperate for information. The letters often stated the date and time of death, the soldier's willingness to accept his destiny, and his final words.[75] Thomas R. Rockhold's letter to Elizabeth Rothwell follows this script, which aimed to give the Rothwell family some closure by detailing the circumstances of Rothwell's death. Good death rhetoric sought to provide some emotional consolation for grieving families. Simultaneously, good death messages honored the manhood of dead USCT soldiers and helped their contribution as citizens to be recognized by their families and possibly the nation.[76]

Deaths on the frontlines brought the Civil War to the home front.[77] In many cases, the sudden restructuring of families emotionally devastated surviving kin. Relatives soon learned that, according to cultural practice, family members were expected to mourn dead soldiers for specific lengths of time, depending on their connection to him. For example, a soldier's mother and his children were expected to grieve for about a year. On the other hand, the "appropriate" mourning period for a widow was one and a half to two years.[78]

African American families did not always have the same opportunities to publicly weep over their dead kin in the same way that many white families did. Some white families grieved by participating in public organizations that honored the soldier's sacrifices. Others adorned clothing that publicly exemplified their mourning and loyalty to the departed.[79] Many African Americans did not have the luxury of participating in this "Cult of Mourning," most likely due to financial constraints and limited public remembrances for deceased USCT soldiers during the war.[80]

In addition to grieving over the death of a soldier, some families began requesting economic relief, in the form of dependent pensions, from the U.S. government. Some USCT families chose to apply for a Civil War dependent's pension out of financial necessity. Perhaps others sought a pension as a way of insisting that the federal government recognize the lasting impact of Civil War military service on their families. Their collective effort to receive compensation for the loss of their male kin, as later chapters show, illustrates their desire to maintain a relationship with the federal government after military service.

As previously mentioned, the 1862 pension law's expansion of pension eligibility to some of a deceased veteran's dependents profoundly impacted many Americans of all races. Unlike the 1861 pension policy, the 1862 law authorized a monthly payout to legal widows and minors. Widows could not remarry if they wanted to remain a pensioner. In the absence of a widow and minor children, the U.S. Congress authorized pensioning either a biological mother or minor sister.[81] Because race was never explicitly specified in the 1862 law or later modifications of it, nonwhites qualified for pensions.

The 1862 law constricted accessibility to the pension rolls as well.

More specifically, the federal pension law removed Confederates, their sympathizers, and their dependents, who were on the pension rolls for previous international wars, including the Mexican-American War.[82] Their removal should not be surprising since Confederates committed treason when they seceded from the Union, therefore negating any claims to a federal pension. By removing Confederates from the pension rolls, the United States rewarded pension-eligible African Americans for their present loyalty and punished now disloyal whites by ignoring their past sacrifices.

Twenty-eight men (or 15 percent) of this study's sample died in service, including from combat wounds.[83] For comparison, 20 percent of the white soldiers from Deerfield, Massachusetts, never returned home.[84] Both cases illustrate that local communities felt the effects of the war in tragic ways. Northern African American families understood that it was necessary to channel their sorrow into the quest for economic restitution for lives lost.

One consequence of military service was that it created war widows. The wives of the five soldiers in legal marriages generally had the easiest pathway to getting a pension. From 1863 to 1865, all but one (Mary E. Griggs) applied for and received a widow's pension of eight dollars per month. Applicants, including Charlotte Streets, supplied copies of their marriage licenses.[85] When documents were unavailable, witness testimony, preferably from the officiant, sufficed. By providing this evidence, legally wed widows were able to receive money from the federal government.

The wives in common-law marriages were automatically deemed ineligible to receive a pension. The Bureau of Pensions believed that a legal marriage could impose domesticity on wives and enforced white Christian ideals of civility on African Americans, men, and women alike.[86] Couples who, for differing reasons, preferred common-law marriages could not become pensioners. The U.S. Congress eventually revised the pension law in 1864 to make common-law wives in states where enslaved people could not legally wed provide testimony from at least two witnesses to become pension eligible. However, in states where marriage was legal for African Americans, "the usual evidence shall be required."[87] The 1864 pension law referred to formerly enslaved couples in southern states where bondsmen and bondswomen could not legally wed. By making freedwomen pension eligible, the U.S. Congress sought to provide economic assistance to some destitute people.[88] Unfortunately, northern African American women in common-law marriages from states like Pennsylvania still did not qualify. Therefore, the federal government was more likely to accept common-law marriages from former slave states than from free states.

Maintaining a widow's pension was extremely difficult for women of all races. The federal government mandated that widows could never remarry if they wanted to continue on the pension rolls. The Bureau of Pensions claimed that remarried widows immediately became dependents of their new spouses and therefore were disqualified.[89] From a racialized standpoint, the Bureau of Pensions thus sought to make African American women conform to white societal notions of patriarchy.[90] At the same time, it is plausible that this policy effectively incentivized common-law marriages for a subsequent relationship. By viewing wives only as dependents to their husbands, the Bureau of Pensions imposed gender notions by requiring widows to remain reliant on their deceased spouses to survive financially.[91]

Minor children of deceased USCT veterans could also apply for a pension.[92] Only one child from a legal marriage, Ella Irene Deets, received a minor's pension in this sample. Like many other children, she received two dollars per month until she was sixteen years old. Records provide no rationale about why eight other children from legal marriages never had applications filed on their behalf. One might speculate that their mothers were unaware that their children qualified. However, Charlotte Streets, Elizabeth Rothwell, and Martha Ann Jackson all had widow's pensions. None of the women worked full-time wage-earning jobs, and Charlotte Streets and Elizabeth Rothwell each had three minors. These mothers could have undoubtedly used the two dollars per month that each child was eligible to receive, but the women did not apply.

Children from common-law marriages could get a pension, but the process was difficult.[93] Pension agents, who were often white men, made judgments about some northern African American families because of the marital practices of the minor's parents. In Jerome Davis's case, the pension agent only approved the application after multiple witnesses testified that Benjamin had publicly claimed his son.[94] Since Mary Leighton (later Williamson) gave up guardianship of Jerome due to financial hardships, his grandparents managed his monthly pension until he was sixteen years old.[95]

Deceased soldiers' mothers sought pensions as well. During the war, three mothers of soldiers examined here applied for a pension. To receive a pension, a mother had to demonstrate her economic dependency on her dead son before, during, or after his service.[96] The cases of mothers receiving pensions after their veteran sons died highlight the fact that some dependent pensions were not predicated on the son dying while in service. The mothers of George Henderson, Alexander Robinson, and Andrew White all emphasized their previous dependency when applying. Before their deaths, all of the men were the primary wage earners in their households, and this continued during the war—though some of these soldiering sons were unsuccessful in sending money home. Jane Robinson stated that after Alexander "went in the [U.S.] army he never sent his mother any money as he never received any."[97] Ultimately, the opportunity never came for Robinson, which left his mother, who was already poverty stricken, in an even worse situation after his death. Meanwhile, Sarah Reeves testified that she had become financially dependent on her local community's charity to survive. Reeves testified, "After my son's death and for many years, a great portion of my support was contributions by the kindness of neighbors and without which I would have become a charge on the public."[98] Wealthy Gross, Henderson's mother, successfully received a pension after demonstrating economic dependence on her son while he lived.[99] Dead sons had a profound financial impact on mothers who had previously heard calls to sacrifice their children.[100] In the end, the women had their applications approved, and they each received eight dollars per month in pensions.

When the Bureau of Pensions approved a dependent's pension, the federal government became a key contributor to each household. Still, each payment was a reminder of how the war contributed to lasting financial insecurity. At the same time, pension approvals demonstrated to surviving kin that the federal government had not forgotten their wartime sacrifices. Upon receiving a dependent's pension, family members had to persevere with money rather than with the help of their male kin. Financial disbursements, while valuable economic contributions, served as a constant reminder of the men's absence.

The pension process never occurred privately. Lawyers, pension agents, medical examiners, witnesses, claimants, members of a local community, and state and federal government officials all took part in the process. Therefore, every approved application meant that a USCT family member received financial compensation for their wartime sacrifices. Furthermore, the federal government illustrated to these pensioners that white amnesia toward USCT service did not necessarily occur within the Bureau of Pensions. In doing so, African American pensioners became part of the public discourse about memorializing dead soldiers.

By supporting their family members in service, African American women challenged discrimination based on race, gender, and humanity while traveling to and from military grounds. Not all USCT soldiers' families supported their decision to enlist, as kin expressed fears that their relatives could die in service and their household would have difficulty making ends meet without a crucial wage earner. The U.S. Army's decision to delay demobilization of USCT regiments furthered the financial and emotional hardships endured by soldiers' families. For the dependents of USCT veterans, Civil War pensions became an important way for African American families to demand economic restitution for their deceased relative and request that the federal government document how the war impacted their lives. Unfortunately, their family strain persisted into the Reconstruction era.

CHAPTER FIVE

Reconstructing the Northern African American Family

The Reconstruction era is rightly considered a defining moment in American history, filled with dramatic, contested elements, including the liberation of enslaved people and fundamental change in American politics, economics, as well as racial and gender ideologies. The federal government focused most of its attention southward as it sought to reintegrate ex-Confederate states back into the United States, but not before forcing its defeated foe to acknowledge the new status and rights of formerly enslaved people and submit to the authority of the U.S. government. Meanwhile, the United States turned its attention westward to resume its objective of forcefully removing Indigenous peoples from their lands in the name of nation building. In short, the national priority was reunification and national expansion.

Previous Reconstruction-era scholarship has focused largely on the hardships of formerly enslaved families in the South who sought to reform or create households in freedom.[1] However, turning the focus northward presents a starkly different and important story of African American life after the Civil War. Freeborn Philadelphian USCT veterans and their families fought every day to stay intact, just as they had during the war, against various forms of racial discrimination.

As America evolved rapidly following the war, northern USCT veterans and their families faced reunification challenges as they sought to reestablish some semblance of stability within their homes. For some USCT veterans, their occupational status was improved because they could now reenlist in the military. For veterans who did not reenlist and their kin, some experienced economic stagnation or deterioration, ultimately creating many problems for their families.

The Reconstruction era is an important historical marker often used to highlight dramatic changes to American society. For African Americans, the transition from enslavement to freedom is a vital story that usually dominates the historical narrative. Conversely, freeborn northern African Americans were focused on the desire to attain full equality, but their battles do not garner equal attention.

Numerous USCT veterans dealt with employment problems, primarily due to occupational racial discrimination, which limited the types of jobs available to African American men. In some ways the postwar period narrowed African Americans' choices. Many USCT veterans did not see any improvement in their occupational status in comparison to their pre-service jobs.[2] Others suffered from wartime disabilities that kept them from regularly working. Unfortunately, both employed and underemployed USCT veterans discovered that their pay was almost always lower than that of white men working the same jobs, which further hindered any expectations of establishing economic stability for themselves or their families. Meanwhile, some disabled and unemployed USCT veterans turned to state almshouses and various branches of the National Home for Disabled Volunteer Soldiers (NHDVS) for assistance.[3]

The kin of surviving veterans not only witnessed firsthand the various postwar problems of their male relatives, but they also suffered. Some USCT veterans dealt with various emotional, psychological, and mental issues, which led to physical abuse of the people close to them. Additionally, some family members, including women and parents of veterans, assumed responsibilities either as the primary or secondary full-time wage earner in their homes. Their financial contributions, both big and small, were essential to the survival of their families.

From 1866 to 1877 USCT veterans and their kin also discovered that it was extremely challenging, if not impossible, to acquire a pension, partly due to limited legislation. The immediate postwar period marks a transition in the pension process after the U.S. Congress passed two federal policies that made applying for and receiving a pension more accessible for veterans and some of their dependents. Becoming an invalid pensioner was difficult since the federal government stipulated that a veteran's inability to perform remunerative labor had to be a direct result of his military service. Thus, veterans who did not have documented cases of suffering from wartime injuries or disease were ineligible, and the receipt of a pension could not possibly have figured into their hopes for economic solvency.

To make matters worse, racial discrimination and a highly bureaucratic application process prevented or deterred pension-eligible USCT veterans and their kin from applying. Some people discovered that their financial challenges made it nearly impossible for them to afford lawyer fees, travel for interviews with Bureau of Pensions officials, or locate records and witnesses.

Successful receipt of a pension still did not assure the pensioner's financial prosperity, especially if she or he had others who were dependent on the monthly payments. Pension rejections and approvals financially impacted Philadelphian USCT families. It also created conversations over whether their wartime sacrifices and postwar struggles would be recognized by the federal government during a period when white society minimized the role played by African American military servicemen. Moreover, many white Americans and ex-Confederates began interpreting the significance and meaning of the Civil War in ways that excluded USCT soldiers' role, the impact of the war on their kin, and the importance of emancipation to the war.[4]

Regardless of how anyone viewed their military service, veterans needed work. Soldiers wanted to return home to their families and resume earning wages outside of the military.[5] Between September and December 1865, all three regiments examined here received the order to demobilize.[6] As the demobilization of African American and white regiments occurred, many civilians voiced their concerns about reintegrating U.S. soldiers back into civilian society.[7] After all, more than one million soldiers were coming home with no guarantees of an improved life or any chance of establishing economic stability. In the opinion of the American public, one of the most pressing needs was finding jobs for demobilized veterans, both white and African American. Civilian uneasiness toward unemployed veterans stemmed from the fear that veterans would become financial drains on both the state and federal governments. Furthermore, some civilians believed veterans might prefer living off social welfare rather than becoming financially independent men.[8] This questioning of U.S. Army veterans' work ethic meant that some civilians had little sympathy for veterans' wartime sacrifices and potential postwar struggles.

Northern newspapers recognized that there was a growing employment crisis for recently demobilized veterans.[9] On June 16, 1865, the *New York Times* notified locals that "thousands of discharged soldiers are now in this city seeking employment."[10] Veterans needed to find jobs for their families' survival. Meanwhile, the *Weekly Anglo-African* used its prominent position among northern African Americans to advocate for USCT veterans. On May 17, 1865, an anonymous author proclaimed, "Let our doors and heart[s] be open to receive [them]. . . . Above all let us not forget to have doors [open] for them to enter into any employment or business they may desire."[11] In the author's opinion, employers had a responsibility to hire USCT veterans. Perhaps the author rationalized veteran preference in hiring because civilian businessmen continued operations, and in some cases profited from the war, as soldiers sacrificed their lives in service. By privileging employment opportunities for USCT veterans, the author of the *Weekly Anglo-African* article, possibly unknowingly, jeopardized chances for civilians finding work, especially if they were in direct competition with veterans.

Northern industrialists, manufacturers, and railroad companies had indeed benefited from the wartime mobilization of industry.[12] The Frankford Arsenal, located in Philadelphia, saw its operations, employee numbers, and munitions productions flourish thanks to its contract with the Ordnance Department of the U.S. Army.[13] For instance, the arsenal hired over one thousand workers during the war.

Wage earning accomplished an important goal for veterans: it allowed them to provide for (or at least contribute to) their families.[14] USCT veterans were not alone in their desire to find work. A collection of 250 unemployed white veterans marched through downtown New York City on August 11, 1865, calling upon local officials and businesses to provide employment assistance. Veterans displayed a banner that spoke to their financial crisis, which impacted their families; their perceived masculine identity as the breadwinner; and how they saw themselves as part of the American citizenry: "GIVE US EMPLOYMENT TO SUPPORT OUR FAMILIES," the banner stated, "Our last employers were Grant, Sherman, Sheridan, Meade, Hancock, and Hooker[.] WE ARE NOW THE SOLDIER CITIZENS."[15] Their banner reveals that the veterans believed postwar employment was a critical element in recognizing their status as "soldier citizens." This public event sought to have civilians recognize that veterans wanted to work rather than become dependent upon social welfare or be public adulation recipients. Even though the USCT men examined here were not part of this event, it is highly plausible that they would have agreed with their white compatriots.

Experiencing a decline in one's occupation status was not a universal experience for all USCT veterans. Some USCT veterans saw an improvement, sometimes dramatically, in the types of positions that they held. Five of the men were laborers prior to the war. Afterward they worked either semiskilled or skilled occupations, including working as a porter, barber, domestic servant, and farm laborer.[16] Other veterans successfully transitioned from having semiskilled jobs to becoming skilled workers. Before the war, James Ellsbury was a waiter, Samuel Crawford was a servant, and Francis Fausett was a tradesman. Later, Ellsbury became a shoemaker, Crawford was a barber, and brickmaking became Fausett's profession.[17] Perhaps some of these veterans learned new skills in the army, including reading and writing, which could prepare them for different postservice careers.[18]

Henry S. Harmon arguably had one of the most impressive postwar employment and political careers after the Civil War, not only for the men examined here but perhaps among USCT veterans in general. Rather than returning to Philadelphia, he remained in Gainesville, Florida, after the Third USCI demobilized. Perhaps he wanted to avoid returning to work as a sailor and found jobs in county and state politics more appealing. Throughout the Reconstruction era, Harmon worked various professional occupations, including working as an Alachua County registrar and clerk of court; serving in the House of Representatives for Florida at the state level; and practicing law as the first African American to pass the bar in Florida.[19] His impressive postwar employment career was in part due to his political networking and intelligence. Additionally, Harmon benefitted from residing in a state where the Reconstruction Acts of 1867 empowered African Americans with new civil and political rights. Since the Reconstruction Acts of 1867 focused on ex-Confederate states, African Americans living in Philadelphia did not have the same layers of protection for their rights (civil or political). Even though Harmon was an anomaly compared to other men examined here, his example shows that possibly any USCT veteran could significantly improve his employment opportunities, even if it was outside of his native city.

Across the country, some USCT veterans, including Philadelphian

USCT veterans, found employment in skilled occupations.[20] However, their experiences were not representative of the postwar lives of the rest of their comrades. For example, most of the Seventy-Ninth USCI, the Fourteenth United States Colored Heavy Artillery, the Thirty-Fifth USCI, the Thirty-Sixth USCI, the Thirty-Seventh USCI, and the Twenty-Ninth USCI veterans continued working as laborers and farmers.[21] Some veterans in the regiments studied here continued working as unskilled laborers due to whites' racial discrimination. The veterans who found skilled occupations were the exceptions.[22]

African American Philadelphians had expected their service to make a significant difference in their postwar lives. As historian W. E. B. Du Bois argued, African American Philadelphians believed that their wartime participation and patriotism would end societal racism. "After the war and emancipation great hopes were intertwined by the Negroes for rapid advancement," Du Bois wrote, "and nowhere did they seem better founded than in Philadelphia."[23] Maybe African American Philadelphians thought that their invaluable contributions during a national crisis might change whites' views.

Occupational racism remained prevalent across the reunified nation.[24] Many African Americans in northern cities earned low wages working unskilled jobs.[25] For instance, 47 percent of African Americans in Harrisburg, Pennsylvania, were laborers in 1870.[26] Some northern African Americans lost employment opportunities when in direct competition with Irish Americans. To make matters worse, the rise of labor organizations supported occupational racial segregation to protect white workers.[27] Thus, northern African Americans lived in locations where racism remained pervasive, and whites continually worked to hinder African American families' economic stability.

Civilian life seemed little better for African American Philadelphians during these postwar years. Fourteen USCT veterans, of those who could find work, saw no change in their employment status during the Reconstruction era. Eight of the men returned to their pre-service unskilled and semiskilled work. Henry Thompson, Solomon Flemmer, Henry Johnson, and George Roland's continuance as laborers was not surprising since white Philadelphians used racial discrimination, such as barring African Americans from employment, to ensure white superiority and economic dominance.[28] Being a Philadelphian laborer did provide an advantage in the summers for some African Americans who traveled to the Jersey Shore, where they successfully demanded and received better wages.[29] Perhaps some of the veterans examined here, who worked as laborers, took advantage of this employment opportunity. Meanwhile, Samuel Brown, Thomas C. King Sr., Robert G. Parker, and Wesley Maloney resumed their semiskilled employment as a fisherman, farm laborer, waiter, and driver, respectively. Three other men—George H. Buck, Isaac Becket Jr., and William Henry—changed occupations but continued working semiskilled professions, including as ferryman, stevedore, and teamster.[30] Unfortunately, semiskilled African American workers often earned three to four dollars less per month than their white counterparts.[31]

Other men continued working their pre-service skilled occupations after the war. Seven Philadelphian USCT veterans were barbers. Their numbers were not unique since they compromised a significant group of financially stable and sometimes affluent African Americans. Nevertheless, potential white clients often insisted that African American barbers practice racial segregation among their customers by not serving African American clients. If the barbers hoped to maintain business with whites, then these skilled African American men had to discriminate against those of their own race for economic stability.[32] At least three hundred barbershops with countless employees were operating in Philadelphia in the late nineteenth century.[33] Most likely, many African American barbers did not own their barbershops and instead rented space. Perhaps the USCT veterans who worked as barbers were thankful that the war had not taken away their ability to have highly skilled occupations.[34]

Edward Davis, meanwhile, worked as a sailor. His decision to remain a civilian sailor was crucial to his family's financial well-being. After returning home, Davis briefly attempted to work as a horseman, but he found himself back on a whaling ship working for Captain Edward Kelly and going on whaling expeditions to the Arctic Ocean.[35] Maybe Davis went back to working at sea because it was one of the few racially integrated workspaces. For instance, it was not uncommon for white and African American men to earn the same wages as whalers.[36] Arretta Davis, Edward's wife, recalled that he wrote her from Portland, Oregon, noting his sailing experiences and his capacity to earn money. Arretta testified, "Capt. Kelly offered him grand wages. . . . He provided well for me and treated me 'beautifully.'"[37] His duties aboard the ship determined how much Davis could make. For example, an experienced seaman could earn nearly $300 or higher annually if the crew had a profitable yield.[38] Her comments about Edward's earnings meant that he was somehow able to earn decent wages during a period when rising costs in petroleum oil, a declining number of employees, and treacherous work led to a decline in the whaling industry.[39]

However, delayed payments, possibly due to financial mismanagement from Captain Kelly or a slow whaling season, angered Edward Davis to the point that he contemplated quitting his profession altogether. "I am giving one [more] season of six months in the Ar[c]tic [Ocean] and when I get back to San Francisco I think I will give up whaling and return home and go somew[h]ere that I can earn some money. . . . I think I can earn more money on shore than I can sailoring," Davis wrote.[40] In the end, even African Americans working semiskilled occupations struggled to establish economic stability even if their circumstances differed. Moreover, their economic struggles reverberated to their families.

Davis's work frequently took him away from his wife for lengthy periods. Charles H. Lee, a family friend, confirmed his long absences. "He would be away 1, 3, or 4 years at a time," Lee stated.[41] For Davis, the extended separation began to weigh on him as he agonized over not seeing or being near his wife. "I am dreaming about you," he wrote, "and not only then but when I am awake I am thinking about you. And I wish I was with you again for I am get[t]ing sick [and] tyred [*sic*] of whaling."[42] Davis was undoubtedly angry about the infrequency of his payouts, either due to financial mismanagement by Captain Kelly or limited whaling opportunities. His letter also implies that living apart influenced his thoughts on whether he should change occupations because his physical and emotional desires began to outweigh the job's benefits. Additionally, Davis's letter denotes that he most likely had a companionate marriage, a relationship where both partners openly showed mutual affections.[43]

Sadly, Davis would not survive his final excursion in the Arctic Ocean; he went missing while at sea. Back in Philadelphia, rumors began swirling over what may have happened to him. Some people, including Sarah Jane Hayes (his sister), suspected foul play since Davis had recently written his mother stating that he would be home soon.[44] James Jackson, a friend, believed that Captain Kelly was the perpetrator after hearing some uncorroborated stories. Jackson testified, "Captain Kelly told John, Edward's brother, that he left him on an island in the sea and that was the last he ever heard of him."[45] Captain Kelly might have abandoned Davis in a desolate area since Davis vocalized his displeasure with his employer. "I want to tell you that a man on shore is a tyrant at sea. . . . He gives us 10 hours liberty on a barrow rock if he went from Heave[n] to Hell. He could not find a worse place," Davis bemoaned.[46] Captain Kelly did little to quell any suspicions or ingratiate himself to Arretta, who desperately sought answers about her husband's whereabouts. When asked, Captain Kelly stated to Arretta that he "would give no satisfaction."[47] In the end, no one ever discovered what happened to Edward Davis, and his family suffered emotionally and financially.

Some USCT veterans, similar to many other African Americans, experienced a decline in their occupational status, including being unemployed.[48] At least twenty-two Philadelphian USCT veterans experienced either under- or unemployment following the Civil War.[49] Isaac D. Henderson and William Smallwood no longer worked their skilled jobs as umbrella maker and barber. Formerly semiskilled workers, such as Joseph Green, Samuel Derry, Jacob Purnell, James Richmond, William Woodson, and Charles Brown, never resumed their pre-service occupations. All of these men previously worked as either laborers, domestic servants, waiters, or porters. Throughout the postwar era, white U.S. veterans could be more selective in choosing their employment opportunities, as race never limited their work.[50] USCT veterans, unfortunately, were among the many victims of workplace racism that created economic crises for many African American families.

On at least one occasion, the *Christian Recorder* displayed a lack of sympathy for the economic disparity between skilled workers and unskilled laborers. In 1873 the paper printed a one-sentence declarative statement deriding wage-earning parity. "To have the pay of the laborer, equal the pay of the artisan, would be to undermine civilization itself," the article stated.[51] The author's callous tone ignored the fact that countless African American men with skills, including USCT and regular army veterans, were laborers. Furthermore, claiming that the very fabric of "civilization" would crumble meant that the author cared little, if at all, for the families of laborers, who desperately needed the money the men acquired. Ultimately, the article highlights that even a prominent northern African American press failed to recognize employment hardships driven by racism for African American laborers.

Some northerners also believed that laborers made more than they deserved. As Philadelphia and other northern cities saw their industries and manufacturers flourish, there was a clear need for workers.[52] In 1865 Sidney George Fisher, a wealthy white Philadelphian, claimed that white laborers were abounding with high wages and limitless opportunities. "The demand for labor is so great that it injures the laborers by rendering them independent, indifferent, & careless. . . . This cause is acting on the whole laboring class throughout the country," Fisher wrote, "& its effects are constant demands for high wages & less work."[53] Perhaps Fisher's assertion held for some whites, including Irish Americans, but meanwhile, many African Americans remained unemployed or underemployed.[54]

Not all instances of underemployment were the result of racism. Some Philadelphian USCT veterans could not return to their skilled pre-service employment because of physical disabilities incurred in service. For instance, Hezekiah Wilson suffered a gunshot wound and subsequently had his pinky finger amputated. He lost movement in two fingers on his right hand, making it nearly impossible to perform skilled work, so he became a laborer.[55] Other veterans, such as Joseph Anderson, Henry Harley, George Roland, Ephraim Maloney, Samuel Derry, Charles Tobias, and Hiram Waters, struggled to find work throughout the Reconstruction era due to their military-related disabilities. For instance, Tobias, who formerly worked as a shoemaker, suffered greatly from a rupture that plagued him for the remainder of his life.[56] Derry suffered from piles, which kept him from regularly working.[57] Sadly for these and many other veterans, their brief tenure in the U.S. Army caused long-term economic consequences for the previously able-bodied men. Upon returning to their civilian lives, amputees who depended on their physical labor for wages experienced dramatic changes to their conception of their manhood. Unfortunately for Civil War veterans, the federal government did not establish work programs to reintegrate disabled men into the workforce.[58]

Whether USCT veterans' injuries resulted from combat or performing fatigue duty, men such as James Crippen, Edward Brown, John Short, George Henderson, John Thompson, and George Stiles all remained unemployed. Vertigo and frequent headaches plagued Crippen, which made continuing as a laborer nearly impossible.[59] For Stiles, a ruptured pelvis, brought on after a cannonball struck him, created lifelong physical pain as he had a "great deal of pain in his *privates*."[60] Stiles's disabilities also hindered his ability to work. A medical examiner noted, "He is incapacitated from performing manual labor."[61]

Friends, who were also USCT veterans, verified that war-related physical ailments were the direct cause of some USCT veterans' unemployment. Third USCI veterans Joseph Preston and William Summers enlisted and served together in the same company as their friend Edward Brown and testified that he suffered from catarrh (or excessive mucus in the nose or mouth), which gave him "misery in his head."[62] Brown confirmed that he also had chronic diphtheria, which, with catarrh, made working unlikely.[63] Edward Purnell Jr. emphasized that John Thompsons's family also suffered financially due to John rheumatism and piles. Purnell testified, "He is not able to do any manual labor enough to support himself and family[.] He is a sick man at the present time and not being able to earn money to buy medicine."[64] Charles H. Freemen and Henry Anderson were both Third USCI veterans who knew Samuel Derry prior, during, and after their military service. Both veterans stated that piles routinely prevented Derry from working after the war.[65] Sixth USCI veteran William Ingraham reported that he served with John Short, who suffered from vision issues that impeded his ability to acquire a job. Ingraham recalled, "He is not able to work hard or to do much on the account of his eyes."[66]

The war took a physical and financial toll on USCT veterans. Their bodies, already ravaged by their military service, never recovered from their time as soldiers. The hardships of the Civil War ultimately created lasting and damaging effects on their bodies and their finances as they struggled, and sometimes failed, to reestablish their work and income. Perhaps these USCT veterans believed that they could not live up to the late nineteenth-century masculine ideal of being self-reliant, independent men.[67]

Some USCT veterans believed that staying in the military was their best option for steady employment after the war. After the issuance of the Army Reorganization Act of 1866, which created new racially segregated infantry, cavalry, and artillery regiments, the U.S. Army employed thousands of African Americans.[68] The federal government refocused its attention on westward expansion, including building transcontinental railroads, extrapolating gold from western territories, protecting the "rights" of homesteaders, and creating new states from newly formed territories.[69] Doing so meant that the military officials used African American men to remove various Native American tribes from their lands directly. In short, the regular army needed African Americans.[70] As a result, African American soldiers were integral to the United States' national expansion objectives despite persistent racism in the military.[71]

Perhaps the regular army's regulated pay motivated some USCT veterans to serve. From 1864 to 1902, African American soldiers earned thirteen dollars per month (which now equaled white soldiers' pay), meaning their yearly salary was $156.[72] Therefore, since the Civil War, African American soldiers made less than unskilled day laborers, who, on average, earned $300 annually.[73] However, unlike unskilled laborers, African American soldiers also received food, housing, uniforms, and even access to education, which were unquantifiable benefits, in exchange for their service and sometimes their lives. Limited civilian employment opportunities possibly influenced some African Americans to enlist in peacetime. Perhaps other men developed a comradery or even familial bonds with fellow service members that influenced their desire to serve. One stark difference between enlisting in the regular army and USCT regiments was that the former did not provide bounties for recruits. Thus, there was no immediate financial compensation for African American soldiers serving after 1865, which undoubtedly affected their households. Perhaps what mattered more to African American soldiers was the knowledge that they would have consistent employment, whereas their civilian counterparts struggled to find steady work.[74]

Enlistment of African Americans into the regular army was slow, however.[75] Since African American men were not flocking to enroll, the regular army depended heavily on USCT veterans to join.[76] Included among reenlisting USCT veterans were Jacob Thornton, Charles Penn, Lorenzo George, and Francis Hawkins (all of whom served in the Third USCI). Because of the great need to fill the rank and file positions, doctors performed cursory medical examinations on these potential recruits.[77] During a medical examination that required Lorenzo George to strip naked, the medical doctors, either in a rush or due to incompetence, failed to diagnose his gunshot wound that caused a hip disability. Perhaps more alarming, examiners did not disqualify him from reenlisting, even though George was completely deaf in his left ear and partially deaf in his right ear.[78] However, a doctor discovered that George still suffered from piles, but after a discussion, and possibly a plea with the doctor, George returned to the military. "The surgeon who examined me said I had the piles but I told him [that] I wanted to go and he passed me," George testified.[79] George never expounded on what pressed him back to soldiering.

The reintroduction to military service quickly reminded USCT veterans that little had changed for the rank and file. Performing physically grueling work in locations with dry weather, limited access to clean water, and unbalanced food diets led to a rise in diseases that paralleled numerous USCT soldiers' hardships.[80] While serving in the Tenth U.S. Cavalry, Francis Hawkins suffered from gastrointestinal issues due to drinking impure water. When Alexander W. Brown, his comrade, inquired what was wrong with Hawkins, he tapped his stomach. "I don't feel well here," Hawkins declared.[81] John H. Little, another Tenth U.S. Cavalry soldier, stated that limited access to water and "a rough army diet" kept Hawkins from regularly performing his military duties.[82] Hawkins's medical problems suggest that the regular army remained inept at providing nutritional food and clean water to soldiers willing to sacrifice their lives for the nation.

The return to military service sometimes ended in desertion when African American men were not content. From 1867 to 1877, African American soldier desertions in the regular army serving along the Mexican border ranged from 935 (in 1867) to 1,112 (in 1877), with a peak of 1,871 (in 1870).[83] Desertions were, in some ways, similar to labor strikes. USCT soldiers were essential workers for the U.S. Army, and the regular army depended on African American men to serve during peacetime.[84] Deserters directly challenged oppressive and racially discriminatory conditions and thus sought to reclaim ownership over their individuality. By deserting, African American soldiers asserted their right to quit—a fundamental right that free labor ideology promised workers. For African Americans, however, desertion also had other negative implications. Absconding from military service would ultimately lead some people to question a soldier's patriotism and manhood.

Desertion remained a problem for the regular army throughout the late nineteenth and early twentieth centuries. White men left the ranks more often than African Americans, however.[85] For example, in 1910 the desertion rate of African American soldiers was one-third that of their white comrades in arms.[86] Thus, race was a factor in whether soldiers fulfilled their citizenship duties and demonstrated their manhood as soldiers or whether they deserted.

African American soldiers, such as Lorenzo George, still left the regular army regardless of the potential consequences. George had not deserted during his time in the Third USCI, but he abandoned his post–Civil War regiment. In 1868, after only being in the Fortieth USCI for a year, he left the ranks in Raleigh, North Carolina. Perhaps George departed from Raleigh because he became a target of ex-Confederate violence for his role in protecting freedpeople, which threatened their notions of white superiority. Alternatively, maybe he simply wanted to get out of the military.[87] George soon returned to Philadelphia and resided with his parents while working at his father's lumberyard.[88] He later fled from Philadelphia to Kingston, Canada, for a year before returning home. George gave no information on what led to his desertion or flight from the United States. Regardless, it was clear that the initial zeal that brought him back to the military quickly dissipated for George.

On October 10, 1873, President Ulysses S. Grant issued a proclamation pardoning any deserter who returned to the army to finish out their contract, and Lorenzo George rejoined the regular army that same year.[89] Grant's proclamation shows that the regular army continued struggling to fill its regiments with soldiers, and that desertion amnesty became a tactic for rectifying the matter. As a result Lorenzo George reenlisted, but he enrolled under the alias William L. Green for unknown reasons.[90] Later, the military discovered that Lorenzo George and 721 other soldiers used false names.[91]

George's third stint in the military did not include an act of desertion; he remained in the ranks until he received an honorable discharge at Fort Clinch, Florida, on November 30, 1874.[92] He somehow continued performing his duties even though he had aural problems and a hip injury. However, piles plagued him, and it sent him to the hospital toward the end of his term. During his hospitalization, George openly contemplated whether he should return to civilian life rather than remain in the military. Maybe the physical toll of regular army life, coupled with low wages and the permanence of racial discrimination, influenced his debate. His commanding officer sought to dissuade George from leaving. "I told the Captain that I was unfit for duty and [that I] wanted to come home," George professed, "but he persuaded me to reenlist and remain in the service."[93] Multiple disabilities, weariness of soldiering, a desire to be home, and maybe the hope of reconnecting with kin did not matter to George's captain. What mattered more was keeping a disabled veteran with over six years of military experience in the regular army.

Some soldiers, like Lorenzo George, repeatedly deserted, even though they knew the potential consequences. His fourth term lasted about two months, and he deserted for a second time in April 1876.[94] In doing so, George performed a second labor strike to demonstrate his dissatisfaction with his federal employer. It is plausible to believe that his collective disabilities and low wages necessitated a change. His actions also show that desertion forgiveness did not hinder a repeat offense. In 1883 authorities eventually found and arrested George in Chicago, Illinois, where he worked as a cook.[95]

Familial Formation and Troubles

Postwar life and its various hardships did not dissuade USCT veterans from finding partners and establishing new relationships. During the Reconstruction era, twenty-six of the veterans in this study married. Twelve of those relationships were common-law unions where the couples, for undisclosed reasons, chose this less formal bond. One explanation is the fact that it was common practice in this era for African American women to establish independence by rejecting legal marriages and the related notion that a woman must submit to a man.[96] Edward Davis and Charity Gilmore's common-law union ended once she began seeing another man.[97] What led their relationship to disintegrate is unknown, but it does demonstrate that women like Gilmore exercised their choice about whether to stay in relationships or not.[98] At the same time, four of the common-law marriages involving USCT veterans yielded seven children—three daughters and four sons. As later sections will detail, these families would face long-term economic consequences because of their choice to forego a legal wedding.

In the case of Henry Thompson, his wartime disabilities hindered him from marrying. Before serving, the able-bodied Thompson worked as a laborer and began a relationship with an unnamed woman. According to Mary Taylor, a friend of Thompson's, the two planned to wed after he got his military discharge. Upon Thompson's return home, his partner soon discovered that he had noticeable rheumatic pain in his knees that made finding work difficult. As a result, the unnamed woman refused to wed Thompson because his crippling physical disability would make it, in her opinion, harder for him to provide for her financially.[99] Hearing the news must have devastated Thompson, especially since he incurred the physical ailment by risking himself for the nation and protecting formerly enslaved people.[100] Unfortunately for Thompson, his former partner valued the man as a breadwinner over the man as a soldier.

In Philadelphia, prominent African American figures orchestrated a church marriage campaign in the hopes of convincing couples to publicly demonstrate that they conformed to social conventions of marriage. Fifteen legal marriages for the USCT veterans in this sample occurred inside various Presbyterian, AME, and Baptist churches in Pennsylvania, New York, New Jersey, and Virginia. Meanwhile, Richard John and Malinda Orr were the only couple to legally marry outside of the church during this period.[101] For the couples who married in churches, their collective decision reveals the communal significance of African American churches at the time. Maybe their preference for a church marriage had to do with their involvement in the church itself.[102] It is also feasible that the politics of respectability influenced their wedding locations. For instance, the *Christian Recorder*, a newspaper connected to the African Methodist Episcopal Church, often published marriage notifications for its readers.[103] Religious leaders believed that marrying within the church meant that couples would conform to conventional standards of respectability for several reasons. First, religious leaders and some community members celebrated each couple for "proving" that African Americans could adhere to white standards, which were used to judge African Americans. Second, each marriage recognized the feminine religious piety of African American women. Third, it "legitimized" the spouses and any of their progeny in the eyes of elite African Americans (and the federal government). Finally, church marriages reinforced the social ideals of masculine piety and domination over one's kin.[104] At least in the Reconstruction era, the church marriage campaign was effective among numerous USCT veterans and their partners.

A legal marriage did not necessarily assure spousal fidelity, however. Some legal marriage advocates recognized that both individuals had to display genuine affection for each other. The *Christian Recorder* published an article urging spouses to be more passionate and caring to each other. "Married people should treat each other like lovers all their lives then they would be happy. Bickering and quarreling would soon break off love affairs; consequently," the article stated, "lovers indulge in such, only to a very limited extent."[105]

The author's advice did not seem to resonate with Robert G. Parker and Emeline Murray, who wed on January 18, 1869, at an unnamed Philadelphian Methodist church. The Parkers eventually separated due to Robert's infidelity, but the couple never filed for a divorce. Four years later, in September 1874, Parker legally wed Mary M. Parker at St. Mary's AME Church. However, marital discord soon materialized once Robert again failed to remain faithful, causing the couple to separate. Mary M. Parker stated that she knew about Robert's unfaithfulness. "I do know, as a matter of fact that he run around with other women a great deal," Parker testified, "and that was the cause of our separation more than anything else. He went after other women all the time."[106] Robert's brother, and fellow Third USCI veteran, William H. Parker knew full well his brother's philandering ways. "I can tell you as a matter of fact that my brother used to go with many women. Whether he was ever married to any woman but this claimant I have no means of knowing. I do know however," William H. Parker noted, "that he was pretty fast after women."[107] Marriages, including legal ones, did not stop problematic relationships from forming among the veterans and their families. While marriage advocates would have celebrated legalized church unions, they undoubtedly disapproved of the instances of infidelity.

Marital problems were not exclusive to legally wed couples. The common-law marriage of Wilson and Margaret Day was volatile due to his violent outbursts and mood swings caused by a mental illness that he evinced even before his Civil War service (though it is quite possible that his military service worsened his already troubled state, as was the case for white veterans too).[108] After the war, Sarah A. Fisher, a family friend, stated that Wilson "would become violent and overtaken with bouts of insanity."[109] Unfortunately for his wife and children, his chaotic mental state led to violent outbursts. Mary Elizabeth Crawford, a neighbor, testified, "She heard cries for help and 'murder' and hurriedly sent her husband to Margaret Day's assistance, for she thought said Wilson Day insane."[110] Crawford then reported that Wilson "attempted [to take the] life of said Margaret Day choking her unconscious."[111] Furthermore, she stated, "This was only one of many instances in which said Wilson Day acted in an insane manner, different times threatening the lives of [the] children and wife."[112] Violence was, sadly, a common occurrence in the Day household. On a separate occasion Day attempted to burn his children on the stove.[113]

Unfortunately for many other family members of Civil War veterans like Day, both white and African American, physical violence toward the individuals who regularly interacted with, and in many cases cared for, them was common.[114] Even though no soldier examined here received a diagnosis of or treatment for mental illness, scholars note that among USCT soldiers there were roughly 12.1 cases of mental illness in every 10,000 servicemen, which sometimes lasted long after their service ended.[115] While the prevalence of domestic violence among African American couples is unknown, it is clear that marriages were not always blissful.[116] For many men, domestic violence allowed them to reestablish patriarchal control over their families.[117]

The mental states of some veterans continued to deteriorate long after the conflicts ended.[118] And in some examples, their war-related mental instability led to suicide attempts.[119] George H. Buck became mentally unstable after a shell fragment became permanently lodged in his cranium. While Buck did not, at least not according to available records, have suicidal thoughts, he was mentally disturbed afterward. He permanently wore a bandage on his head to cover the wound that never properly healed and caused him great pain for the rest of his life. Joshua James, a lifelong friend, testified that Buck's mental state dramatically changed after the war as he seemed almost "completely insane."[120] Buck eventually found work as a ferryman and later drowned accidentally. Some acquaintances maintained that Buck's mental problems most likely led to his death.[121] Sadly, his death had a profound impact on his family.

For some mentally unstable and physically disabled veterans, living in a state or federal institution became a viable option, especially when their spouses realized that they were incapable of tending to the men's needs. Margaret Day, for example, had Wilson Day placed in two different institutions—the Blockley Almshouse in Philadelphia and the Dauphin County Almshouse in Harrisburg—because of his mental illness.[122] Testimony later revealed that Day went missing in 1878 and was never heard from or seen again. Before he vanished, Day escaped once from the Blockley Almshouse to be arrested and returned to the facility.[123] After a lengthy investigation, the Bureau of Pensions concluded that Day died, from unknown circumstances, after escaping a second time.[124]

While Wilson Day was the only USCT veteran residing in the Blockley Almshouse during the Reconstruction era, another Philadelphian USCT veteran would reside there in the late nineteenth century. William F. Gray also stayed at the institution, though the reason for his residence is unknown. He would eventually die at the facility on April 13, 1892. During his time at Blockley Almshouse, his family, including his daughter, Louisa, did not visit him, perhaps due to familial discord.[125] While the circumstances of Gray's death remain unclear, his time at the institution did not improve his health.

This was true for male patients all across northern almshouses, where they had to stay in overcrowded and dilapidated buildings. Patients, especially African Americans and European immigrants, sometimes engaged in violence (even homicides) against each other.[126] "With those in the single rooms, the case is still worse, for they not only breathe a highly vitiated air, but they are in danger from the destructive propensities of one another. If homicide is not committed every night in the year," a visitor noted, "it certainly is not for lack of fitting occasion and opportunity."[127] Throughout the nineteenth and early twentieth centuries, almshouses and insane asylums enforced racial segregation of patient wings on the belief that race mixing might lead to violence. For instance, African American patients in the Blockley Almshouse resided in the institution's attic, where they kept warm during the cold months by huddling together and burning anthracite near common stoves.[128]

The existence of horrid conditions for almshouse patients was not unique to Pennsylvania; it was a national problem. Most institutions featured unsanitary bathrooms and washing facilities.[129] Of the patients, many, if not all, received inadequate treatment from understaffed and poorly trained employees. Some nurses showed little empathy or sympathy for their patients, whom they viewed as annoyances.[130] Mentally ill patients experienced horrific treatment that included forceful restraints against their will.[131] In extreme cases, patients handled the medical care of one another. "The worst feature, however, is the fact nursing care, the feeding of bed patients, and the many tasks that illness imposes are done after a fashion by other inmates,—nearly always by the mentally defective," a report stated, "because they are the able bodied."[132] Almshouses were able to keep such deplorable conditions because inspections only occurred annually by state board representatives with little interest in the almshouse's conditions.[133] It was in these circumstances that some disabled USCT veterans lived after the war. Perhaps these factors contributed to Wilson Day's eventual disappearance.

William Butler was the only veteran in this study's sample to stay at a branch of the National Home for Disabled Volunteer Soldiers (NHDVS) during the Reconstruction era. All NHDVS branches welcomed honorably discharged veterans with housing, either temporary or permanent, and medical care. To gain entrance to an NHDVS branch, veterans had to pass a rigorous medical examination to prove that they had a physical need to warrant their stay. Until 1884, only disabled veterans could live at the NHDVS.[134] From 1867 to 1869, Butler successfully passed his medical examination since he had an amputated right thigh, which allowed him to live at the central branch in Dayton, Ohio. He eventually left and returned to Philadelphia to comfort his ailing mother.[135]

In total, three men studied here—William Butler, Lorenzo George, and Samuel Brown—lived at the NHDVS as they aged. Brown stayed in Hampton, Virginia, from 1904 to 1907. Meanwhile, George resided in Dayton, Ohio, from 1887 to 1895.[136] Even though George and Brown do not disclose the exact reasons for their stay at the institution, their collective experiences highlight, for differing reasons, that race did not determine one's ability to reside at a branch of the NHDVS. Maybe Butler, and others, chose the central branch because it was the closest to Philadelphia. It is also feasible that he chose the central branch because he would receive more support and protection there from other veterans than he could expect to receive from most civilians.[137] In Butler's case, his short stay at the NHDVS was not unusual. Some veterans used the institution as informal hostels during brief periods of homelessness or economic hardship.[138] The NHDVS forced residents to adhere to elements of military discipline again. Some men viewed these policies as challenges to their manhood because it forced the veterans to conform to rigid military structures that suppressed their individuality, similar to their time in the military.[139]

Still, there were several benefits to living at the NHDVS. For one, veterans received medical treatment. Some residents also received vocational training, for instance, by learning telegraphy, so that the men could work a trade after they left the facility.[140] Some veterans residing at NHDVS branches also worked at the facilities, performing various forms of manual labor that might have allowed them to feel useful and receive income.[141] Becoming a resident also allowed veterans to cohabitate with other veterans who could empathize with each other's hardships.[142]

However, while residing in the NHDVS, many USCT veterans encountered racial discrimination from white veterans and administrators. White and African American veterans ate and slept in informally segregated spaces, even though the NHDVS had no official policy enforcing segregation.[143] White veterans may have demanded these discriminatory practices.[144] Maybe experiencing racism at the institution partly influenced William Butler's decision to leave. Even so, residing at the NHDVS allowed veterans to revel in idealized notions of manhood by remembering their military service even decades after the war had ended.[145] Nevertheless, by including USCT veterans into various NHDVS branches, these spaces also became shelters where they received medical and emotional support, as racial discrimination remained pervasive throughout American society.[146]

Other Philadelphian USCT veterans continued residing in domiciles with nuclear and fictive kin. Some USCT veterans, such as Nathaniel Logan Sr. and James Ellsbury, returned to their families after military service to raise their children with their spouses while also opening their homes to individuals who became fictive kin through cohabitation. Both men were skilled workers—Ellsbury was a shoemaker, and Logan was a carpenter, and their wives contributed to their households through their essential unpaid labor, including tending to the needs of the two Ellsbury and four Logan children. Both families continued housing female fictive kin, who had lived with them during the prior decade.

Emma Costa (a fictive kin residing with the Ellsburys since 1860), who was sixteen years old in 1870, was working as a domestic servant, most likely for a white Philadelphian family.[147] Costa's occupation, due to workforce racism, was a profession that many white women considered both a denigration of their self-worth and a "fitting" place for African American women. Sadly, white employers showed minimal concern for their domestic employees, which led to African American women working in horrid conditions, usually for meager wages of four to eight dollars a month, if they received any payments at all.[148] Costa's employment situation was undoubtedly physically and mentally draining, as domestic workers remained under their employers' constant supervision. Costa's wage-earning work was necessary since Catherine Ellsbury remained at home raising two infant children.

Meanwhile, fifty-six-year-old Adaline Kelly, who also lived with the Logans in 1860, remained with the family in 1870.[149] Her continued cohabitation was most likely a welcomed addition, as Mary Logan reared three school-age children and one infant. Kelly remained at home, where she may have assisted Mary with childrearing responsibilities. Maybe she found work outside of the home temporarily to contribute economically to the household. However, even without her potential addition as a wage earner, Kelly's presence was critical to a young family with multiple children.

Both cases illustrate that different circumstances led to African American women becoming fictive kin in the homes of USCT veterans and their families. Moreover, their continued cohabitation in these homes highlights that they were more than interlopers or boarders. They were vital to families that needed the varied contributions that these women made in their households.

Two USCT veterans—William Butler and Joseph Green—also became fictive kin during the Reconstruction era. Both men began living with an eclectic group of white and African American Philadelphians. While working as a domestic servant, Butler resided with Alexander and Jane Elligood and Maggie Reagan, an unemployed white woman.[150] Alexander worked as a laborer, while Jane was a domestic servant. Joseph Green, meanwhile, was a domestic servant, and Richard Smith (who was white) was a hostler. Both Green and Smith resided with their employers, the Garmins, a wealthy white family.[151] Green's employment was crucial for the Garmins, who most likely depended on his work to keep the household running smoothly.

The employment of both Green and Butler as domestic servants reveals that two USCT veterans experienced a gendered paradox. On the one hand, both men were able to resume their postwar lives as wage earners, which allowed them to demonstrate their manhood during a period when civilians questioned the masculinity of unemployed veterans.[152] On the other hand, these USCT veterans worked an occupation that African American women dominated (though never exclusively).[153] Therefore, Green and Butler might have developed a complicated understanding of their gender identity through their immediate postwar employment. However, it is also feasible that neither man cared about public perceptions of gender, instead focusing on their material realities. Both households were examples of interracially mixed residences during a period of racial violence.[154]

Most USCT veterans moved back home with their blood-related kin immediately following the war. Eight of the USCT veterans examined here returned to their parents' residences, though for different reasons. Except for Charles Tobias, all of these eight USCT veteran sons had full-time wage-earning occupations that their families undoubtedly appreciated. Isaac Becket Jr. intermittently found work as a stevedore, which could pay up to twenty cents per hour, though finding regular work was more difficult.[155] Along with his three brothers, Samuel Crawford worked as a barber in a household that had eighteen other family members, including nine children. Their significant household size necessitated that all inhabitants take responsibilities and contribute, whether domestically or financially, to keep their household together.

Even though USCT veterans resumed living in their parents' residences, it was highly likely that many parents needed their sons' economic contributions. Wesley Maloney's work as a teamster was undoubtedly a welcome financial injection to his parents' home, especially since Solomon Maloney was a seventy-two-year-old cook.[156] Having his son home was perhaps helpful to Solomon, who might have been unable to work the physically demanding job consistently.[157] For the Parker brothers, William H. and Robert G., the ability to have semiskilled work as a butcher and porter became of great benefit to their parents since their father was a laborer.[158] Previous scholarship argues that Civil War veterans believed their military service elevated their familial role, from being a dependent to having equal standing with their parents.[159] Alternatively, maybe some USCT veterans were most concerned about coming together to keep their families cohesive in a turbulent period. Regardless, these men collectively worked to assure some financial stability for their parents.

Battling the Bureau of Pensions

As previous chapters discussed, the Civil War pension system became an important vehicle for the federal government to provide economic compensation for U.S. veterans and their nuclear dependents.[160] During the Reconstruction era, the U.S. Congress enacted pension laws—in 1866 and 1873—to increase pay disbursements to all invalid pensioners. The payouts rose (depending on the disability rating) to eighteen dollars, twenty-four dollars, and thirty-one dollars and twenty-five cents.[161] By providing increases to pensions, the federal government recognized that physically disabled veterans, especially formerly enlisted men, needed more than eight dollars per month to survive financially.[162]

Meanwhile, the 1873 pension law recognized, for the first time, illnesses and diseases as pension-eligible disabilities. Some Americans derided the 1873 policy for, in their opinion, awarding unseen medical ailments.[163] But USCT veterans greatly benefitted from the pension revision because many African American soldiers contracted various illnesses during their time in the U.S. Army. Furthermore, the 1873 law acknowledged that the Civil War caused lingering internal physical problems for men defending the nation.

The federal government still required widows and minors to provide legal documentation or witnesses to corroborate their "legitimate" relationship to the veteran to receive pension benefits. If there was no wife or child to claim a pension, then a biological mother or sister could benefit. Mothers or sisters, however, had to demonstrate their previous financial dependence on the deceased veteran.[164]

The U.S. Congress enacted two additional policies addressing veterans' dependents. By 1868, legal minors (under sixteen years old) were eligible for two dollars monthly if their mother was a pensioner. Biological fathers also qualified for a pension. Later, the 1873 pension law permitted legal minors an extra two dollars per month if the pensioner's mother recently died.[165] Both policies highlight that the federal government was expanding the pension program to protect more dependent disbursements, for qualified surviving biological kin, upon a pensioner's death. As a result, the federal government created ways to ensure that Civil War veterans' family members continued on the pension rolls.

From 1866 to 1877, five new invalid applications examined in this study arrived for the Bureau of Pensions to review. Three veterans—Robert Johnson, Jacob Thornton, and George Stiles—all had their pensions approved. Stiles got one dollar per month; Johnson received two dollars per month; Thornton collected fifteen dollars per month.[166] Their combined acceptance into the pension rolls meant that Philadelphian USCT veterans continued agitating for pension benefits well after the war. Moreover, they maintained their sense of national belonging as they applied for pensions.

Meanwhile, two veterans—Charles Brant and Charles Tobias—had their applications rejected. After an extensive examination, including testimony from a former lieutenant colonel, Loren Burritt, who affirmed that Brant received an injury during the Battle of Olustee, the

Bureau of Pensions rendered no decision (a de facto rejection) on the case.[167] Therefore, having a former officer as a witness, at least in this case, did not assure an invalid application's success. Tobias chose, for unstated reasons, to abandon his case even after he had asked men to testify on his behalf.[168] Their two cases highlight that acquiring an invalid pension did not come easily for some USCT veterans due to the Reconstruction era's stringent pension policies.

Becoming an invalid pensioner still did not ensure economic stability for a veteran's family, however. Four married men—Robert Johnson, George Stiles, James Crippen, and John Short—had wives dependent upon money supplied by the federal government. Wives and other household inhabitants needed the monthly payouts, especially when the men could not resume working.

Meanwhile, Nathaniel Logan Sr. was an invalid pensioner, husband, and a father to thirteen children.[169] His four dollars per month pension barely allowed for the survival of their sizeable family. Perhaps his low pension, coupled with his many children, forced him to find work. Luckily for his kin, Logan became a carpenter.[170] Therefore, he provides an example of an invalid who did not become wholly reliant on payments from the federal government.

Applying for an invalid pension presented veterans with another battleground over their manhood. Advocates of enlistments previously argued that Civil War military service proved that African Americans were now, in fact, men.[171] However, the gendered battle over African American manhood continued after the war. Throughout the Reconstruction era, U.S. Army veterans became "living monuments" (referring to Americans using veterans as visible reminders of the war) as their bodies and minds deteriorated.[172] USCT veterans needed invalid pensions for financial aid and public recognition, especially from the federal government. Each payment assured that the invalid pensioner had his manhood and wartime sacrifices honored after the war.

As previously mentioned, Civil War and Reconstruction era pension laws collectively provided benefits to legal widows because they conformed to the Bureau of Pensions' definition of a "legitimate" marriage. By opening the possibility of a widow's pension to the wives of deceased USCT veterans, the federal government allowed African American women to legitimize their own gender identity and rights as a citizen. After all, African American widows had gained access to the same privileges as white Union widows and now shared their status as patriots. When orphans received pensions, too, the federal government recognized the African American family within the nation's imagined community.[173] However, the federal government's acknowledgment of African American womanhood and the African American family's status only occurred when women and children pushed for it and endured the rigors of the application process.

The widows of Jacob G. Jackson and George Glascow both had their applications assessed during the Reconstruction era, with different outcomes for each woman. Martha Ann Jackson became a widow pensioner at eight dollars per month, beginning in 1866. As part of her application, she supplied a copy of their marriage license.[174] Additionally, Jacob Jackson, who died in the war, sent Martha Ann his military enlistment document while stationed at Camp William Penn. On the back, he wrote: "Ann[,] this you must keep and if I should get kill[ed] you can draw all the money that is coming to me. Do not lose it."[175] Thanks to Jackson's forethought and a clear understanding of his mortality, he provided his wife with evidence that would later help her widow's application.

In contrast, Margaret Glascow struggled throughout the pension process because of documentation problems. Though Samuel Dill and John Clark testified about seeing her husband George die, she failed to prove their marriage.[176] Margaret needed witnesses to confirm their marriage, but no one came forward to assist her. Ultimately, the Bureau of Pensions never decided (a de facto rejection) on her case. Therefore, even with USCT veterans' testimony, at least in this case, without the necessary information, a widow was not assured a spot on the pension rolls. Margaret died on November 5, 1871, impoverished and leaving behind a daughter, also named Margaret.

Four children in this study had mothers or guardians submit minor's applications on their behalf immediately following the war. Every one of these children became pensioners, even though their circumstances for approval differed. Though her mother never received a pension, the younger Margaret Glascow joined the pension rolls in 1871.[177] Similarly, Victoria Jackson joined the pension rolls in 1866, two years after her mother, Martha Ann Jackson, did.[178] In the end, the Jackson family experience in the pension system denotes that dependents who were pension eligible did not always pursue the process, which had the potential to create lasting financial consequences on the family.

Mary E. Grigg's remarriage, in 1867, to Benjamin L. Tyler immediately nullified her widow's pension.[179] From the federal government's perspective, widows had to remain unmarried and continue mourning their deceased husbands, potentially for the remainder of their lives, to remain on the pension rolls.[180] By remarrying, Griggs gained a new male breadwinner in the eyes of the federal government. This indicates that the federal government used pension eligibility to criticize and police the sexual and moral behavior of widows—white and African American.[181] Mary's decision to move on thus created economic consequences for her family while allowing her to reclaim her individuality and agency over her intimate relationships. In doing so, she and her new husband quickly recognized that the two children from Mary's first marriage—Maria Louisa and Emeretta—needed to apply for pensions. Both girls received approvals for their applications. Maria Louisa's remained until 1877, and Emeretta's ended the next year.[182]

Throughout the Reconstruction era, and arguably long afterward, the children of deceased veterans learned that they were part of a battle over the public memory of the Civil War. The children of dead Confederate soldiers in Virginia at the Male Orphan Asylum, for example, symbolized, at least to the institution's administrators, the hardships of the war on white families.[183] Conversely, the minors of deceased U.S. soldiers and veterans, as long as they were "legitimate," gained access to the pension rolls for a limited period. In doing so, the federal government demonstrated, theoretically, a racially egalitarian policy that not only recognized the wartime sacrifices of the children's parents but also included the minors in the national memory of the Civil War.

Many African Americans used USCT soldiering to push their various agendas to acquire full citizenship rights. Nevertheless, the families examined here focused their attention on finding and maintaining wage-earning employment and working to keep their households stable. Civil War pensions became potential sources of money, medical care, and recognition for the wartime sacrifices of African Americans. But gaining pension approval was an arduous process that did not always happen for eligible African Americans. Even so, the families examined here continued their lifelong fight to keep their households together.

CHAPTER SIX

USCT Families in an Industrializing Nation

The rapid advance of industry by the late nineteenth century proved to be a prosperous time for Philadelphia's manufacturers, businesses, and industries.[1] Textile businesses were, arguably, some of the most important in the city.[2] For instance, by 1880, 21.6 percent of Philadelphia's laboring population worked in the textile industry.[3] The city's industries benefitted from its shipping ports, railroads connecting to far-reaching markets, roads, and a sizeable labor pool.[4]

However, Philadelphian USCT veterans and their families seeking employment learned that the industrialized workplace often excluded them. A majority of manufacturers refused to hire African Americans by enforcing de facto segregation hiring practices. Midvale Steel, in 1890, was the only local manufacturer that openly hired African Americans. By 1900 Midvale Steel employed twelve hundred African Americans, which provided the company with an accessible labor supply.[5] In short, American "progress" did not assure that occupational racial discrimination ended.

By comparison, employed whites and various labor organizations fought a two-front battle. On one side, laborers fought against businesses and state and federal governments for safer working conditions, the right to unionize, and other issues.[6] On the other side, white workers battled to restrict African Americans from certain occupations and equal participation (if any at all) in labor organizations. Employers understood these racial tensions among laborers and used these divisions to their advantage. More specifically, during labor strikes African American "scab" workers filled the void created by whites seeking better benefits. In some instances, employers openly threatened to hire African Americans, who would take lower wages than white workers.[7] This made a volatile situation even worse as violence could, and did, occur.[8]

As the United States industrialized and modernized, new employment opportunities were not available to many African Americans.[9] By the 1890s African American Philadelphians were the least likely workers to find regular employment. "Every one know[s] that in a city like Philadelphia[,] a Negro does not have the same chance to exercise his ability or secure work according to his talents as a white man," historian W. E. B. Du Bois noted.[10]

It was within this racialized milieu that the families studied here had to navigate the workplace. From 1878 to 1900, twenty veterans in this sample remained regularly employed. Other veterans no longer worked either due to death or advanced age. Some veterans may have been unemployed because of rampant discrimination.

Seven of the men were laborers, which was typical for many African Americans.[11] It is worth noting that census enumerators who categorized men as "laborers" did not always recognize that sometimes men performed a myriad of other forms of work (semiskilled and skilled), but whites denied them the chance to claim either the title or the compensation for more complex employment.[12] Thomas C. King Sr., for instance, occasionally found skilled work as a builder, coal miner, and bricklayer. Conversely, the U.S. Census stated in 1900 that he was a day laborer.[13] Racial discrimination most likely kept him from obtaining permanent employment in his chosen fields. Perhaps USCT veterans, like Jacob Thornton and Charles Brown, found their new positions depressing because of the collective denigration of their occupational status. Before the Civil War, Thornton was a brickmaker; Brown was a farmer. However, by 1880 both men performed unskilled labor similar to hundreds of thousands of other African American men.[14]

Even in the face of persistent, and in many cases effective, occupational racial discrimination, some veterans found semiskilled, skilled, and professional work. Their jobs included that of porter, butcher, railroad porter, driver, turnkey, plasterer, waiter, farm laborer, and barber. Others found work in professional jobs as a train engineer, lawyer, clerk of court for Alachua County, cabinet maker, U.S. deputy collector of revenue in Florida, and as secretary of the Florida State Republican Executive Committee (the final three occupations were held, at different times, by one veteran).[15] By 1880, working as a porter was not uncommon for African Americans across the country.[16] However, rarely, if ever, did African American men work as train engineers, showing that industrialization and access to public transportation did not cease occupational racial discrimination.[17] Perhaps some African Americans hoped that a modernizing nation would consider racism an ancient practice, but such hopes did not come to fruition.

Three USCT veterans continued working as barbers, which remained the most common semiskilled or skilled position for African American men.[18] African American barbers had a choice between cutting the hair of only African American men and sustaining an important community space for Philadelphia's African American community or allowing white men in too—which brought more income but would change the social dynamics of the barbershop itself.[19] At the same time, their profession permitted them to engage in political discussions with their clientele—white and African American.[20]

Working as a barber did not assure that one remained stationary. Some barbers had to travel in order to continue working.[21] For instance, in order to find work, Francis Hawkins left his wife (Sarah) and their two children as he plied his trade in numerous states, including California, Kansas, Nebraska, Missouri, New Mexico, Washington State, Oregon, Montana, and Indiana, which caused a strain on the couple because of limited communication and physical distance.[22] Travel did not always ensure work. During his travels, Hawkins intermittently became a porter (once for the Northern Pacific Railway), highlighting his ability to adapt to his situation to earn money.[23]

Hawkins also found that his occupation allowed him to continue emphasizing his military service. William James, a fellow barber in Missouri, testified that Hawkins, in 1893, routinely wore a military badge and talked with others about the Civil War. William recalled, "I heard old soldiers talk to him in the shop, and he always said that he had been in the [U.S.] army."[24] Hawkins confirmed that customers knew of his military service. "At Pettyfare's shop[, in Kansas City, Missouri,] they all called me old soldier," Hawkins said.[25] His ongoing discussions about his service meant that at least one veteran traveled the country and used his profession to challenge the growing national white amnesia about the exploits of USCT regiments. Of course, this also meant that his family had to live without his presence.

Hawkins's extended separation put a significant strain on his family, especially in times of crisis. Sarah pleaded with her husband to send money home when one of their children was sick and needed a doctor. "I sent her $5 all the money that I had," Hawkins stated.[26] In addition to financial and medical troubles, the couple struggled with a lack of regular communications over the years. "We corresponded after I came [out] West but after a time[,] she ceased to answer my letters," he testified.[27] Hawkins's stress was heightened when a letter that he previously sent two years earlier came back unopened.

Limited communications perhaps raised concerns of infidelity.[28] Though in Hawkins's case, sparse correspondence led Sarah to believe that Francis had died. "He must be dead," Sarah claimed, "as he had never forgotten to write me regularly before that, every other week."[29] Under this assumption, Sarah applied for a widow's pension. Little did she know (as later sections will detail) he was still alive. In the end, the Hawkins family story reveals that an eagerness to find work and a desire to emphasize USCT veteranhood (possibly to attract customers) had financial and emotional consequences for his family.

In the late nineteenth century, some USCT veterans improved their occupational status. Prior to the war, William H. Parker, Francis Hawkins, and James Crippen were laborers. However, by 1880 Parker was a butcher, Hawkins mainly worked as a barber, and Crippen was a waiter.[30] John Thompson, who was previously a waiter, also worked as a barber.[31] Their collective improvement in occupational status was not unique; it was not an anomaly as some nonveteran African Americans living in Steelton, Pennsylvania, also saw an improvement.[32]

Two USCT veterans were successful in sustaining their employment in skilled and professional class occupations. From 1860 to 1880, Charles W. Jones was a barber.[33] Samuel Benson continued working as an engineer, his pre-service job, in 1880.[34] Benson's ability to persevere at this particular occupation was essential to African Americans across the country.[35] For example, during an American Missionary Association event on July 4, 1878, Colonel Preston depressingly told the audience that some prized occupations were a white man's domain. "There is . . . no room for them among the whites as doctors, lawyers, professors, engineers, architects, or artists. By other pursuits they must gain their livelihood," Preston lamented.[36] While Preston's comment was undoubtedly true for most African Americans, it did not hold with Benson.

Some Philadelphian USCT veterans changed jobs and did not see a denigration in their occupational status as they remained in skilled and professional occupations. Henry S. Harmon provides a fascinating example as he continued practicing law in Florida, where, by 1880, he served as the secretary of the Florida State Republican Executive Committee. He later became the U.S. deputy collector of revenue in Florida as well.[37] As previously noted, perhaps Harmon chose to remain in Florida to exercise more political and civil rights in a state under the federal government's oversight in the immediate postwar period. Harmon's sustained involvement in politics and law were both highly impressive feats that show various professional occupations were available outside of Pennsylvania. Eventually, Harmon lost his political influence and clients as a lawyer after white conservative Democrats regained control of the state government and began instituting Jim Crow laws, which led to his work as a cabinetmaker.[38]

Making and Keeping Families Together

Some USCT veterans saw their intimate relationships blossom after 1877. Seven USCT veterans and their spouses legally married during the period. Five couples had twelve children collectively.[39] Charles and Grace Brown's marriage came four years after the birth of their firstborn child, Mary. The Browns' premarital sexual relationship and offspring demonstrate that their intimate private interactions ran counter to social mores that abhorred such activities. By getting a legal marriage, the Browns' union and progeny became legitimate in the federal government's view.

Mary Allen learned that having a child outside of wedlock left an individual open to public derision, sometimes from the Bureau of Pensions. Even though Mary and Edward Purnell Jr. legally wed, during her pension examination she had to provide detailed information about her sexual encounter with Frank Williams, a previous lover. "It was at Atlantic City[, New Jersey,] that said Williams had carnal intercourse with me. And this is all there is to the Frank Williams affair except that I had a child," Allen testified.[40] Having to share her personal, intimate history with federal government representatives must have been a genuinely humiliating event for a woman seeking a widow's pension.

Meanwhile, four USCT veterans and their partners preferred

common-law marriages. Joseph and Mattie Woodson had six children, even as they remained unmarried in the eyes of the law.[41] By not getting a legal marriage, both spouses maintained their independence and individual legal identity. However, this choice also had consequences for the women and children who were not pension eligible. White society disparaged these men and women for failing to "legitimize" their relationships. However, their collective decision to have common-law marriages highlights northern African Americans' long-standing history of ignoring legal marriage advocates to emphasize their gender relations, family, and marriage concepts.[42]

Extended kin remained ever present in the homes of veterans. Surprisingly, or perhaps not, USCT veterans with semiskilled and skilled occupations were more likely to cohabitate with relatives. In 1880 James Crippen, his wife Ellen, and their daughters opened their residence to James's mother-in-law, brother, and two nephews. Since his brother, Allen Crippen, and nephew, Samuel Williams, both worked as hotel waiters and his other nephew was a laborer at a brickyard, it was undoubtedly helpful to the entire family to pool their resources together. Even though Crippen's mother-in-law did not have a regular wage-earning job, she possibly helped rear her seven-year-old granddaughter, Carrie.[43] Meanwhile, there was one instance of three USCT veterans, all blood related, living together in 1880. William H. and Robert G. Parker and their cousin, John Thompson, and William H.'s and John's wives (Sarah and Elizabeth, respectively) resided in the home. Robert G.'s situation stands out because, unlike his male relatives, he was an unskilled divorcee.[44] Being divorced meant, to some African Americans, that he failed as a husband, lacked morality, and may have been spiritually corrupt.[45] Still, his family chose to maintain its bonds to avoid potentially squalid living conditions for Robert G. Parker.

Families remained ever essential to the survival of USCT veterans. Lorenzo George and Charles W. Jones took up residence with various family members. George's nephew, Daniel Benn, his niece-in-law, and George's sister welcomed him into their home. Benn's employment as a laborer was most likely insufficient to provide for their family, which would have made George's income as a barber beneficial.[46] Charles W. Jones chose to move back in with his parents and his seven siblings. The Jones family was unusually successful as Charles and his father, Robert, both worked as barbers. Robert Jr. was a waiter. All of the adult

Jones daughters had full-time wage-earning occupations. Sarah was a mantua-maker (a seamstress), while Anna and Maria were both public school teachers.[47] All three women successfully defied the nationwide systematic racial barriers that put hundreds of thousands of African American women into domestic laboring positions, including working as cooks and servants.

By avoiding such work, this small group of women did not endure the domestics' hellish experiences. Employers of domestic servants demanded long work hours from their employees (sometimes twelve- to thirteen-hour shifts) and paid meager wages that were sometimes infrequent. Some white employers chose in-kind payments rather than paying cash. To make matters worse, physical and sexual assaults were also a reality, especially for those living at the residence.[48]

Some adult children continued living with their USCT veteran fathers. USCT veteran Richard Carter and his wife, Hannah, allowed their adult son, John, to remain in their residence. In 1880, John, who was twenty-six years old, worked as a barber, which certainly helped his family since only Richard regularly worked as a driver.[49]

White middle-class societal standards for the time held that men like John Carter—an adult bachelor working in a semiskilled occupation—should create their own families. By comparison, the mean age for marriage for African American men in Montgomery County, Virginia, was 24.6 years old, which meant that John Carter's continued bachelorhood might have been considered an oddity if he lived there.[50] However, such a judgment ignored the critical contribution, both financial and emotional, that he regularly provided to his parents. The Carters successfully worked together to keep their two-generation household afloat in the face of racial discrimination.

Other USCT veterans and their spouses also allowed their progeny and extended kin to live with them. Both Marshall Price and Nathaniel Logan Sr. were examples of USCT veterans who kept their residences accessible to family members in need. In 1880 Price and his wife Emily permitted their daughter, Isabella H. Crook, her husband, John, the couple's two-year-old daughter, Eva, and their one-month-old daughter, Mary, to reside with them.[51] The U.S. Census, unfortunately, and for unknown reasons, does not provide any details on their employment information. Still, one can hypothesize that the young Crook family could not afford to live independently, given the fact that they had a toddler and an infant. Perhaps the Prices wanted to assist in rearing their grandchildren. Nathaniel Sr. and Mary Logan had their son R. P., daughter U. E. Westwood, and son-in-law Charles W. Westwood in their domicile. All of the men had full-time wage-earning work. Logan was a porter, Westwood was a driver, and R. P. worked as a laborer.[52] Their combined employment and regular incomes were, in 1900, critical for the five family members, especially since the women did not have full-time wage-earning jobs. Perhaps veterans permitted extended kin to reside with them to establish supplementary incomes, provide a safe space for their progeny, or support the navigation of the complexities of adulthood, all while living in a racially oppressive society.

There were seven school-age children (three males and four females) in at least five USCT veterans' homes who attended school. The near-equal distribution of male and female pupils meant that some USCT veterans and their wives believed in gender equality in educational opportunities. Perhaps these families hoped that the children's scholastic pursuits could improve their chances for better employment.[53] The parents may have agreed with M. Louise Taylor (an education advocate), who argued that educated youths received character training. "Of what use is an education? What means such assiduous efforts for the eradication of the mind?. . . . An education," Taylor claimed, "most assuredly refines the morals if it has no further use."[54] In Taylor's opinion, these four USCT households recognized the value of educating African American youths' intellect and morality.

Four other USCT veteran households, for undisclosed reasons, did not send their six school-age youths (three males and three females) to school. John Smith worked as a farm laborer in 1880, and none of his three children were in school. The census enumerator cataloged Grant, his eleven-year-old son, as "at home."[55] It is possible that the Smith children assisted their father with his work. It is also plausible that they received informal schooling at home from a parent or relative. James Crippen, Jacob Purnell, and Thomas C. King Sr. each had one child who attended school and one who did not at the same time. King Sr. and his thirteen-year-old son, Thomas King Jr., were unique from the other fathers and offspring because both Kings worked as day laborers in 1900, possibly alongside each other. For undisclosed reasons, King Sr. and Alice King chose to send their nine-year-old son, Earl, to school. Ultimately, each decision came after parents deliberated whether the long-term goals of education or immediate need for incoming money was more important to their households.

Perhaps some African American families could not afford their child's schooling. Cash-strapped African American parents already scraping by would have to set aside additional money to pay for school supplies and clothing, which a *Christian Recorder* article recognized as a factor in their decision to keep children out of school. "[Some] are so poor that they find it difficult to get the proper outfit for their children, while numbers aside from these are blind to the value of education and wilfully [*sic*] rob the little ones of their mental birthright," the article stated, "or indulge all manner of excuses for keeping the children at home."[56] The article acknowledged the economic plight of African Americans and claimed that parents seemed to ignore the potential benefits of going to school. Maybe familial issues, such as a limited household income, the need to assist in rearing a sibling or relative, or the loss of a parent kept them from becoming students.

From 1878 to 1900, thirteen wives of the veterans in this study did not acquire full-time, wage-earning work. Census enumerators often stated that these women were "keeping house," which failed to acknowledge how invaluable their unpaid labor was to their entire household. By labeling these African American women as "keeping house," the census enumerators did not see them, at least in their brief assessments, on the same terms as white women.[57] Even so, these women sometimes engaged in short-term employment that the census enumerators ignored.

On the other hand, from 1878 to 1900, ten wives of other veterans in this sample worked full-time. Collectively, the women had various jobs that ranged from laundress, to washerwoman, domestic servant to laborer.[58] In the case of the laborers, it is feasible that the women were domestic laborers or performed various types of tasks, including watching children, sewing, weeding, and other duties. Four women—Anna Fausett, Mary Purnell, Arretta Davis, and Patience Buck—were able to find employment cleaning clothes, which was preferred by many African American women over domestic work because it allowed them to remain at home and receive pay for their labor. In Purnell's case, she earned four dollars per week for her work, the same amount an African American cook could earn working in a white household.[59] While they both earned the same wages, Purnell avoided the constant oversight of her employer and thus maintained her freedom. Working as a laundress may have given African American women control of their personal space, but their job was still very physically taxing, and they worked long hours.[60]

The Continued Fight with the Bureau of Pensions

The federal pension system's highly rigid guidelines for veterans seeking to become pensioners came under fire in the late nineteenth century. The Grand Army of the Republic (GAR), an organization composed of Civil War veterans, continually lobbied for the pension system's liberalization because its policies kept veterans from becoming pensioners, including Philadelphian USCT veterans.[61]

Grover Cleveland's presidency, in the late 1880s, became a significant roadblock in U.S. veterans' pursuits for expanding pension eligibility, however. Soon after becoming president, Cleveland (a Democrat who paid his way out of serving in the Civil War) criticized the multiple pension laws, which he considered unnecessary, for leading to a ballooning federal budget. For instance, Cleveland vetoed 228 proposed pension bills during his time in office.[62] Due to this antipension stance, he rejected the proposed 1887 pension law that wanted to make any U.S. soldier who served at least ninety days and earned an honorable discharge eligible for a pension.[63] Part of Cleveland's reasoning stemmed from his desire to move away from Civil War passions and toward "a 'spirit of conciliation' toward the South."[64] And yet, even though Cleveland claimed there was a "veteran problem," he made repeated overtures to ex-Confederates, including returning their captured battle flags.[65] As a result of President Cleveland's hardline antipension position, many Philadelphian USCT veterans and their families suffered as their lives became part of a contested national debate.

Within this political context, the Philadelphian USCT veterans and their kin attempted to navigate the pension system, including finding and supplying documentation, hiring a lawyer, finding witnesses, and providing testimony to pension agents. Some individuals were successful with their pension applications, even in this restrictive period of the pension system. A number of them soon learned that pensions did not guarantee economic stability, especially if a family was dependent on the monthly disbursements. Other people, unfortunately, discovered that becoming a pensioner was extremely difficult, if not impossible. Even so, numerous Philadelphian USCT veterans and their families refused to accept the Bureau of Pensions' rejections and continued fighting to join the pension rolls and earn the financial and symbolic benefits that came with it.

USCT veterans and their families learned that the federal government, through awarding pensions, could recognize how military service continued to affect their bodies, finances, and families. Through the maintenance of a pension system and dispensation of monthly payouts to individuals on the pension rolls, the federal government acknowledged that the toll of military service lingered long after the war ended.[66]

The approval of each invalid application became more significant as time passed. Over time, witnesses either aged or died. For others, the passage of days, years, and generations hazed their memories. Another obstacle came with the loss of documents that applicants once possessed and were still necessary for proving their case. Limited literacy and finances hindered the application process too. Moreover, even if one waded through those hurdles, pension representatives' racism further affected the process.

Seven USCT veterans who began receiving a pension in 1865 or later continued to do so afterward. Success in obtaining a pension did not assure financial stability. George Stiles, who began receiving one dollar per month in 1876, never received more than two dollars per month. For Stiles, the money was helpful, but it was ultimately insufficient due to his inability to work.[67] John Short saw his 1865 monthly payment of six dollars per month double thirty-five years later. His loss of a right thumb and retinal issues made finding any work nearly impossible, which meant that his pension was his only income.[68] James Crippen, who still suffered from a minié ball injury to the head (for which he received two dollars monthly in 1865), saw his pension increase to six dollars a month in 1884.[69] Unfortunately for George Roland, he suffered from a severe facial deformity that caused severe pain and mastication difficulties. By 1888, his monthly pension of four dollars doubled again.[70] While Roland was grateful for the economic aid that continued for twenty-two years, the money could never alleviate the lifelong pain and anguish that he suffered every day. All four cases demonstrate that there was no uniformity in pension disbursements for USCT veterans receiving invalid pensions. In the end, the varied medical assessments for disabled veterans meant that the federal government assessed the severity of USCT veterans' physical ailments differently.

Henry Thompson and Nathaniel Logan Sr. were two examples of USCT veterans who started receiving pensions in 1865 but experienced multiple setbacks in their quest for a pension increase. In his invalid applications, Thompson consistently emphasized that his right leg's rheumatic pain worsened as he aged, sometimes making it very hard for him to work. For instance, with his 1886 increase request, Thompson informed the Bureau of Pensions that his body was deteriorating, which impacted his ability to earn money. His medical doctor stated, "His knee is growing weaker and lamer and more painful. He is unable to perform ordinary manual labor one half the time on account of his wound."[71] In his 1890 invalid pension increase application, Thompson informed the pension agent that the federal government owed him more money for his military disabilities. "He claims that he should have a higher rating for by reasons of said disabilities he is a great suffering," the pension agent noted, "greatly disabled for the performance of manual labor and as he grows older his condition steadily gets worse."[72] His nearly annual demand for more money frequently garnered rejections because medical examiners did not believe Thompson's injuries worsened. Only three of Thompson's requests received approvals and led to increases in his pension, topping out at fourteen dollars monthly in 1891. Nevertheless, even with these successes he received more rejections than approvals. While likely frustrating, Thompson's persistence, and each application he submitted, forced the federal government to remember his suffering and sacrifice.

When applying for a pension increase, Nathaniel Logan Sr. received approvals and rejections. Seven times he requested more money, as his physical disability made him unable to work.[73] During an 1891 medical examination, the doctor stated that Logan's gunshot wound was still debilitating to him, in addition to his intensifying ocular problems. Even with a doctor's confirmation, the Bureau of Pensions rejected the increase after it deemed the records "unacceptable," ending the application.[74] The following year, Logan stated that his ailments kept him from regularly working. Though the 1900 U.S. Census noted he was a porter, which meant that his physical issues did not stop him from working entirely, he may have had to perform his duties while dealing with pain to survive financially.[75] At four different times the Bureau of Pensions, due to new pension laws passed by the U.S. Congress, increased his pension.[76]

In 1924 and 1927 Logan noted that his advanced age, inability to work or even leave his residence, deteriorating body (including use of crutches, failing kidneys, and vision loss), and dependency on his daughter, U. E. Westwood, who since 1920 had provided him full-time medical care, made him eligible for an increase.[77] Ultimately, his medical issues led to Logan receiving ninety dollars per month. Unfortunately, he died not long after his final approval in 1927. In some ways Nathaniel Logan Sr. was more successful than other USCT veterans, such as Henry Thompson. However, both veterans knew that receiving more money required an applicant's resolve in the face of the federal government's scrutiny.

Five other USCT veterans—Edward Purnell Jr., Edward Brown, John Thompson, Thomas C. King Sr., and Lorenzo George—applied for their first pensions between 1885 and 1889. None of their applications were approved due to the Bureau of Pensions either not rendering a decision or rejecting their disability claims outright. As previously mentioned, Grover Cleveland's administration focused on limiting access to pensions.[78] Thus, his presidency directly impacted the inability of these five USCT veterans to become invalid pensioners.

King emphasized to his pension agent that gastrointestinal issues caused him to maintain a strict diet of pies, milk, and crackers since particular foods, such as eggs, caused him to experience fever and chills. His stomach issues intermittently caused him to leave work. His limited wages as a day laborer made it hard for him to afford medical care regularly. "I could not afford to pay a doctor," he stated.[79] After an examination, the doctor confirmed his ailments, but the Bureau of Pensions rejected his claim since the disability occurred outside of his military service. Ultimately, in 1890, the federal government approved his application for lumbago and a "diseased rectum." He received a monthly pension of eight dollars, which continued for the remainder of his life.[80] The awarding of an invalid pension did not mean that veterans were content with the payments, as was the case with King. He attempted, in 1902, to get an increase for his weak heart and vertigo, which were due to his elderly age, but the Bureau of Pensions denied his request.[81]

Edward Purnell Jr.'s initial rejection in 1887 did not dissuade him from trying again. Nine years later, after the 1890 pension law passed, his application was successful after the Bureau of Pensions' doctor noted that Purnell used a cane because he had rheumatic issues in both knees. He also noted conjunctivitis in his eyes. The federal government awarded him eight dollars per month. Perhaps winning his nine-year battle to receive a pension brought joy and assured him that the nation had not forgotten his military service. Nevertheless, the victory was short lived, as he died later that year.

Edward Brown had his applications denied four times before finally receiving a pension in 1899. During his time as a pensioner, he earned numerous increases that eventually reached twelve dollars per month in 1912.[82] Brown's twelve-year journey navigating the pension process was not easy. Ultimately, he joined the hundreds of thousands of disabled veterans receiving compensation. In the end, a USCT pensioner was a soldier in the battle for Civil War memory, fighting widespread disregard for their military service.

Lorenzo George would have to wait a year after his first application, in 1889, before he would get a pension of ten dollars per month. He attempted to acquire a better payout for the next fourteen years, but he had no success. The Bureau of Pensions never outright denied him. Instead, it chose to avoid rendering a decision.[83]

Successes and Failures with the Expansion of Pensions

After Benjamin Harrison, Indiana's Republican senator, became president in 1889, U.S veterans discovered that they had a powerful ally. Unlike his predecessor, Harrison supported the pension system's liberalization to expand invalid and legal dependent eligibility and monthly pension payouts.[84] Since Harrison was a former U.S. Army officer and a GAR member, it did not surprise many people that he wanted to improve the pension system to benefit his former comrades and their kin for their previous wartime sacrifices. As a result, President Harrison signed the 1890 Dependent and Disability pension law, a policy that Grover Cleveland vetoed three years earlier.[85] President Harrison, unlike Cleveland, publicly stated that he valued the wartime sacrifices of U.S. veterans and their families. Harrison made it clear, during an 1889 speech as the president-elect, that he still remembered the importance of USCT military service. He "praised the Negro race generally, and especially soldiers, veterans, and other blacks."[86] Harrison's words and actions revealed that USCT veterans and their kin were more likely now than ever before to become pension-eligible and possibly get approval for pensions.

By enacting the 1890 pension policy, the federal government demonstrated to U.S. veterans and some of their kin that it recognized that the Civil War impacted people, individually and collectively, long after the war's end. For veteran applicants, the new law removed the military service-related physical disability requirement. The 1890 law instead had three conditions for a veteran to qualify for a pension. First, the veteran had to have served at least ninety days. Second, the veterans must have acquired an honorable discharge. Finally, the veterans must have a physical ailment, developed either during or after military service, that kept them from performing manual labor consistently.[87] Personal wealth, previous income, or current living conditions no longer impacted an invalid claimant.[88] Thus, the removal of two application conditions stimulated first-time and previously rejected applicants to file claims.

Dependents also benefitted from the liberalized pension law. Legal widows of qualifying veterans could receive a pension. Furthermore, the Bureau of Pensions emphasized that widows must illustrate their prior economic dependence on their veteran husbands, a requirement which the federal government removed in 1900.[89] Regardless of when the U.S. Army veteran incurred his disability or death, the policy permitted legal widows and minors to apply for a pension. However, the federal government still mandated that widows stay unmarried and sexually chaste for the remainder of their lives if they wanted to remain on the pension rolls. The pension policy against women of all races meant that the federal government sought to effectively deny widows the ability to establish new romantic partnerships.[90] Thus, a widow's pension became a tool that attempted to control the sexual activities of women.[91]

When the 1890 pension law passed, the number of new invalid applications exploded. For instance, invalid pensions spiked from 244,201 in 1885 to 520,158 in 1891.[92] The rise in pension applications occurred when invalid applicants no longer had to link their disability to military service.[93] Additionally, the 1890 law negated the character clause in the 1882 pension law that had stipulated invalid pension eligibility only for a "moral and deserving veteran."[94] As a result, the 1890 pension law made applying for a pension easier and the possibility of success more likely.

From 1890 to 1895, thirteen Philadelphian-born USCT veterans formally applied for their first invalid pension. By 1895, 735,338 total Civil War veterans were on the pension rolls.[95] Among those were Marshall Price, Edward Brown, Henry Harley, and Robert G. and William H.

Parker, whose monthly pensions ranged from six to ten dollars. After the passage of the 1907 pension act, which stated that honorably discharged veterans who were over sixty-two years old were pension eligible, Robert G. Parker's pension rose to twelve dollars monthly in 1909. The same law also allowed William H. Parker's pension to increase to thirty dollars per month due to a total disability in 1919.[96] Collectively, the new wave of pension applications demonstrates that the 1890 law allowed more veterans to receive aid from the federal government. It also showed USCT veterans that their service was still remembered twenty-five years after the Civil War.

The dramatic expansion of pension eligibility did not assure that the claimants earned approvals. Numerous veterans and their kin, for differing reasons, did not become pensioners. Some USCT veterans discovered that they did not meet all three conditions to qualify as pensioners, in the opinions of pension agents. Various dependent applicants, for a multitude of reasons, also did not join the pension rolls. Even so, some applicants remained resolute and continued resubmitting claims with eventual success. By refusing to accept the Bureau of Pensions's decision, these African Americans demonstrated their tenacity in the ongoing fight for cultural citizenship, economic aid, and acknowledgment of the war's impact on them.

Other African American claimants, however, decided to give up on their pension applications. For some individuals, perhaps the lawyer fee of ten dollars (per the 1878 pension law) was too high.[97] Maybe some African Americans, already dealing with limited finances, could not afford the cost of travel to and from local Bureau of Pensions offices. Sadly, the loss of documentation or an inability to find a witness hindered other applicants. The mental, physical, and psychological deterioration of claimants still deterred others from applying. It is possible that one or multiple issues made it impossible for some of the African American families studied here to become pensioners.

The 1890 pension law stipulated that a U.S. veteran who served for at least ninety days and earned an honorable discharge qualified for a pension.[98] Six veterans who met the criteria had their applications rejected because they did not have a physical disability keeping them from performing wage-earning work. By deeming their invalid claims unqualified, the federal government demonstrated that it would not make exceptions for USCT veterans hoping to receive a pension.

Seeking an invalid pension and receiving a rejection frustrated USCT veterans. It may have been worse for invalid claimants who never heard back from the Bureau of Pensions. William Tallman pointed out that his multiple physical disabilities made work unfeasible. After sacrificing his body for the war, Tallman's ability to earn wages for himself was impaired. Much to Tallman's dismay, the Bureau of Pensions never responded, which led him to abandon the case after two years of failed attempts.[99] Even with crippling rheumatic pain in both knees, Franklin Viney did not become a pensioner.[100] George Henderson abandoned his pension application for an unknown reason.[101] Henderson's friend, John B. Nedary, attempted to write the Bureau of Pensions, noting his character: "[I] know him to be a good and honorable citizen," Nedary stated, "and in his old age is much in need of any help the [federal] government might be willing after an examination of his claim."[102] The heartfelt letter did not lead to Henderson's acceptance as an invalid pensioner, however.

After eight rejected invalid applications, Joseph Anderson likely felt disappointed and disillusioned. Anderson remained in contact with Francis Hawkins, who was a pensioner.[103] Knowing that his friend was able to acquire an approval must have angered Anderson, who may have questioned why he was not on the pension rolls too.

Other USCT men abandoned active applications as well. For instance, Joseph Harris gave up on his pension claim, even though he suffered from a gunshot wound in his right thigh.[104] Perhaps the costly endeavor of filing a pension stopped him from reapplying. Alternatively, maybe his inability to find witnesses to prove his claim influenced his decision. Either way, Harris's case reveals that the 1890 pension law in no way guaranteed veteran's automatic acceptance to the pension rolls.

Denials of first-time invalid pension applications did not stop men from eventually becoming pensioners. Both Joseph Woodson and Charles Penn became pensioners on their second attempt. Woodson, in 1898, got six dollars per month, and it rose to thirty dollars per month in 1919. Penn eventually received twelve dollars per month in 1908.[105] Their assertiveness over the years shows that they refused to accept the initial judgments of the Bureau of Pensions' representatives. By ultimately becoming pensioners, it made them part of an exclusive group that did not include all of their fellow USCT veterans.

Acquiring an invalid pension did not alleviate the pain and other health problems that they suffered. Marshall Price attempted in six different years to obtain a pension increase by stating that his rheumatic pain worsened. In 1893 a medical examiner detailed Price's mental and physical degradation in great detail. "[Price] stoops and walks with evident pain. There is crepitus in [his] right shoulder joint; [He] is incapable of elevating [his] shoulder (right) above horizontal without great pain.... The pain over [the] left side of [his] body," the doctor reported, "and back is rheumatic so also is the pain in [his] lower extremities.... The senility is, in addition to rheumatism, cause[s] much disability."[106] And yet, the Bureau of Pensions did not approve his application for an increased pension.

USCT veterans fought with the federal government to have their noncombat disabilities awarded pensions. Henry Harley (who initially received a pension in 1890) applied for a pension increase in the hopes of receiving compensation for his afflicted lungs. By picking and choosing which disability would be the basis for awarding a pension and ignoring some of the ailments claimed, the federal government's assessment implied that some veterans were not "honorable" men who lied about their disabilities. Eight different medical examinations occurred, all with similar results, even with multiple witnesses confirming Harley's disabilities as legitimate. The nearly annual rejections must have angered ailing veterans like him who demanded the federal government's benefits.[107] Eventually, however, the Bureau of Pensions increased Harley's monthly pension to twelve dollars.[108]

Unfortunately for Francis Hawkins, however, his lingering disabilities, inability to work, and lack of pension compounded his difficult situation. Hawkins testified that he only applied for a pension once and was unable to work. To make matters worse, between August 15, 1895, and September 18, 1896, he was "absolutely destitute and without the means to secure medical advise or treatment."[109] It would take fifteen years from Hawkins's initial application submission before he received his first pension payment when his 1907 invalid application received an approval. He then received multiple increases over the next thirteen years, reaching fifty dollars per month in 1920.[110] Hawkins refused to accept the initial rejections from pension agents. His persistence was driven by his lack of consistent work, money for food, and medical treatment, as well as the needs of a spouse who had become his unofficial nurse.[111]

Like Hawkins, other elderly USCT veterans depended on family members for medical care. By 1927 Nathaniel Logan Sr. could no longer clothe or feed himself. His daughter, U. E. Westwood, gave him full-time medical care.[112] Hawkins's and Logan's differing experiences with receiving treatment show that family members assumed essential life-sustaining responsibilities for their aging male kin. Monthly pensions undoubtedly helped the families, especially the women who were unable to maintain full-time wage-earning work as they assumed informal roles as nurses.

Excluded from the Bureau of Pensions' judgments in invalid pension applications examined here were USCT veterans who emphasized a mental, emotional, or psychological disability. Generally, medical examiners focused on actual physical ailment(s) that could be examined.[113] Veterans claiming nonphysical disabilities experienced skepticism from pension agents, who possibly considered mental, emotional, and psychological issues to be mere excuses from men who were unwilling to work.[114] When veterans, similar to civilians, received a diagnosis of insanity, society viewed them negatively, just as paupers were.[115] And yet, the Bureau of Pensions, from time to time, did award pensions to veterans and dependents with unseen disabilities.[116]

Whether or not the Bureau of Pensions wanted to believe it, numerous veterans suffered from various nonphysical disabilities. According to the 1890 U.S. Census, 2,900 U.S. Army veterans were "insane."[117] During the war soldiers struggled with familial separation. Others experienced punishments (physical, psychological, and emotional) for demonstrating their individuality through desertions and other forms of military disobedience. Some soldiers could not recover, both mentally and psychologically, after witnessing the horrors of war. And after the war, numerous veterans had a hard time finding consistent wage-earning employment. Other veterans, meanwhile, discovered that some civilians did not care about the hardships of war once the war ended. These were just some of the factors that could cause mental, emotional, and psychological disabilities for veterans.[118] Addiction to narcotics and alcohol often resulted and continued to be an issue for veterans after returning to civilian life.[119] Some veterans suffered from depression; some attempted suicides, and some succeeded.[120]

The USCT veterans investigated here assuredly dealt with various mental, emotional, and psychological ailments throughout their lives. However, none of the men tried making any such claim in their pension applications. Therefore, it is feasible that a number of USCT veterans examined here dealt with nonphysical ailments, but they did not include them in their pension applications. By keeping their mental and emotional struggles private, their enduring nonphysical ailments did not get chronicled in the historical record.

The families of these veterans relied on pensions for more than the coverage of day-to-day expenses. Once the veteran passed away, there were new costs that arose. Shortly after James Ellsbury's death, his daughter Katherine Ellsbury, on seven occasions between November 4, 1921, and September 5, 1922, wrote to the Bureau of Pensions. In her letters, she first notified them that her father had died. Then she forwarded the undertaker's bill, including burial, casket, burial suit, hearse, and card costs, for a combined $136. She also sent a bill of $100 for a doctor's visit Ellsbury had before dying. Katherine stated that she paid $116 toward the two bills but demanded that the Bureau of Pensions pay the remainder. Additionally, she stated that her father never received his October payment (even though he died in September), and she wanted it. After a lengthy nine-month correspondence that included frustrated replies from both parties, the Bureau of Pensions agreed to pay the debt, as it authorized a payment of $183 toward the physician, nursing care, undertaker's bill, and livery.[121]

Katherine Ellsbury's assiduousness was successful in getting the federal government to subsidize the medical and funeral expenses of James Ellsbury. In doing so, this USCT veteran's kin contended that the federal government owed them financially for her father's wartime sacrifices, even in death. To the Bureau of Pensions' credit, it honored that debt. Despite the challenges some African Americans faced navigating the pension system, Ellsbury's example reveals that even if amnesia surrounded USCT regiments in many Americans' memories, the Bureau of Pensions had not forgotten some African Americans for their wartime sacrifices.

Pensioner dependents also came into conflict with the Bureau of Pensions in the late nineteenth century. Pension agents questioned the mothers of Alexander Robinson and Andrew White, for example, because they believed the women were defrauding the federal government. One pension agent wanted to know if Jane Robinson, a widow and the mother of Alexander Robinson, had remarried while remaining on the pension rolls. By remarrying, the Bureau of Pensions reasoned, a woman's dependency transferred from the federal government to her new husband. Robinson's case quickly closed once the Bureau of Pensions learned that she had recently died.[122] In the case of Sarah Reeves, Andrew White's mother, the pension agent wanted to know if her husband and Andrew's stepfather, James, was still alive. If so, then he wanted to know if James's previously noted disabilities prevented him from working in the nineteen years after her initial pension got approved. Reeves informed the Bureau of Pensions of James's death in 1874.[123] Witnesses testified that even with her pension, Reeves was poverty stricken. H. Powell stated that Reeves was heavily reliant on the charity of friends.[124] Henry Gamble made a similar statement while adding that Sarah Reeve's son, George, gave her money, and she also earned a small amount of cash from selling candy.[125] In the end, Sarah Reeves maintained her mother's pension, which later rose to thirty-three dollars per month in 1896.[126]

From 1878 to 1889, seven dependents of dead USCT veterans sought to become first-time pensioners. Sarah Brown, William Brown's widow, joined the pension rolls in 1886, gaining eight dollars per month.[127] Daniel Brown's wife, Margaret, and their two children, Annie and Marion, successfully earned approvals in 1884 for a widow's pension of eight dollars per month and two dollars for each minor until they turned sixteen years old in 1889 and 1897, respectively.[128] Unfortunately, in 1893 the Bureau of Pensions rejected Brown's family pensions on a technicality of Daniel's disability: "on the ground that 'the evidence failed to connect the fatal disease[, consumption,] with any cause arising in the service and [the] line of duty.'"[129] The testimonies of USCT veterans Samuel Benson and Edward Purnell Jr., however, recalled that Daniel's illness originated during his time in the military from drinking impure water.[130] The Bureau of Pensions believed otherwise and rejected their applications. Thus, the Browns (after not reapplying) lost both their pensions.

Sometimes witholding a decision was enough discouragement for a dependent to give up on their application. For instance, Priscilla Waters, Hiram Waters's mother, hoped to establish some economic stability in 1882, nine years after her son died. She noted that she had no real estate or personal estate, a repeated statement for many USCT dependents.[131] According to the records, the Bureau of Pensions did not respond. Upon Priscilla's death in 1891, her family felt that it was necessary to notify the federal government that she died an indigent.[132] Perhaps her family relayed the tragic news as one parting shot to the Bureau of Pensions for not even investigating their mother's pension claim.

The passage of time created problems for other applicants, especially when it came to having documentation. Solomon Hoff's widow, Anna Eliza, learned this fact during her 1881 pension application. The presiding pension agent promptly rejected her case "on the ground of the claimant[']s neglect and apparent inability to furnish proof showing origin, continuance, date, and cause of death, date of marriage, cohabitation, dates of birth, widowhood, and identity."[133] Either due to feeling vexed or resigned to the point where she could not provide any documentation, she abandoned her claim. Whatever the circumstances that led to an individual's abandonment of a dependent application, the result was not becoming a pensioner.

Of the pre-1890 dependent applications, George H. Buck's widow, Patience, had arguably the most invasive and tumultuous investigation into her personal life. From 1879 to 1883, the pension agent first wanted to know about the origins of George's head injury; he had heard that Buck's drowning was due to a lingering head wound that he may have received in the war. Two USCT veterans, Joshua James and George W. Green stated that Buck's mental state was never the same after a cannon shell struck his head.[134] The Bureau of Pensions ruled that Buck's death was accidental, however, and not due to an injury he incurred during his military service.[135] Such logic refused to recognize that a cannon hitting a soldier's head would disrupt and dramatically change his mental faculties. Thus, the decision left Patience without a pension because the federal government refused to accept responsibility for the mental injury to a formerly able-bodied African American man. Patience Buck would not accept the Bureau of Pensions' decision, and she applied again in 1890. On her second attempt, she earned a widow's pension of eight dollars a month, and there was no explanation in the record as to why the decision changed with the second application.[136]

A year later an investigation began questioning Patience Buck's morality and sexual history. And over the next five years, the Bureau of Pensions conducted an invasive inspection that included a special examination. Special examinations, which became more frequent after 1890, required applicants and witnesses to provide further information, sometimes over many years, to either confirm or contradict previous statements.[137] Unfortunately for Buck, the special examination brought forth accusations and judgments from her neighbors.

Multiple witnesses collectively stated that Buck was a washerwoman and also a prostitute. For instance, James P. Levin made it clear that she was a career criminal because of her sex work. "She is a public prostitute," Levin claimed, "of the trash[i]est sort. . . . Patience is keeping a lewd house that is notoriously known."[138] Levin pointed to the fact that Patience went to jail on several occasions to affirm his thesis.[139] John Wright also made a similar statement about Patience: "She is a terrible character[.] She is often in jail. . . . She is a public whore," Wright testified.[140]

Others disputed the salacious claims against Patience. Flowers Dorsey, who lived with Patience, noted that she made her money legally as a washerwoman.[141] Reuben Gardner, Buck's neighbor for six years, had only heard rumors about her having sex for money after George's death. However, Garner never saw any actual evidence to substantiate the claim.[142] Susie Battle, Buck's coworker, outright refuted the claims as baseless conjecture. "I have lived nex[t] door to her, and during the nin[e] year[s] that I have known her she has not adulterer[,] nor notorious adulteras . . . with men," Battle said.[143] In the end, the pension agent rejected Buck's case on the belief that she was "a notorious adulterer," even though no one provided any concrete evidence of a sexual relationship with a married man.[144] Even so, the pension agent wanted to make it known that he considered her a "public prostitute."[145] Maybe the Bureau of Pensions was looking to cut off any "unworthy" pensioners to trim down excess federal costs.

William F. Gray's widow, Susan, had to discuss her dead husband's infidelity after applying. The special examiner discovered that they separated, and after their split he began a common-law marriage with Henrietta Woodyard. Susan knew that Woodyard was not the first woman he committed adultery with, and Susan made it clear that she loathed him. She also noted that they were still legally married. Susan stated, "We were never divorced[. He] deserted me and took up with Rachel Hatfield who was a woman of ill reputed [character]."[146] Susan and William seemed to have a tempestuous relationship where they had long spells of no communication until he needed something from her. Rebecca Dolliver, Susan's friend, recalled, "The soldier deserted the claimant, that he is went away from her; . . . he would come back once in a while and stay . . . with the claimant as he was taken sick."[147] Susan must have been angered that William openly had sexual relationships with women while simultaneously using his wife and her resources when it suited him. To make matters worse for Susan, Gray's philandering, along with the couple never divorcing, led to her rejection. Thus, she was denied a pension for a husband's unfaithfulness and continued to suffer because of Gray's choices.

Over time pension expansions benefitted some of the deceased veterans' dependents too. Mothers, for example, did not need to demonstrate complete economic reliance on their sons or provide extensive documentation anymore.[148] Sisters and fathers also became pension eligible. Widows could receive twelve dollars monthly, which was an increase from eight dollars a month.[149] As a result of the dependent expansion, amidst a wave of new, first-time applications from 1890 to 1895, thirteen dependents applied. Six individuals were successful in becoming pensioners. The widows of George Stiles, Solomon Flemmer, Franklin Viney, and Francis Fausett all gained twelve dollars per month.[150] Getting a pension was necessary for a woman like Anna Fausett, who desperately needed money to cover her regular living expenses, including six cents for firewood to avoid freezing in the cold months.[151] Viney's son, Alphonso, received two dollars per month for a minor's pension from 1892 to 1895.[152] And James Gray's father, Henderson, also received twelve dollars per month.[153]

Six other pension applicants either never got a decision from the Bureau of Pensions or received outright rejections. The widow of Robert Johnson and the mother of William Smallwood abandoned their cases for unknown reasons.[154] In the case of Hannah Thomas, the widow of Joseph Thomas, the Bureau of Pensions never made a ruling after it failed to acquire her correct address, even while attempting to contact her from 1892 to 1893, 1895 to 1899, and in 1901.[155] Correspondence difficulties led to Francis Hawkins's wife, Sarah, getting denied after a special examination discovered that he was still alive.[156] Regardless of the circumstances, these cases ended without the applicants' inclusion in the pension rolls.

From 1896 to the 1920s, thirteen dependents filed various first-time pension applications. All of these claimants were widows. Ten of the applicants successfully earned approvals. Most began receiving a rate of either eight or twelve dollars per month, and some ended at rates between twenty to fifty dollars monthly.[157]

As part of their investigations, numerous witnesses testified that these women had legally wed USCT veterans. Some women supplied their marriage certificates to the Bureau of Pensions while making it clear that they wanted their documents back after their examinations concluded. Alice King notified the Bureau of Pensions, "As for the marriage cert. that I hand[ed] you, and which I desire to have returned to me by the Pension Bureau when [it's] through with it."[158] Meanwhile, Elizabeth Poulson, in a letter, stated, "Sir. You have on file in your Office my Marriage. Certificate[,] which I would like to have you Return [in] the same to me you have Had it in your Office several years as . . . Pruf to get my Pension, this Property I would Like very much to have Return[ed] to me."[159]

Their collective, defiant statements illustrate that they treasured the records documenting their unions. Sadly, the Bureau of Pensions informed Poulson that the certificate became a public record for her case and never returned it.[160]

Applying for a widow's pension did not mean that the women were without money. In two instances widows collected life insurance policies. Elizabeth Anderson, formerly the widow of Alfred Rothwell, received thirty-four dollars monthly after her second husband, Robert Anderson (who was also a USCT veteran), died.[161] Meanwhile, Alice King amassed a combined $224 in policies from Prudential and German-Armenian Mutual Benefit for her husband, Thomas C. King Sr.[162] These one-time cash injections temporarily alleviated expenses; however, bills remained. Elizabeth M. Becket, Isaac's widow, had a house worth $2,000 and made an income of $250 a year from renting out a room.[163] Some USCT veterans owned homes, such as Robert Anderson and Isaac Baynard, ranging in value from $100 to $400.[164] All three cases are examples of marriages where the women attempted, even if only temporarily, to earn money after their husbands died.

Widows learned that pension agents obsessed over the legality of their unions. Margaret Parker, William H. Parker's widow, had her application rejected due to her inability to supply any evidence of their marriage.[165] The pension agent did not let Parker's desperate plea for a pension impact his decision, even though she neglected her own serious medical issues to care for the ailing veteran. "I broke my health waiting on him day or night[.] . . . [I] am very weak and can hardly get about," Parker testified.[166] Her rejection left her confused a year later, in 1894, when she again noted her medical issues. "Why that I am not entitled to a pension as I am his lawful wife and the only one that he ever had[?] I would like to hear from you," she demanded, "with full information why[,] and what reason that I am not recognized in the pension bureau[.]"[167] Furthermore, she stated, "I have broke myself down trying to take care of [him] whilst he was sick[.]"[168] In the end, Margaret Parker did not receive a widow's pension because the pension agent did not believe that she was William H. Parker's legitimate widow.[169]

Investigators found that Rose (maiden name unknown) never divorced her first husband and began a common-law marriage with Henry Harley. Meanwhile, Edward Davis remained wed to Charity Gilmore and later married Arretta Davis. Both women had their cases rejected.[170]

Other widow pensioners experienced scrutiny about the legitimacy of their marriages. Margaret (maiden name unknown) lost her pension after an examination found that her husband, Wilson Day, never divorced his first wife, Kate. Even though Day's marital status was unknown to Margaret, it automatically disqualified her from the pension.[171] Afterward, the pension agent felt it necessary to critique Margaret's character. In the pension agent's opinion, she was foolish for not knowing about her husband's past. "This claimant is an ignorant colored woman," he wrote, "who begs for her livi[n]g and by reason of her dense ignorance is unreliable."[172]

Mary M. Parker, Robert G. Parker's widow, lost her pension after the Bureau of Pensions learned that he never divorced his first wife, Emeline Murray. The news shocked Mary, who had no idea about his past. "That is all news to me and a great surprise to me also. It is strange that he never told me of that marriage," Mary testified, "especially as he was given to throwing up things at me when he was mad and I wonder [why] he never told me of that in one of his ugly fits of temper."[173] Meanwhile, Ida Rebecca Nolan, a friend of Mary's, testified that Robert G. Parker came and went as he pleased even after leaving Mary. "I know that he treated her very bad but I do not know the cause of their separation. He went away," Ida remembered, "and left her. . . . He used to come and see his wife whenever he felt like but never did anything for her in the way of support."[174]

During their time apart, William H. Parker, a fellow USCT veteran, and Robert G. Parker's brother, recalled that Robert was "pretty fast after women."[175] Nevertheless, on his deathbed, Robert G. Parker wanted to see Mary. None of the Parkers' relationship complications concerned the pension agent. All that mattered in the Bureau's eyes was that Robert G. was a habitual adulterer, and Mary was guilty of sleeping with a married man.[176]

The politics of marriage legality was a problem for many African Americans, even more so when a dependent applied for a Civil War pension.[177] For many African Americans, the likelihood of their family receiving an approved pension application was more challenging, given the (racist) tendency of the pension agents to judge their relationships harshly. The federal government supported legal marriages as an avenue to have African American men, especially the formerly enslaved, establish and maintain patriarchal control over their nuclear family members.[178] While the Bureau of Pensions would eventually enact a policy that allowed formerly enslaved women to receive pensions without providing legal documentation, no such law pertained to free African Americans. For the Bureau of Pensions, legality was a critical aspect for widows and minors to get and remain on the pension roll. And without such evidence, or a failure to acquire a divorce, the federal government sullied African Americans' character, in particular that of women.[179] In doing so, the Bureau of Pensions refused to consider that many African Americans could not afford divorces or that their cultural marital practices, at times, differed from white societal standards. As a result, African American women fought against the Bureau of Pensions over competing notions of marriage.

❧

For the Bureau of Pensions, the efforts of women such as Mary M. Parker were futile. Whether they knew it or not, the women were not always the legal wives of the USCT veterans. Therefore, from a legal standing, their widow's applications were viewed as illegitimate. And yet, these African American women refused to adhere to the federal government's static framing of what comprised a family. With each of their claims, these wives attempted to force the Bureau of Pensions to recognize that the reality for some African American families did not adhere to the limited conception imposed by the federal government. Moreover, the repeated submissions of widow applications demonstrate their persistence in pursuing legal recognition of their families as legitimate. Even their failed pension applications reveal the contested definitions of family and the struggles that some USCT widows experienced while attempting to acknowledge their cultural citizenship.

EPILOGUE

Throughout the 1930s, the lingering effects of the Great Depression ravaged the nation. The fight for survival as starvation, homelessness, illnesses, and the combined loss of jobs and personal savings became a reality for millions of Americans. By 1939 the national unemployment rate was over 17 percent, which created dire living situations for many.[1] Sadly, racial discrimination remained a staple of American society, and the economic crisis made their lives even worse.[2] African Americans often felt the brunt of the financial hardships due to an unofficial policy of "last hired, first fired" among white employers.[3]

Many Americans looked to Franklin Delano Roosevelt and Eleanor Roosevelt for assistance in their quest to make ends meet. Perhaps some people felt a personal connection to the president because of his fireside chats. He spoke directly to an audience desperate for hope. Additionally, his New Deal programs sought to alleviate the various hardships that Americans experienced. Eleanor, meanwhile, interacted directly with African Americans in her mission to denounce racial discrimination. For instance, she condemned Bull Connor (the Birmingham commissioner of public safety) for threatening to arrest attendees at an interracial civil rights event in Alabama. She also gave African American institutions money and brought African American children to social gatherings at the White House.[4]

Perhaps these, and other examples, influenced Edmonia Woodson's decision, on September 18, 1939, to write to the first lady for some advice on a Civil War dependent pension application. She began by apologizing for any possible intrusion into the critical work that the Roosevelts were doing to rebuild the nation's economy and improve race relations. And yet, Edmonia expressed her gratitude for their racially egalitarian efforts to improve the lives of "poor people regardless to race[,] creed[,] or color."[5] Afterward, she wondered if the first lady might know why her mother, Julia, never received a widow's pension after William Woodson died in 1885.[6] The Bureau of Pensions, forty-two years earlier, had rejected Julia's pension application. Edmonia did not understand why it happened, especially since her parents were legally married.[7] She then discussed her family's struggles after her mother, and then she herself, battled cancer. To make matters worse, she was unable to find regular employment. At the end of her letter, she offered prayers and gratitude to the first family and hoped for a reply.[8]

Seven days later, the Department of Veterans Affairs (VA) responded to Edmonia Woodson. It acknowledged receiving her letter, "addressed to Mrs. Roosevelt," regarding her mother's application.[9] The VA stated that it needed her father's name to investigate the matter further. The organization never said how the personal correspondence made its way to them. Even so, someone in the White House received and dispatched the document to the proper channel on Edmonia's behalf.

On October 3, 1939, Edmonia wrote another letter to the first lady. She opened by confirming that she received Eleanor's reply.[10] "Your letter was rec' a few days ago[,] which I thank you kindly."[11] Edmonia then stated that she answered numerous questions from federal government representatives about her father's service and her mother's application. Doing so made her frustrated since many potential witnesses and "friends have passed away that knew him."[12] After venting, she closed her letter by thanking Eleanor for her graciousness. Nine days later, Edmonia's message, under the first lady's direction, reached the VA.

After continued pressure from Eleanor Roosevelt, the VA rendered a decision on Edmonia's case on October 17, 1939. E. L. Bailey, director of the Dependents Claim Service, notified Edmonia that Julia's rejection occurred because William Woodson never received an honorable discharge.[13] Bailey did not explain that William deserted from Camp William Penn on December 20, 1863. Nor did Bailey state that after William's capture he served six months while performing hard labor.[14] Since William and Julia wed in 1875, maybe he never told his family about his time as a soldier, especially since it did not end honorably. Ultimately, his decision to desert had lasting effects on his family that continued seventy-four years after the Civil War.

Woodson's case provides one of the most compelling stories of the long-term hardships and perseverance in their fight for recognition and possible economic restitution for the sacrifices of their male kin. Their story, however, is not a tale of victimization. Instead, it is a story of empowerment and persistence as African Americans demanded and sometimes received federal government assistance despite societal racism. The Woodsons illustrate a refusal to submit to the constant pressures of anti-Blackness in America.

❧

USCT soldiers and their families waged battles against racial discrimination throughout northern society. Before the war, whites imposed barriers on employment, education, access to transportation, and other avenues to oppress African Americans and champion white supremacy. When the war came, soldiering made the living situations for African Americans more difficult. By choosing enlistment, African American men, such as Benjamin Davis, prioritized the nation's needs over their obligations to their families. Deciding whether to serve was a highly complex decision that every northern African American man had to make. Those who advocated enlistment promised that service would be worthwhile because it would uplift these men as individuals and their race. Yet the removal of African American men from northern households to fulfill social obligations to the nation threw their families into economic disarray. Mary Leighton (later Williamson) knew this point firsthand when she said, "They[, the U.S. Army,] drafted men, and left me no means of support to work ourselves."[15]

Military participation placed USCT soldiers and their families in a new environment, one in which they still fought racial discrimination in various ways while serving. Their additional hardships as soldiers stemmed from one reason—because they were African American. The indignities that USCT soldiers experienced also impacted their families on the home front, where they eagerly waited for their male kin to return home safely. Some northern African American families never recovered after their male kin served in the U.S. Army but failed to return home.

Military service had long-term negative consequences on the economies, familial dynamics, and relationships of USCT veterans and their families. Reconstructing their families was difficult. Some of these costs affected all veterans, African American and white, but because of the marginalized social and economic status of USCT veterans and their families, the effects were catastrophic. Numerous USCT soldiers died while serving, and their deaths reverberated to the home front. The families of deceased USCT soldiers were thrust into economic disarray once they lost their vital wage earners. Those who came home experienced difficulty finding or maintaining full-time, wage-earning employment. The soldiers who survived often went home with wartime disabilities—psychological, physical, and emotional—that affected the veterans and their families alike. Their short tenure in military service left numerous northern African American families without economic stability and, in some cases, without male kin.

Working-class northern African American familial dynamics and marital practices became another battleground for USCT veterans and their families. White ideals of manhood championed legal marriage as the only respectable, legitimate type of union. White judgments of African American gender roles and marital practices also materialized whenever USCT veterans and their family members applied for pensions. The Bureau of Pensions penalized African American couples who had chosen to forgo legal marriage by making USCT veterans' widows and minor children ineligible for pensions. The marital practices of working-class northern USCT veterans and their families faced critiques, but this criticism led to economic instability after the war, even though USCT veterans sacrificed their lives in the service and had families who supported them from the home front.

APPENDIX I

Methodology

Rather than conduct a random sample, I examine Philadelphian-born African American men who either served in the Third USCI, the Sixth USCI, or the Eighth USCI, which totals 185 soldiers. By including their families, I detail the lives of nearly one thousand people. I am not claiming that this specific group of people is representative of the African American experience. Unlike other African American Philadelphians, this group of individuals had a unique relationship with the federal government and U.S. Army as Civil War service potentially gave them access to federally sponsored social welfare and a way to have their lives, including various hardships, documented in federal governmental records. Ultimately, USCT soldiers are only the beginning point to truly understanding the complexity of northern African American families over this study's seventy years.

This book is based on in-depth research of a wide variety of archival records. Though none of these families left behind substantial personal paper collections, I could identify them and learn about their experiences by examining federal government records. To be clear, I am not simply studying USCT soldiers. This is an investigation of their working-class (and/or working-poor) families. Due to their financial constraints and the pervasiveness of racism, these people rarely (if ever) cataloged their lives in first-hand accounts. And yet, even with this limitation, I uncovered information about their lives by turning to military records. First, I investigated USCT regimental books and Compiled Military Service Records. Both sources denote an individual's name, age, birthplace, civilian occupation, date of enlistment, payment records, and possible injury or punishment. Even with this sizable body of material, both sources provide minimal qualitative information on the soldiers. Since some soldiers provided misinformation and enlisting officers did not regularly check for accuracy, neither source is precise. When cross-referenced with each other, both sources are the ideal starting point for uncovering who served in a specific regiment, as well as snapshots of the lives of soldiers before enlisting and during the war.

Next, examining the U.S. Census provided details on veterans and their families' households and personal lives. Created each decade, the U.S. Census only yields information on the birthplace, occupations, age, marital status, literacy, ownership of real and personal estate, disabilities, and whether school-age children attended school. With Census data, it becomes possible to discover more about the veterans' familial dynamics before and after the war that other available records do not disclose.

The U.S. Census is not without its flaws due to how gender and racial biases impacted census enumerators' collected data. Historically, census enumerators devalued unpaid labor, for example, since women did not regularly have full-time wage-earning employment.[1] This book, however, recognizes that women were vital to their household economies through their various household contributions.[2] I recognize that this source historically diminished women's labor, but census enumerators' limited understanding of women's contributions to their homes does not influence me. Instead, I am using these sources to catalog the various inhabitants, marriage documentation, ages of children, and birthplaces of all residents that do not always get noted in other available primary sources.

Investigating relevant Civil War pension records provided the richest material on enlisted men's military service and civilian lives. Pension applications offer detailed information on how service impacted the men's finances, minds, bodies, and personal relationships with family and community members.[3] Additionally, Civil War pensions highlight that veterans and dependents hoped the federal government would recognize their wartime sacrifices by providing medical aid to invalid veterans and giving financial compensation to family members. The federal government's highly bureaucratic process mandated that applicants and witnesses substantiate claims of disability, unemployment, avoidance of "immoral activity," or familial dependency. It was also not uncommon for witnesses to provide personal information about themselves while testifying a case. Pension records provide us with the words from these historical subjects, even if dictated to a federal government clerk. And in many cases, these are the only sources providing firsthand narratives of their lives. Even though these narratives were often recorded long after a man's military service, which raises the possibility of faulty memory, there is no reason to believe that pension records are any more problematic than other historical sources—all of which must be read with a critical eye. Therefore, as numerous scholars note, pension documents become avenues for learning about the sampled families and their larger communities.[4]

Meanwhile, the *Weekly Anglo-African* and *Christian Recorder* were influential northern African American newspapers, and both publications were integral to this study.[5] Both presses published editorials submitted by various USCT soldiers describing their lives on the frontline.[6] Numerous USCT enlisted men used these newspapers to describe how they felt about their military service to a northern African American audience.

Even with these sources, there are noticeable gaps, for countless reasons, in the documented lives of families examined here. Therefore, whenever possible, I incorporate the histories of other northern freeborn USCT soldiers and their families to denote their hardships and successes. Selectively combining them allows me to speculate on how this study's sample experienced events similar to other African American soldiers. I accomplish this by relying on published memoirs and correspondences between USCT soldiers and their families to uncover how various northern African Americans traversed through life.

By investigating all of these sources, it is evident that one can uncover detailed sketches of USCT soldiers, their families, and their local communities. Collectively, these sources make it possible to survey African American Philadelphian families' survival strategies and to uncover the myriad ways that the Civil War disrupted their lives. Carrying the project into the early twentieth century allows us to see the long-term impact of military service on the descendants of USCT veterans.

APPENDIX II

Philadelphian-Born United States Colored Infantry (USCI) Soldiers

Philadelphian-Born Third USCI Soldiers

Name	*Age*	*Enlistment date*	*Precivilian occupation upon enlistment*
COMPANY A			
1. George Allen	19	June 26, 1863	Laborer
2. John F. Diamond	19	June 26, 1863	Butcher
3. Wilson Day	23	July 18, 1863	Wagoner
4. Jeremiah Hill	20	June 26, 1863	Laborer
5. David Hawkins	19	June 26, 1863	Waiter
6. Richard Johnson	22	June 26, 1863	Coachman
7. David Murray	20	June 26, 1863	Butcher
8. Joseph Perkins	34	June 26, 1863	Laborer
9. Edward Purnell Jr.	22	June 26, 1863	Porter
10. David Smith	19	June 26, 1863	Waiter
11. John Thompson	19	June 3, 1863	Waiter
12. Hiram Waters	20	June 26, 1863	Baker
13. George White	19	June 26, 1863	Baker
14. John Bailey	33	June 26, 1863	Waiter
15. William B. Johnston	21	June 26, 1863	Shoemaker
COMPANY B			
1. Joseph Thomas	19	June 30, 1863	Laborer
2. Henry Harley	22	June 30, 1863	Laborer
3. Thomas King	18	June 30, 1863	Laborer
4. William F. Gray	20	June 30, 1863	Laborer
5. Henry S. Harmon	25	June 30, 1863	Laborer
COMPANY C			
1. Harten Foreman	40	July 2, 1863	Porter
2. Alfred Henderson	22	July 3, 1863	Laborer

Name	*Age*	*Enlistment date*	*Precivilian occupation upon enlistment*
3. Richard Lee	20	July 3, 1863	Laborer
4. William H. Parker	20	July 3, 1863	Butcher
5. John Ross	21	July 3, 1863	Laborer
6. C. W. Sewell	28	July 3, 1863	Loafer
7. Charles Tobias	21	July 3, 1863	Shoemaker
8. John Wharton	31	July 3, 1863	Teamster
9. James Grey	20	July 3, 1863	Laborer
10. Thomas Williams	19	July 3, 1863	Sailor
11. John Forman	17	July 3, 1863	Laborer
12. David Murray	22	June 26, 1863	Hostler
COMPANY D			
1. Samuel Benson	28	July 4, 1863	Engineer
2. Daniel Brown	18	July 4, 1863	Coachman
3. Samuel Brown	32	July 4, 1863	Fisherman
4. Draper Brown	18	July 4, 1863	Coachman
5. Edward Brown	19	July 4, 1863	Boatman
6. George K. Buck	20	July 4, 1863	Carpenter
7. Samuel Derry	23	July 4, 1863	Farmer
8. James Gray	19	July 4, 1863	Farmer
9. Crawford Hardy	20	July 4, 1863	Waiter
10. Solomon Hoff	25	July 4, 1863	Sash maker
11. Joseph Hooper	18	July 4, 1863	Brickmaker
12. Alfred Rothwell	25	July 4, 1863	Fisherman
13. John Stuart	26	July 4, 1863	Mason
14. Theodore Smith	18	July 4, 1863	Carpenter
15. Joseph Wilson	25	July 4, 1863	Blacksmith
16. John Wilson	21	July 4, 1863	Musician
COMPANY E			
n/a	n/a	n/a	n/a
COMPANY F			
1. Joseph Green	17	July 8, 1863	Farmer
2. Lorenzo George	22	July 9, 1863	Longshoreman
3. Francis Hawkins	16	July 3, 1863	Porter
4. Richard Howard	20	July 8, 1863	Bricklayer
5. Alexander Jackson	34	July 11, 1863	Brickmaker
6. Henry Lawrence	45	July 10, 1863	Bootblack
7. Henry McDonald	30	July 11, 1863	Farmer
8. John Parker	38	July 10, 1863	Laborer

Name	Age	Enlistment date	Precivilian occupation upon enlistment
9. Charles Penn	21	July 11, 1863	Laborer
10. Jacob Purnell	37	July 11, 1863	Baker
11. James White	27	July 11, 1863	Teamster
12. James Henderson	34	July 11, 1863	Laborer
13. John Parker	38	July 10, 1863	Laborer
14. James Songo	21	July 11, 1863	Laborer
15. Pierce Brown	20	July 11, 1863	Brickmaker
COMPANY G			
1. Henry Johnson	19	July 11, 1863	Laborer
2. Joseph Williams	25	July 13, 1863	Laborer
3. William Yates	20	July 14, 1863	Farmer
4. Isaac Becket	21	July 13, 1863	Waiter
5. Richard Black	25	July 14, 1863	Seaman
6. James B. Williams	34	July 13, 1863	Farmer
7. George Potts	16	July 14, 1863	Unknown
COMPANY H			
1. George Crosberry	24	July 17, 1863	Farmer
2. Peter James	18	July 17, 1863	Waiter
3. William Cooper	30	July 18, 1863	Sailor
4. Richard Drisberry	20	July 20, 1863	Waiter
5. Samuel Lewis	22	July 18, 1863	Wagoner
COMPANY I			
1. Joseph Anderson	21	July 20, 1863	Musician
2. Isaac Byron	21	July 21, 1863	Farmer
3. Abel Drummond	21	July 21, 1863	Laborer
4. John Lee	23	July 22, 1863	Laborer
5. Alexander Manly	18	July 21, 1863	Farmer
6. Joseph Watkins	27	July 22, 1863	Seaman
7. Peter Wilson	18	July 21, 1863	Coachman
8. John H. Poulson	21	July 21, 1863	Laborer
9. Jacob Thorn	19	July 21, 1863	Brickmaker
COMPANY K			
1. James Ennis	27	July 17, 1863	Laborer
2. Isaac D. Henderson	18	July 23, 1863	Laborer
3. James Hogan	19	July 24, 1863	Farmer
4. Robert H. Lee	18	July 23, 1863	Barber
5. Isaac H. Roach	22	July 24, 1863	Baker
6. Moses Schenck	25	October 5, 1864	Laborer

Philadelphian-Born Sixth USCI Soldiers

Name	*Age*	*Enlistment date*	*Precivilian occupation upon enlistment*
COMPANY A			
1. Richard Carter	26	July 27, 1863	Farmer
2. Solomon Flemmer	31	July 28, 1863	Laborer
3. Nathaniel Logan Sr.	29	July 27, 1863	Carpenter
4. David Meads	27	July 25, 1863	Laborer
5. Thomas Moore	20	July 28, 1863	Huckster
6. Alexander Young	32	July 27, 1863	Laborer
7. William Brown	23	July 27, 1863	Assistant Engineer
8. Joseph Harris	18	July 28, 1863	Huckster
COMPANY B			
1. Malachi Bird	26	February 5, 1865	Porter
2. George Glascow	27	July 13, 1863	Farmer
3. Jeremiah B. Griggs	25	August 1, 1863	Laborer
4. Thomas Johnson	31	July 31, 1863	Farmer
5. John W. Jackson	31	July 30, 1863	Brickmaker
6. Daniel Robinson	28	July 14, 1863	Laborer
COMPANY C			
1. William Butler	33	August 3, 1863	Farmer
2. Lewis Cork	18	August 7, 1863	Farmer
3. George Elliot	31	August 7, 1863	Barter
4. Wesley Maloney	32	July 15, 1863	Driver
5. Marshall Price	29	August 7, 1863	Farmer
6. Alexander Robinson	21	August 5, 1863	Barber
7. Lewis Smith	16	August 5, 1863	Carpenter
8. William Tallman	23	March 21, 1865	Barber
9. John Wallen	25	June 27, 1865	Coachman
COMPANY D			
1. Josiah Allen	23	July 15, 1863	Laborer
2. William Ballet	24	August 10, 1863	Steward
3. Richard Bryant	23	August 10, 1863	Laborer
4. Samuel E. Crawford	24	July 15, 1863	Servant
5. Nathaniel Danks	25	August 10, 1863	Laborer
6. Richard Duffey	32	August 10, 1863	Laborer
7. Francis Fausett	19	August 10, 1863	Tradesman
8. David Gould	18	August 10, 1863	Servant
9. Mark Hamilton	34	August 13, 1863	Sailor
10. Ephraim Maloney	25	July 13, 1863	Laborer

Name	Age	Enlistment date	Precivilian occupation upon enlistment
11. Miles Parker	26	August 10, 1863	Laborer
12. James Richmond	26	August 11, 1863	Journeyman
13. John Richmond	22	August 10, 1863	Laborer
14. Andrew White	21	August 12, 1863	Laborer
15. Thomas Dye	25	August 18, 1863	Boatman
COMPANY E			
1. Benjamin Davis	28	August 15, 1863	Barber
2. William Henry	18	August 20, 1863	Waiter
3. Peter Marsh	24	August 15, 1863	Laborer
4. William Smallwood	19	August 22, 1863	Barber
5. William Griffin	18	September 13, 1864	Boatman
6. John Turner	41	August 4, 1864	Porter
7. Alfred Crosier	18	August 22, 1863	Laborer
8. John Ditton	19	August 18, 1863	Laborer
COMPANY F			
1. Charles Brown	29	August 24, 1863	Farmer
2. James Crippen	21	August 26, 1863	Laborer
3. John Richmond	27	August 10, 1863	Butcher
COMPANY G			
1. Edward Davis	26	December 30, 1864	Unknown
2. James H. Ellsbury	29	August 29, 1863	Servant
3. William H. Parker	21	September 2, 1863	Waiter
COMPANY H			
1. William Barrett	35	July 18, 1863	Miner
2. Isaiah Elsbury	22	August 3, 1863	Coachman
3. Shedwick Johnson	21	September 9, 1863	Laborer
4. Edward Lloyd	35	September 7, 1863	Laborer
5. Joseph Piner	21	August 29, 1863	Laborer
6. Robert G. Parker	18	September 4, 1863	Laborer
7. George Roland	22	September 3, 1863	Laborer
8. Franklin Viney	25	September 2, 1863	Coachman
COMPANY I			
1. John Brown	28	November 11, 1864	Sailor
2. Charles H. Deets	25	September 10, 1863	Boatman
3. Charles W. Jones	22	July 29, 1863	Barber
4. Robert Johnson	32	September 11, 1863	Farmer
5. Henry Richardson	29	June 23, 1863	Laborer

Name	Age	Enlistment date	Precivilian occupation upon enlistment
6. James Robinson	24	September 3, 1863	Laborer
7. George M. Shorter	20	August 12, 1863	Laborer
8. Hezekiah Wilson	33	June 23, 1863	Laborer
9. George Henderson	20	September 4, 1863	Waterman
COMPANY K			
1. John Short	28	September 12, 1863	Laborer

Philadelphian-Born Eighth USCI Soldiers

Name	Age	Enlistment date	Precivilian occupation upon enlistment
COMPANY A			
1. William Edward	20	September 18, 1863	Laborer
2. James Burk	28	August 13, 1863	Barber
3. George P. Miller	22	September 16, 1863	Brickyard hand
4. Samuel Savall	28	July 28, 1863	Seaman
COMPANY B			
n/a	n/a	n/a	n/a
COMPANY C			
n/a	n/a	n/a	n/a
COMPANY D			
1. Jacob G. Jackson	20	October 5, 1863	Farmer
2. Henry Thompson	38	August 14, 1863	Laborer
3. Joseph Woodson	19	October 1, 1863	Barber
COMPANY E			
1. Robert Streets	22	October 5, 1863	Laborer
2. Frank Herbert	31	October 5, 1863	Laborer
3. John Hazard	37	October 5, 1863	Laborer
COMPANY F			
1. Charles Brant	28	October 22, 1863	Laborer
2. Charles A. Early	30	October 8, 1863	Laborer
3. Thomas Short	20	October 13, 1863	Laborer
4. John H. Smith	27	July 13, 1863	Driver
COMPANY G			
1. George Butler	30	July 16, 1863	Farmer

Name	*Age*	*Enlistment date*	*Precivilian occupation upon enlistment*
COMPANY H			
n/a	n/a	n/a	n/a
COMPANY I			
1. John W. Young	19	November 20, 1863	Boatman
2. Henry Cary	34	July 28, 1863	Barber
3. David (Daniel) Derry	24	August 28, 1863	Seaman
4. William Wharton	21	July 28, 1863	Laborer
5. John Young	25	July 20, 1863	Brickmaker
6. George Stiles	32	July 29, 1863	Laborer
COMPANY K			
1. George Willett	20	November 28, 1863	Farmer
2. William Woodson	36	July 28, 1863	Hackman
3. John Wilson	40	November 28, 1863	Farmer
4. Samuel Robinson	23	November 29, 1863	Waiter

NOTES

INTRODUCTION

1. Deposition of Mary Williamson, on April 8, 1884, in Benjamin Davis, Sixth USCI, pension file, National Archives and Records Administration, Washington, D.C. (hereafter pension file).

2. For various studies on the experiences of USCT soldiers, see Ira Berlin, Joseph P. Reidy, and Leslie S. Rowland, eds., *Freedom's Soldiers: The Black Military Experience in the Civil War* (Cambridge: Cambridge University Press, 1997); Edward G. Longacre, *A Regiment of Slaves: The 4th United States Colored Infantry, 1863–1866* (Mechanicsburg, Pa.: Stackpole Books, 2003); Steven Hahn, *A Nation under Our Feet: Black Political Struggles in the Rural South from Slavery to the Great Migration* (Cambridge, Mass.: Harvard University Press, 2003); Aaron Sheehan-Dean, ed., *The Cambridge History of the American Civil War*, vol. 1: *Military Affairs* (Cambridge, Mass.: Cambridge University Press, 2019); Paul D. Escott, *Paying Freedom's Price: A History of African Americans in the Civil War* (New York: Rowman & Littlefield, 2017); Howard C. Westwood, *Black Troops White Commanders and Freedmen During The Civil War* (Carbondale: Southern Illinois State University Press, 1992); William A. Dobak, *Freedom by the Sword: The U.S. Colored Troops, 1862–1867* (New York: Skyhorse Publishing, 2013); Carole Emberton, *Beyond Redemption: Race, Violence, and the American South after the Civil War* (Chicago: University of Chicago Press, 2013); Brandi Clay Brimmer, *Claiming Union Widowhood: Race, Respectability, and Poverty in the Post-Emancipation South* (Durham, N.C.: Duke University Press, 2020); Kelly D. Mezurek, *For Their Own Cause: The 27th United States Colored Troops* (Kent, Ohio: Kent State University Press, 2016); Edward A. Miller Jr., *The Black Civil War Soldiers of Illinois: The Story of the Twenty-Ninth U.S. Colored Infantry* (Columbia: University of South Carolina Press, 1998); Ian Michael Spurgeon, *Soldiers in the Army of Freedom: The 1st Kansas Colored, the 63–64, The Civil War's First African American Combat Unit* (Norman: University of Oklahoma Press, 2014); Richard M. Reid, *African Canadians in Union Blue: Volunteering for the Cause in the Civil War* (Kent, Ohio: Kent State University Press, 2014); Ira Berlin, Joseph P. Reidy, and Leslie S. Rowland, eds., *Freedom: A Docu-*

mentary History of Emancipation, 1861–1867, 2 vols. (Cambridge: Cambridge University Press, 2010).

3. Chandra Manning, *What This Cruel War Was Over: Soldiers, Slavery, and the Civil War* (New York: Alfred A. Knopf, 2007), 130; Leslie A. Schwalm, *Emancipation's Diaspora: Race and Reconstruction in the Upper Midwest* (Chapel Hill: University of North Carolina Press, 2009), 176–184.

4. The following studies examine a mixture of working poor and middle-class northern USCT soldiers. However, their families' lives are not the focuses of the projects. Each project is critical to better understanding the complexity of northern society and USCT soldiers' experiences. Please refer to the following studies: Edythe Ann Quinn, *Freedom Journey: Black Civil War Soldiers and The Hills Community, Westchester County, New York* (Albany: State of New York University Press, 2015); Keith P. Wilson, *Campfires of Freedom: The Camp Life of Black Soldiers During the Civil War* (Kent, Ohio: Kent State University Press, 2002); Douglas R. Egerton, *Thunder at the Gates: The Black Civil War Regiments That Redeemed America* (New York: Basic Books, 2016); William Seraile, *New York's Black Regiments during the Civil War* (New York: Routledge, 2001); Edwin Redkey, ed., *A Grand Army of Black Men: Letters from African-American Soldiers in the Union Army, 1861–1865* (Cambridge: Cambridge University Press, 1992); John David Smith, ed., *Black Soldiers in Blue: African American Troops in the Civil War Era* (Chapel Hill: University of North Carolina Press, 2002); Judith Giesberg, *Army at Home: Women and the Civil War on the Northern Home Front* (Chapel Hill: University of North Carolina Press, 2009); Mezurek, *For Their Own Cause.*

5. My work aligns with other scholars dealing with the war and its meaning for racial justice. Please refer to the following studies for examples that discuss this particular topic: Wilson, *Campfires of Freedom*; Brimmer, *Claiming Union Widowhood*; Donald Shaffer, *After the Glory: The Struggles of Black Civil War Veterans* (Lawrence: University of Kansas Press, 2004); Elizabeth Regosin, *Freedom's Promise: Ex-Slave Families and Citizenship in the Age of Emancipation* (Charlottesville: University of Virginia Press, 2002); Andrew K. Diemer, *The Politics of Black Citizenship: Free African Americans in the Mid-Atlantic Borderland, 1817–1863* (Athens: University of Georgia Press, 2016); Jim Downs, *Sick from Freedom: African-American Illness and Suffering During the Civil War and Reconstruction* (Oxford: Oxford University Press, 2002); Martha S. Jones, *Vanguard: How Black Women Broke Barriers, Won the Vote, and Insisted on Equality for All* (New York: Basic Books, 2020); Brian Taylor, *Fighting for Citizenship: Black Northerners and the Debate over Military Service in the Civil War* (Chapel Hill: University of North Carolina Press, 2020); Christian G. Samito, *Becoming American under Fire: Irish Americans, African Americans, and the Politics of Citizenship During the Civil War Era* (Ithaca: Cornell University Press, 2009); Carole Emberton, "Unwriting the Freedom Narrative: A Review Essay," *Journal of Southern History* 82, no. 2 (May 2016): 377–394.

6. Bruce Dorsey, *Reforming Men and Women: Gender in the Antebellum City* (Ithaca: Cornell University Press, 2002), 20, 26–27, 62, 75.

7. Shaffer, *After the Glory*, 123–132; Larry M. Logue and Peter Blanck, *Race, Ethnicity, and Disability: Veterans and Benefits in Post–Civil War America* (Cambridge: Cambridge University Press, 2010), 113–114; Brimmer, *Claiming Union Widowhood*, 2–7.

8. To date, southern formerly enslaved African Americans have garnered the most scholarly attention. Of the extensive research on USCT soldiers, few have focused on the lived experiences of soldiers' families. Studies on African Americans in the Civil War include Chandra Manning, *Troubled Refuge: Struggling for Freedom in the Civil War* (New York: Alfred A. Knopf, 2016); Tera W. Hunter, *Bound in Wedlock: Slave and Free Black Marriage in the Nineteenth Century* (Cambridge, Mass.: Belknap Press of Harvard University Press, 2017); Noralee Frankel, *Freedom's Women: Black Women and Families in Civil War Era Mississippi* (Bloomington: Indiana University Press, 1999); Shaffer, *After the Glory*; Regosin, *Freedom's Promise*; Stephanie McCurry, *Women's War: Fighting and Surviving the American Civil War* (Cambridge, Mass.: Belknap Press of Harvard University Press, 2019); Katherine Franke, *Wedlocked: The Perils of Marriage Equality—How African Americans and Gays Mistakenly Thought the Right to Marry Would Set Them Free* (New York: New York University Press, 2015).

9. William A. Gladstone, *United States Colored Troops, 1863–1867* (Gettysburg, Pa.: Thomas Publications, 1996), 120.

10. The eleven regiments were the Third USCI, the Sixth USCI, the Eighth USCI, the Twenty-Second USCI, the Twenty-Fourth USCI, the Twenty-Fifth USCI, the Thirty-Second USCI, the Forty-First USCI, the Forty-Third USCI, the Forty-Fifth USCI, and the 127th USCI. Lucien Holness, "United States Colored Troops," Encyclopedia of Greater Philadelphia, https://philadelphiaencyclopedia.org/archive/united-states-colored-troops/.

11. Unlike Tremel, I am not examining all counties comprising the modern-day Philadelphia metro area (Bucks, Chester, Delaware, and Montgomery). Andrew T. Tremel, "The Union League, Black Leaders, and the Recruitment of Philadelphia's African American Civil War Regiments," *Pennsylvania History: A Journal of Mid-Atlantic Studies* 80, no. 1 (Winter 2013), 13–36.

12. Andrew Heath, *In Union There Is Strength: Philadelphia in the Age of Urban Consolidation* (Philadelphia: University of Pennsylvania Press, 2019), 19, 50, 105–131; Stuart M. Blumin, "Residential Mobility Within the Nineteenth-Century City," in *The Peoples of Philadelphia: A History of Ethnic Groups and Lower-Class Life, 1790–1940*, eds. Allen F. Davis and Mark H. Haller (Philadelphia: University of Pennsylvania Press, 1973), 42; Bruce Laurie, *Working People of Philadelphia, 1800–1850* (Philadelphia: Temple University Press, 1980), 3–32; J. Matthew Gallman, *Mastering Wartime: A Social History of Philadelphia During the Civil War* (Philadelphia: University of Pennsylvania Press, 1990), 1–3, 7, 28–47.

13. James F. Farley, *Making Arms in The Machine Age: Philadelphia's Frankford Arsenal, 1816–1870* (University Park: Pennsylvania State University Press, 1994), 48, 62–63, 69–70, 73–76, 83–88.

14. *McElroy's Philadelphia City Directory for 1863* (Philadelphia: E.C. & J. Biddle & Co., 1863), 941–944; Theodore Hershberg, Harold E. Cox, Dale B. Light Jr., and Richard R. Greenfield, "The 'Journey-to-Work': An Empirical Investigation of Work, Residence and Transportation, Philadelphia, 1850 and 1880," in *Philadelphia: Work, Space, Family, and Group Experience in the 19th Century*, ed. Theodore Hershberg (Oxford: Oxford University Press, 1981), 142.

15. For comparison, New York City, New York, had a population of 22,000, while Boston, Massachusetts, had a population of 12,500. 1860 United States Federal Census (Washington, D.C.: National Archives and Records Administration, n.d.), accessed via *Ancestry.com* (hereafter 1860 U.S. Census), M324; Karsonya Wise Whitehead, ed., *Notes from a Colored Girl: The Civil War Pocket Diaries of Emilie Frances Davis* (Columbia: The University of South Carolina Press, 2014), 75; Leslie M. Harris, "African-Americans in New York City, 1626–1863," *Emory University Department of History Newsletter*, no. 46 (August 2001), http://history.emory.edu/newsletter01/newsl01/african.htm#:~:text=After%20yea rs%20of%20growth%2C%20New,with%20blacks%20for%20unskilled%20jobs; James Wolfinger, "African American Migration," *The Encyclopedia of Greater Philadelphia*, 2013, https://philadelphiaencyclopedia.org/archive/african-american-migration/.

16. Maxwell Whiteman, *Gentlemen In Crisis: The First Century of the Union League of Philadelphia 1862–1962* (Philadelphia: Union League of Philadelphia, 1974), 48.

17. Nicholas B. Wainwright, "The Loyal Opposition in Civil War Philadelphia," *The Pennsylvania Magazine of History and Biography* 88, no. 3 (July 1964), 294–295, 297–302; Whitehead, *Notes from a Colored Girl*, 100, 120; Kate Masur, *Until Justice Be Done: America's First Civil Rights Movement, from the Revolution to Reconstruction* (New York: W. W. Norton & Company, 2021), 9, 19–22; Carol Wilson, *Freedom at Risk: The Kidnapping of Free Blacks in America, 1780–1865* (Lexington: University of Kentucky Press, 1994), 24–27; Van Gosse, *The First Reconstruction: Black Politics in American from the Revolution to the Civil War* (Chapel Hill: University of North Carolina Press, 2021), 64–69.

18. For examples of studies on the abolition movement in Philadelphia, see Gary B. Nash, *Forging Freedom: The Formation of Philadelphia's Black Community, 1720–1840* (Cambridge, Mass.: Harvard University Press, 1991); Daniel R. Biddle and Murray Dubin, *Tasting Freedom: Octavius Catto and the Battle for Equality in Civil War America* (Philadelphia: Temple University Press, 2010); Julie Winch, *A Gentleman of Color: The Life of James Forten* (Oxford: Oxford University Press, 2003); Manisha Sinha, *The Slave's Cause: A History of Abolition* (New Haven, Conn.: Yale University Press, 2017); R. J. M. Blackett, *The Captive's Quest for Freedom: Fugitive Slaves, the 1850 Fugitive Slave Law, and the Politics of Slavery* (Cambridge: Cambridge University Press, 2018); Paul Goodman, *Of One Blood: Abolitionism and the Origins of Racial Equality* (Berkeley: University of California Press, 1998); David G. Smith, *On the Edge of Freedom: The Fugitive Slave Issue in South Central Pennsylvania, 1829–1870* (New York: Fordham University Press, 2013); James McPherson, *The Struggle for Equality: Abolitionists and the Negro in the Civil War and*

Reconstruction (Princeton, N.J.: Princeton University Press, 1964); Henry Mayer, *All on Fire: William Lloyd Garrison and the Abolition of Slavery* (New York: W. W. Norton & Company, 2008); Kellie Carter Jackson, *Force and Freedom: Black Abolitionists and the Politics of Violence* (Philadelphia: University of Pennsylvania Press, 2019), 98–103; William C. Kashatus, *William Still: The Underground Railraod and the Angel at Philadelphia* (Notre Dame, Ind.: University of Notre Dame Press, 2021), 56–59.

19. Collectively, their studies provide information on the various forms of systematic racial oppression that directly impacted the finances of African American Philadelphians' households for generations. W. E. B. Du Bois, *The Philadelphia Negro*, (Philadelphia: University of Pennsylvania Press, 1899; rpt., 1996); Theodore Hershberg, "Free Blacks in Antebellum Philadelphia: A Study of Ex-Slaves, Freeborn, and Socioeconomic Decline," in *African American in Pennsylvania: Shifting Historical Perspectives*, eds. Joe William Trotter Jr. and Eric Ledell Smith (University Park: Pennsylvania State University Press, 1997), 126–133; Roger Lane, *William Dorsey's Philadelphia and Ours: On the Past and Future of the Black City in America* (Oxford: Oxford University Press, 1991); Roger Lane, *Roots of Violence in Black Philadelphia 1860–1900* (Cambridge, Mass.: Harvard University Press, 1986).

20. Herbert G. Gutman, *The Black Family in Slavery and Freedom, 1750–1925* (New York: Patheon Books, 1976), 137, 202–204, 211–213; Dylan C. Penningroth, *The Claims of Kinfolk: African American Property and Community in the Nineteenth-Century South* (Chapel Hill: University of North Carolina Press, 2003), 7–8, 11, 13–15, 21–22, 24–25, 27–36; Dylan C. Penningroth, "The Claims of Slaves and Ex-Slaves to Family and Property: A Transatlantic Comparison," *American Historical Review* 112, no. 4 (October, 2007), 1044–1059.

21. Previously, studies refer to fictive kin as nongenealogical individuals who developed bonds (real and imagined) with families. Scholars denote that people, over various historical periods, incorporate fictive kin into their families for differing reasons. I will apply this well-established interdisciplinary term to the families examined here to recognize their complex living situations. For examples of studies investigating fictive kin, see Edward Norbeck and Harumi Befu, "Informal Fictive Kinship in Japan," *American Anthropologist* 60, no. 1 (February 1958), 102–117; Linda M. Chatters, Robert Joseph Taylor, and Rukmalie Jayakody, "Fictive Kinship Relations in Black Extended Families," *Journal of Comparative Family Studies* 25, no. 3 (Autumn 1994), 297–312; Libra R. Hilde, *Slavery, Fatherhood, and Paternal Duty in African American Communities over the Long Nineteenth Century* (Chapel Hill: University of North Carolina Press, 2020), 74–75; Steve Mintz and Susan Kellogg, *Domestic Revolutions: A Social History of American Family Life* (New York: Free Press, 1988), 67–69; Karen Cook Bell, *Race, Kinship, and Land in Nineteenth-Century Georgia* (Colombia: University of South Carolina Press, 2018), 31–32.

22. "Anniversary of the Vigilance Committee. On Tuesday Night This," *North*

Star, May 18, 1849; "For Frederick Douglass' Paper. Pursuant to Public Notice, a," *Frederick Douglass Paper*, December 11, 1851.

23. For examples of the intersectional approach, see Kali N. Gross, *Colored Amazons: Crime, Violence, and Black Women in the City of Brotherly Love, 1880–1910* (Durham, N.C.: Duke University Press, 2006), 3; Kimberle Crenshaw, "Mapping the Margins: Intersectionality, Identity Politics, and Violence against Women of Color," *Stanford Law Review* 43, no. 6 (July 1991), 1241–1299. I want to acknowledge that studies on ethnicity and U.S. Army soldiers have previously moved toward an intersectional approach. For studies on ethnicity and U.S. Army regiments, see Susannah J. Ural, *The Harp and the Eagle: Irish-American Volunteers and the Union Army, 1861–1865* (New York: New York University Press, 2006); Ryan W. Keating, *Shades of Green: Irish Regiments, American Soldiers, and Local Communities in the Civil War Era* (New York: Fordham University Press, 2017); William B. Kurtz, *Excommunicated from the Union: How the Civil War Created a Separate Catholic America* (New York: Fordham University Press, 2016); Susannah J. Ural, ed., *Civil War Citizens: Race, Ethnicity, and Identity in America's Bloodiest Conflict* (New York: New York University Press, 2010).

24. For insight on U.S. Army racial policies about various forms of punishment, pay inequality, recruitment, and the laboring conditions of USCT enlisted men, see Joseph T. Glatthaar, *Forged in Battle: The Civil War Alliance of Black Soldiers and White Officers* (Baton Rouge: Louisiana State University Press, 1990); Margaret Humphreys, *Intensely Human: The Health of the Black Soldier in the American Civil War* (Baltimore: Johns Hopkins University Press, 2008); Joseph P. Reidy, *Illusions of Emancipation: The Pursuit of Freedom and Equality in the Twilight of Slavery* (Chapel Hill: University of North Carolina Press, 2020).

25. For studies on USCT veterans and their families agitating for political rights, demanding Civil War pensions, and gaining access to state and governmental institutions, see Brian Matthew Jordan, *Marching Home: Union Veterans and Their Unending Civil War* (New York: Liveright Publishing Corporation, 2014); Frankel, *Freedom's Women*; Emberton, *Beyond Redemption*; Schwalm, *Emancipation's Diaspora*; Brimmer, *Claiming Union Widowhood*.

26. Richard M. Reid, *Freedom for Themselves: North Carolina's Black Soldiers in the Civil War Era* (Chapel Hill: University of North Carolina Press, 2008), xiv.

27. Ira Berlin and Leslie S. Rowland, eds., *Families and Freedom: A Documentary History of African-American Kinship in the Civil War Era* (New York: The New Press, 1997), 79.

28. James G. Mendez primarily investigates African American women—mothers, wives, sisters, and family friends—directly connected to USCT enlisted men during and immediately following the war. James G. Mendez, "A Great Sacrifice: Northern Black Families and Their Civil War Experiences" (PhD diss., University of Illinois at Chicago, 2011), 2–4, 6; James G. Mendez, *A Great Sacrifice: Northern Black Soldiers, Their Families, and the Experience of Civil War* (New York: Fordham University Press, 2019), 4.

29. The first edition of Dudley Taylor Cornish's monograph was initially published in 1956. Dudley Taylor Cornish, *The Sable Arm: Black Troops in the Union Army, 1861–1865* (Lawrence: University Press of Kansas, 1987), xii–xv; Frederick M. Binder, "Pennsylvania Negro Regiments in the Civil War," *Journal of Negro History* 37, no. 4 (October 1952), 386–390, 393–395.

30. James M. McPherson, *The Negro's Civil War: How American Blacks Felt and Acted During the War for the Rebellion* (New York: Vintage Books, 1965), xvi–xvii.

31. Cornish, *The Sable Arm*, xiv.

32. William Wells Brown, *The Negro in the American Rebellion: His Heroism and His Fidelity* (Boston: Lee & Shepard, 1867), vi.

33. USCT veterans began writing regimental histories, most likely to challenge omissions made by scholars and the public, seeking to reaffirm the historical significance of African American soldiers during the Civil War; Joseph T. Wilson's book originally published in 1887. William J. Simmons, *Men of Mark: Eminent, Progressive and Rising* (Cleveland, Ohio: George M. Rewell & Co., 1887), 6–8; George W. Williams, *A History of the Negro Troops in the War of the Rebellion 1861–1865* (New York: Harper & Brothers, 1888), xi–xiv; Joseph T. Wilson, *The Black Phalanx: African American Soldiers in the War, The War of 1812 and The Civil War* (Hartford, Conn.: American Publishing Company, 1888; rpt., New York: Da Capo Press 1994), 1; *The Forty-Third Regiment United States Colored Troops* (Gettysburg, Pa.: J. E. Wible, printer, 1866), 2; Isaac J. Hill, *A Sketch of the 29th Regiment of Connecticut Colored Troops* (Baltimore: Daugherty, Maguire & Co., 1867), 7; Alexander Heritage Newton, *Out of the Briars: An Autobiography and Sketch of the Twenty-Ninth Regiment Connecticut Volunteers* (Philadelphia: A.M.E. Book Concern, 1910), viii.

34. Jeffrey Aaron Snyder, *Making Black History: The Color Line, Culture, and Race in the Age of Jim Crow* (Athens: University of Georgia Press, 2018), 19–21.

35. Susie King Taylor, *Reminiscences Of Life In Camp with The 33rd United States Colored Troops Late 1st S.C. Volunteers* (Boston: Susie King Taylor, 1902), 11, 14–15.

36. Thomas Wentworth Higginson, *Army Life in a Black Regiment* (Boston: Fields, Osgood, and Company, 1879; rpt., New York: Barnes and Noble, 2009), 3–6; Luis F. Emilio, *History of the Fifty-Fourth Regiment of Massachusetts Volunteer Infantry, 1863–1865* (Boston: Boston Book Company, 1894), viii–x.

37. Simmons enlisted in the Forty-First USCI. Wilson served in the Fifty-Fourth Massachusetts. Williams joined the Thirteenth USCI. Newton and Hill were Twenty-Ninth USCI soldiers. For information on these USCT veterans, see Compiled Military Service Records of Volunteer Union Soldiers Who Served with the United States Colored Troops, National Archives, Washington, D.C. (hereafter Compiled Military Service Records).

38. Wilson, *The Black Phalanx*, 14.

39. Simmons, *Men of Mark*, 6.

40. Ibid., 3.

41. In the wake of the Civil War, a clearer definition of citizenship came with

the Fourteenth Amendment and Civil Rights Act of 1866. Martha S. Jones, *Birthright Citizens: A History of Race and Rights in Antebellum America* (Cambridge: Cambridge University Press, 2018), 5; Emberton, *Beyond Redemption*, 23.

42. Sharon Romeo, *Gender and the Jubilee: Black Freedom and the Reconstruction of Citizenship in Civil War Missouri* (Athens: University of Georgia Press, 2016), 4–7.

43. As the collective scholarship of Elizabeth Regosin, Chandra Manning, and Caitlin Verboon denote, cultural citizenship refers to an individual's pursuit to establish national belonging, in this case, through Civil War military service and its pension system. Elizabeth Regosin, "Toward the Temple of American Liberty: Hudlah Gordon and the Question of Former Slaves' Citizenship," in *The Civil War and Transformation of American Citizenship*, ed. Paul Quigley (Baton Rouge: Louisiana State University Press, 2018), 23; Caitlin Verboon, "Black Firemen, and Citizenship in the Postwar Urban South," in *The Civil War and the Transformation of American Citizenship*, 162; Manning, *Troubled Refuge*, 237.

44. For examples of studies on Civil War pensions, see Logue and Blanck, *Race, Ethnicity, and Disability*; Regosin, *Freedom's Promise*; Frankel, *Freedom's Women*.

45. Brimmer, *Claiming Union Widowhood*, 12, 17.

46. Please refer to the following studies for scholarship on infrapolitics: James C. Scott, *Domination and the Arts of Resistance: Hidden Transcripts* (New Haven, Conn.: Yale University Press, 1992); Robin D. G. Kelley, *Race Rebels: Culture, Politics, and the Black Working Class* (New York: Free Press, 1994).

47. Historian Benedict Anderson used the term "imagined community" to investigate the meaning of a nation and an individual's connection to it. I will use this term to refer to the lifelong struggle that African Americans experienced in an attempt to become part of the United States. Benedict Anderson, *Imagined Communities* (London: Verso, 1991), 3–7.

48. Brimmer, *Claiming Union Widowhood*, 17, 119.

49. Please refer to the following studies for information on U.S. organizations and their involvement in the Civil War pension process: Larry M. Logue, "Union Veterans and Their Government: The Effects of Public Policies on Private Lives," *Journal of Interdisciplinary History* 22, no. 3 (Winter 1992), 411–434; Barbara A. Gannon, *The Won Cause: Black and White Comradeship in the Grand Army of the Republic* (Chapel Hill: University of North Carolina Press, 2011).

CHAPTER 1. The African American Family in the Free North

1. Deposition of Francis Hawkins, on June 22, 1915, in Francis Hawkins, Third USCI, pension file, National Archives and Records Administration, Washington, D.C. (hereafter pension file).

2. Timothy Shortell, "The Rhetoric of Black Abolitionism: An Exploratory Analysis of Antislavery Newspapers in New York State," *Social Science History* 28, no. 1 (Spring 2004), 81; "The Negro in the Metropolis," *New York Herald*, January 25, 1861.

3. Bruce Laurie and Mark Schmitz, "Manufacturing and Productivity: The Making of an Industrial Base, Philadelphia, 1850–1880," in *Philadelphia: Work, Space, Family, and Group Experience in the 19th Century*, ed. Theodore Hershberg (Oxford: Oxford University Press, 1981), 44–45; Daniel R. Biddle and Murray Dubin, *Tasting Freedom: Octavius Catto and the Battle for Equality in Civil War America* (Philadelphia: Temple University Press, 2010), 101.

4. Leslie M. Harris, *In the Shadow of Slavery: African Americans in New York City, 1626–1863* (Chicago: University of Illinois Press, 2003), 228; Craig Steven Wilder, *In the Company of Black Men: The African Influence on African American Culture in New York City* (New York: New York University Press, 2001), 151.

5. W. E. B. Du Bois, *The Philadelphia Negro* (Philadelphia: University of Pennsylvania Press, 1899; rpt., 1996), 142.

6. "Free Blacks," *Frederick Douglass' Paper*, October 19, 1855.

7. John F. Quinn, "The Rise and Fall of Repeal: Slavery and Irish Nationalism in Antebellum Philadelphia," *The Pennsylvania Magazine of History and Biography* 130, no. 1 (January 2006), 59–60; Perry K. Blatz, "Boundaries of Responsibility: Philadelphia, Pittsburgh, and the Pennsylvania Riot Damage Law, 1834–1880," *Pennsylvania History: A Journal of Mid-Atlantic Studies* 78, no. 4 (Autumn 2011), 398–400.

8. Lynda J. Morgan, *Known for My Work: African American Ethics from Slavery to Freedom* (Gainesville: University Press of Florida, 2016), 28.

9. Judith Wellman, *Brooklyn's Promised Land: The Free Black Community of Weeksville, New York* (New York: New York University Press, 2014), 83.

10. Laurie, *Working People of Philadelphia, 1800–1850*, 155–158.

11. Theodore Hershberg, "Free Blacks in Antebellum Philadelphia: A Study of Ex- Slaves, Freeborn, and Socioeconomic Decline," in *African Americans in Pennsylvania: Shifting Historical Perspectives*, eds. Joe William Trotter Jr. and Eric Ledell Smith (University Park: Pennsylvania State University Press, 1997), 376, 382.

12. 1850 United States Federal Census (Washington, D.C.: National Archives and Records Administration, n.d.), accessed via *Ancestry.com* (hereafter 1850 U.S. Census), M432.

13. 1860 United States Federal Census (Washington, D.C.: National Archives and Records Administration, n.d.), accessed via *Ancestry.com* (hereafter 1860 U.S. Census), M653.

14. Hershberg, "Free Blacks in Antebellum Philadelphia," 137.

15. Anna C. Rose, *Victorian America and the Civil War* (Cambridge: Cambridge University Press, 1992), 81–84, 89.

16. Sarah N. Roth, *Gender and Race in Antebellum Popular Culture* (New York: Cambridge University Press, 2014), 47–48.

17. "Girls Should Learn To Keep House," *Christian Recorder*, September 24, 1864.

18. Darlene Clark Hine, "African American Women and Their Communities in the Twentieth Century: The Foundation and Future of Black Women's Studies," *Black Women, Gender + Families* 1, no. 1 (Spring 2007), 4–11; Evelyn Brooks Hig-

ginbotham, *Righteous Discontent: The Women's Movement in the Black Baptist Church, 1880–1920* (Cambridge, Mass.: Harvard University Press, 1993), 14–15, 185–229.

19. Ray Allen Billington, ed., *The Journal of Charlotte L. Forten: A Free Negro in the Slave Era* (London: Collier Books, 1969), 126–128.

20. Rebecca de Schweinitz, "'Train Up a Child in the Way He Should Go': The Image of Idealized Childhood in the Slavery Debate, 1850–1870," in *Children and Youth During the Civil War Era*, ed. James Marten (New York: New York University Press, 2012), 15.

21. 1850 U.S. Census, M432.

22. Nancy Folbre and Marjorie Abel, "Women's Work and Women's Households: Gender Bias in the U.S. Census," *Social Research* 56, no. 3 (Autumn 1989), 547–549; Margaret Coleman, "Homemaker as Worker in the United States," *Challenge* 41, no. 6 (November–December 1998), 76–79. For more information on issues of racism in the U.S. Census, see Paul Schor, *Counting Americans: How the U.S. Census Classified the Nation* (Oxford: Oxford University Press, 2017); Margo J. Anderson, *The American Census: A Social History* (New Haven, Conn.: Yale University Press, 1988).

23. Jeanne Boydston, *Home and Work: Housework, Wages, and the Ideology of Labor in the Early Republic* (New York: Oxford University Press, 1990), 16–17, 20, 38, 40, 97, 123, 126; Seth Rockman, "Women's Labor, Gender Ideology, and Working-Class Households in Early Republic Baltimore," *Pennsylvania History: A Journal of Mid-Atlantic Studies* 66 (1999), 175, 185.

24. Jane E. Dabel, *A Respectable Woman: The Public Roles of African American Women in 19th-Century New York* (New York: New York University Press, 2008), 42.

25. Rockman, "Women's Labor," 175; Patrick M. Horan and Peggy G. Hargis, "Children's Work and Schooling in the Late Nineteenth-Century Family Economy," *American Sociological Review* 56, no. 5 (October 1991), 589.

26. Coleman, "Homemaker as Worker," 77–80; Rockman, "Women's Labor," 185.

27. 1860 U.S. Census, M653.

28. Dabel, *A Respectable Woman*, 82; Jacqueline Jones, *American Work: Four Centuries of Black and White Labor* (New York: W. W. Norton & Company, 1998), 284.

29. Dabel, *A Respectable Woman*, 37–43, 63–67.

30. Mary P. Ryan, *Cradle of the Middle Class: The Family in Oneida County, New York, 1790–1865* (Cambridge: Cambridge University Press, 1981), 147; Nicole Etcheson, *A Generation at War: The Civil War Era in a Northern Community* (Lawrence: University of Kansas, 2011), 72.

31. Roth, *Gender and Race*, 160–161.

32. Laurie and Schmitz, "Manufacturing and Productivity," 62–63.

33. 1850 U.S. Census, M432; 1860 U.S. Census, M653.

34. Records do not state whether these various individuals exchanged goods or services to live in each dwelling, and perhaps they did.

35. 1850 U.S. Census, M432.

36. Ibid.; 1860 U.S. Census, M653.

37. Tamara K. Hareven, "The History of the Family and the Complexity of Social Change," *The American Historical Review* 96, no. 1 (February 1991), 103, 105; Mary Stovall Richards, "All Our Connections: Kinship, Family Structure, and Dynamics Among White Families in the Mid-Nineteenth Century Central South," *Tennessee Historical Quarterly* 50, no. 3 (Fall 1991), 142.

38. Richards, "All Our Connections," 145.

39. From 1851 to 1871 in New Brunswick, New Jersey, recently arrived Irish immigrants were the most common fictive kin in family households. Sheva Medjuck, "Family and Household Composition in the Nineteenth Century: The Case of Moncton, New Brunswick, 1851 to 1871," *The Canadian Journal of Sociology* 4, no. 3 (Summer 1979), 279.

40. Hershberg, "Free Blacks in Antebellum Philadelphia," 133.

41. Eighteen were Marylanders; twelve were Virginians; six were Delawareans; one was a South Carolinian. 1850 U.S. Census, M432; 1860 U.S. Census, M653; 1907 Certificate of Death, in Charles Brown, Sixth USCI, pension file.

42. 1850 U.S. Census, M432; 1860 U.S. Census, M653; 1887 dependent mother's pension, in Hiram Waters, Third USCI, pension file.

43. 1860 U.S. Census, M653.

44. Hasia R. Diner, *Erin's Daughters in America: Irish Immigrant Women in the Nineteenth Century* (Baltimore: Johns Hopkins University Press, 1983), 45–46, 54–55, 57–61.

45. 1850 U.S. Census, M432.

46. Hershberg, "Free Blacks in Antebellum Philadelphia," 137.

47. Barbara J. Beeching, *Hopes and Expectations: The Origins of the Black Middle Class in Hartford* (New York: SUNY Press, 2017), 66.

48. Du Bois, *Philadelphia Negro*, 295.

49. 1860 U.S. Census, M653.

50. Hershberg, "Free Blacks in Antebellum Philadelphia," 129.

51. 1860 U.S. Census, M653.

52. In 1850, the HRCC opened, much to the delight of white Philadelphians who believed that African American delinquents needed "guidance" to avoid vices. Kali Nicole Gross, *Hannah Mary Tabbs and the Disembodied Torso: A Tale of Race, Sex, and Violence in America* (Oxford: Oxford University Press, 2016), 89–94; Cecil P. Frey, "The House of Refuge for Colored Children," *The Journal of Negro History* 66, no. 1 (Spring 1981), 10–20.

53. Frey, "The House of Refuge," 10–20; Letter from the Bureau of Pensions to the House of Refuge, on April 12, 1912, and letter from F. Nibecker, superintendent of the House of Refuge, to the Bureau of Pensions on April 10, 1912, in Charles Penn, Third USCI, pension file.

54. 1860 U.S. Census, M653.

55. Ibid.

56. Jacob E. Clayton owned five thousand dollars' worth in real estate in 1850. 1850 U.S. Census, M432.

57. Ibid.

58. The author uses speculative language on these and other examples because of the limited, or nonexistent, primary sources on historically marginalized people. Please refer to the following text for a deeper discussion on individuals using fragmented material. Marisa J. Feuntes, *Dispossessed Lives: Enslaved Women, Violence, and the Archive* (Philadelphia: University of Pennsylvania Press, 2016), 1–12.

59. Hareven, "The History of the Family," 116.

60. "The Future of the Colored Race in America," *Christian Recorder*, September 13, 1862; "The Amalgamation of Races," *National Era*, September 7, 1854; Dorsey, *Reforming Men and Women*, 150–152.

61. 1850 U.S. Census, M432.

62. Paul A. Gilje and Howard B. Rock, "'Sweep O! Sweep O!': African American Chimney Sweeps and Citizenship in the New Nation," in *A Question of Manhood*, eds. Darlene Clark Hine and Earnestine Jenkins, vol. 1, *"Manhood Rights": The Construction of Black Male History and Manhood, 1750–1870* (Bloomington: Indiana State Press, 1999), 275–277.

63. Records do not reveal the circumstances that led each family to send their children to school or not. 1850 U.S. Census, M432; 1860 U.S. Census, M653; Deposition of Francis Hawkins, on June 22, 1915, Francis Hawkins pension file; Deposition of George H. Wilson, on August 8, 1906, in Isaac Becket, Third USCI, pension file; Deposition of Alice King, on April 29, 1903, in Thomas C. King Sr., Third USCI, pension file; Deposition of Joseph Bevans, on March 7, 1900, in Robert G. Parker, Sixth USCI, pension file.

64. Roger Lane, *William Dorsey's Philadelphia and Ours: On the Past and Future of the Black City in America* (Oxford: Oxford University Press, 1991), 135.

65. "Give children education, and no tyrant will trample on your," *National Era*, April 28, 1859.

66. Andrew K. Diemer, *The Politics of Black Citizenship: Free African Americans in the Mid-Atlantic Borderland, 1817–1863* (Athens: University of Georgia Press, 2016), 166–167.

67. "—," *Provincial Freeman*, June 9, 1855.

68. Harry C. Silcox, "Delay and Neglect: Negro Public Education in Antebellum Philadelphia, 1800–1860," *The Pennsylvania Magazine of History and Biography* 97, no. 4 (October 1973), 463.

69. "—," *Provincial Freeman*.

70. Ibid.

71. Nancy Bertaux and Michael Washington, "The 'Colored Schools' of Cincinnati and African American Community in Nineteenth-Century Cincinnati, 1849–1890," *Journal of Negro Education* 74, no. 1 (Winter 2005), 45–46.

72. Ernestine K. Enomoto and David L. Angus, "African American School Attendance in the 19th Century: Education in a Rural Northern Community, 1850–1880," *The Journal of Negro Education* 64, no. 1 (Winter 1995), 42; Silcox, "Delay and Neglect," 452–453, 456, 459, 463.

73. "Free Persons of Color," *National Era*, November 28, 1850; "Colored Mili-

tary Men and Colored Music—While Massachusetts," *Douglass Monthly* (November 1859).

74. "The Colored People of Philadelphia," *Christian Recorder*, August 15, 1863.

75. "Death of Miss Janes Porter,—Since the publication of our," *Douglass' Monthly* (December 1860).

76. Ibid.

77. "Colored Public School, Sixth St., Philadelphia," *Christian Recorder*, January 23, 1864.

78. Ibid.

79. "Institute for Colored Youth.—The Male Department of the," *Frederick Douglass' Paper*, October 22, 1862; "Institute for Colored Youth," *National Era*, October 7, 1852.

80. "Institute for Colored Youth in Philadelphia. We call attention," *Frederick Douglass' Paper*, September 21, 1855.

81. "Scientific Lectures at the Institute for Colored Youth," *Christian Recorder*, March 2, 1861; "Interesting Meeting at the Institute for Colored Youth," *Christian Recorder*, April 6, 1861; "A Recent Visit to Philadelphia," *Douglass' Monthly* (February 1862).

82. Wellman, *Brooklyn's Promised Land*, 59.

83. "The Examination of the Pupils of the Philadelphia Institute for Colored Youth," *Christian Recorder*, May 11, 1861.

84. Hareven, "The History of the Family," 118.

85. Deposition of Francis Hawkins, on June 22, 1915, Francis Hawkins pension file.

86. John C. McWilliams, "'Men of Color': Race, Riots, and Black Firefighters' Struggles for Equality from Afa to the Valiants," *Journal of Social History* 41, no. 1 (Fall 2007), 107–110.

87. 1850 U.S. Census, M432.

88. Dorsey, *Reforming Men and Women*, 139–140, 149, 151–154.

89. "For the Christian Recorder. To Mothers," *Christian Recorder*, January 24, 1863.

90. "Pleasure of Home," *Christian Recorder*, January 12, 1864.

91. Tera W. Hunter, *Bound in Wedlock: Slave and Free Black Marriage in the Nineteenth Century* (Cambridge, Mass.: Belknap Press of Harvard University Press, 2017), 162–164, 200, 211, 214, 221–226, 293–296; Noralee Frankel, *Freedom's Women: Black Women and Families in Civil War Era Mississippi* (Bloomington: Indiana University Press, 1999), 41.

92. "Domestic News," *Christian Recorder*, February 9, 1861.

93. Michael Grossberg, *Governing the Hearth: Kaw and the Family in Nineteenth-Century America* (Chapel Hill: University of North Carolina Press, 1985), 9–30, 73–82.

94. Donald Shaffer, *After the Glory: The Struggles of Black Civil War Veterans* (Lawrence: University of Kansas Press, 2004), 108–109, 111.

95. Tyler D. Parry, *Jumping the Broom: The Surprising Multicultural Origins of a Black Wedding Ritual* (Chapel Hill: University of North Carolina Press, 2020), 71.

96. Leigh Fought, *Women in the World of Frederick Douglass* (Oxford: Oxford University Press, 2017), 5, 49–52; Romeo, *Gender and the Jubilee*, 4–7.

97. David Doddington, "Manhood, Sex, and Power in Antebellum Slave Communities," in *Sexuality and Slavery: Reclaiming Intimate Histories in the Americas*, eds. Daina Ramey Berry and Leslie M. Harris (Athens: University of Georgia Press, 2019), 147–154.

98. Lane, *William Dorsey's Philadelphia and Ours*, 232–238.

99. Records do not reveal any details on E. Kelly, other than his name.

100. An 1865 document from the Indiana County, Pennsylvania, justice of the peace, in George Glascow, Sixth USCI, pension file.

101. After the colonial era, some native-born whites began to view common-law marriages as outdated, as governmental and religious institutions began championing legal marriages. In 1849 the Pennsylvania Supreme Court noted that a legal divorce could cost upward of twenty dollars for various fees, including a divorce bill and legal paperwork. G. S. Rowe, "Femes Covert and Criminal Prosecution in Eighteenth-Century Pennsylvania," *American Journal of Legal History* 32, no. 2 (April 1988), 139–140; "Marriage. Abolition of Common Law Marriage in Pennsylvania," *Virginia Law Review* 30, no. 4 (September 1944), 674; Charles O'Brien, "The Growth in Pennsylvania of the Property Rights of Married Women," *American Law Registrar* 49, no. 9 (September 1901), 526–529; James Dunlop, *The General Laws of Pennsylvania, from Year 1700, to 1849, Chronologically Arranged: With Notes and References, To All the Directions of the Supreme Court of Pennsylvania Giving Construction to Said Laws: With A Copious and Minute Index* (Philadelphia: T&J.W. Johnson, Law Booksellers, 1849), 366, 1051.

102. Deposition of Elizabeth Bond, on April 9, 1884, in Benjamin Davis, Sixth USCI, pension file.

103. Ibid.; Deposition of Ann Tunnel, on April 19, 1884, Benjamin Davis pension file.

104. Special examiner's notes, on May 31, 1903, in Wilson Day, Third USCI, pension file.

105. Ibid.; Deposition of Michael R. Frederick, on April 24, 1903, Wilson Day pension file.

106. Deposition of Michael R. Frederick, on April 24, 1903, Wilson Day pension file.

107. Diner, *Erin's Daughters in America*, 58–61.

108. Common-law marriages in this study resulted in twenty-two children, while legal marriages yielded sixteen.

109. Deposition of James Ellsbury, on November 11, 1903, in James Ellsbury, Sixth USCI, pension file; 1860 U.S. Census, M653.

110. Jane E. Dabel, "Education's Unfulfilled Promise: The Politics of School-

ing for African American Children in Nineteenth Century New York City," *The Journal of the History of Childhood and Youth* 5, no. 2 (Spring 2012), 203.

111. 1850 U.S. Census, M432; 1860 U.S. Census, M653.

112. *History of the Wages in the United States from Colonial Times to 1928* (Washington: United States Government Printing Office, 1934), 179, 276–277.

113. Clarence D. Long, "Wages by Occupational and Individual Characteristics," in *Wages and Earnings in the United States, 1869–1890*, ed. Clarence D. Long (Princeton: Princeton University Press, 1960), 95–99.

114. Du Bois, *Philadelphia Negro*, 345.

115. *Records of the Adjutant General's Office: Book Records of the Volunteer Union Organizations: Sixth* USCT *Infantry*, Regimental Descriptive Book Companies, National Archives and Records Administration, Washington, D.C. (hereafter Descriptive Book Companies), PI-17, vol. 1, RG 94; Descriptive Book Companies A–E, PI-17, vol. 2, accessed via *Ancestry.com*.

116. 1850 U.S. Census, M432.

117. 1860 U.S. Census, M653.

118. Ibid.

119. Special examiner's notes on August 18, 1916, in Charles Howard, Twenty-Sixth USCI, pension file.

120. Deposition of Charles Howard, on August 16, 1918.

121. Howard P. Chudacoff, *The Age of the Bachelor: Creating an American Subculture* (Princeton, N.J.: Princeton University Press, 1999), 67–70.

122. 1860 U.S. Census, M653.

123. 1850 U.S. Census, M432.

124. Walter Licht, *Getting Work: Philadelphia, 1840–1950* (Philadelphia: University of Pennsylvania Press, 1999), 49.

125. 1850 U.S. Census, M432.

126. Licht, *Getting Work*, 43–45, 47–50, 141.

127. 1850 U.S. Census, M432.

128. 1860 U.S. Census, M653.

129. Chudacoff, *The Age of the Bachelor*, 103; "WARNING TO BACHELORS.—Bachelors Are Much Shorter Lived," *Godey's Lady's Book* (November 1855).

130. 1850 U.S. Census, M432.

131. 1860 U.S. Census, M653.

132. Jones, *American Work*, 253, 255–259; Du Bois, *Philadelphia Negro*, 126–127.

133. Deposition of Julian Ann Watkins and Sarah Ann Gale, on July 26, 1866, in George Henderson, Third USCI, pension file.

134. Deposition of Theresa Thomas and Horace Potter, on March 6, 1865, in Alexander Robinson, Sixth USCI, pension file.

135. 1868 claim for mother's pension, George Henderson pension file.

136. Deposition of Francis Hayes, on September 12, 1889, in Andrew White, Sixth, USCI, pension file.

137. Ibid.

138. Deposition of Henry Hopkins, on September 11, 1889, Andrew White pension file.

CHAPTER 2. The United States Needs African American Men

1. Frederick Douglass, "Another Word to Black Men," *Weekly Anglo-African*, March 17, 1863.

2. Paul Taylor, *"The Most Complete Political Machine Ever Known": The North's Union Leagues in the American Civil War* (Kent, Ohio: Kent State University Press, 2018), 4, 69; Winnifred K. McKay, "Philadelphia during the Civil War, 1861–1865," *Pennsylvania Magazine of History and Biography* 70, no. 1 (January 1946), 4.

3. Jonathan W. White, ed., *A Philadelphia Perspective: The Civil War Diary of Sidney George Fisher* (New York: Fordham University Press, 2007), 84.

4. McKay, "Philadelphia during the Civil War," 5.

5. By applying the imagined community analysis, historian Cecilia Elizabeth O'Leary argues that the Civil War became a pivotal moment for Americans who, through armed conflict, began to define a national identity. Moreover, she asserts that this definition occurred by excluding others. Cecilia Elizabeth O'Leary, *To Die For: The Paradox of American Patriotism* (Princeton, N.J.: Princeton University Press, 1999), 25, 33.

6. See the following sources on Philadelphia violence: John Runcie, "'Hunting the Nigs' in Philadelphia: The Race Riot of August 1834," *Pennsylvania History* 39, no. 2 (April 1972), 190, 197–198, 201; Leonard L. Richards, *"Gentlemen of Property and Standing": Anti-Abolition Mobs in Jacksonian America* (Oxford: Oxford University Press, 1970), 9; *History of Pennsylvania Hall, Which Was Destroyed by a Mob, On the 17th of May, 1838* (Philadelphia: Merrihew & Gunn, 1838), 63, 65, 117, 119, 124, 136; "The Riots," *Pennsylvania Freeman*, July 14, 1844.

7. Gerald F. Linderman, *Embattled Courage: The Experience of Combat in the American Civil War* (New York: Free Press, 1987), 8, 11, 21; William H. Eagle, ed., *Andrew Gregg Curtin: His Life and Services* (Philadelphia: Avil Printing Company, 1895), 50–51, 57, 59.

8. J. Matthew Gallman, *Defining Duty in the Civil War: Personal Choice, Popular Culture, and the Union Home Front* (Chapel Hill: University of North Carolina Press, 2015), 32, 67, 129–135; Jonathan W. White, *Emancipation, The Union Army, and the Reelection of Abraham Lincoln* (Baton Rouge: Louisiana State University Press, 2014), 32–33.

9. James J. Broomall, "Wartime Masculinities," in *The Cambridge History of The American Civil War*, ed. Aaron Sheehan-Dean, vol. 3, *Affairs of the People* (Cambridge: Cambridge University Press, 2019), 3, 6–7; Paul D. Escott, *The Worst Passions of Human Nature: White Supremacy in the Civil War North* (Charlottesville: University of Virginia Press, 2020), 15, 28, 43.

10. O'Leary, *To Die For*, 25–26.

11. Chandra Manning, "A 'Vexed Question': White Union Soldiers on Slavery

and Race," in *The View From the Ground: Experiences of Civil War Soldiers*, ed. Aaron Sheehan-Dean (Lexington: University of Kentucky Press, 2007), 41–45; White, *Emancipation, The Union Army, and the Reelection of Abraham Lincoln*, 69, 75.

12. Ian Michael Spurgeon, *Soldiers in the Army of Freedom: The 1st Kansas Colored, the 63–64, The Civil War's First African American Combat Unit* (Norman: University of Oklahoma Press, 2014), 27.

13. Irvin D. S. Winsboro, "Give Them Their Due: A Reassessment of African Americans and Union Military Service in Florida during the Civil War," *Journal of African American History* 92, no. 3 (Summer 2007), 334–335; Joseph P. Reidy, "The Black Military Service," in *The Cambridge History of the American Civil War*, 222–223; Lisa Y. King, "In Search of Women of African Descent Who Served in the Civil War Union Navy," *Journal of Negro History* 83, no. 4 (Autumn 1998), 302–309.

14. Stephen D. Engle, "Yankee Dutchmen: Germans, the Union, and the Construction of a Wartime Identity," in *Civil War Citizens: Race, Ethnicity, and Identity in America's Bloodiest Conflict, ed.* Susannah J. Ural (New York: New York University Press, 2010), 11, 14–17, 23, 25.

15. Susannah J. Ural, "'Ye Sons of Green Erin Assemble': Northern Irish American Catholics and the Union War Effort, 1861–1865," in *Civil War Citizens*, 105.

16. Ricardo Herrera, *For Liberty and the Republic: The American Citizen as Soldiers, 1775–1861* (New York: New York University Press, 2015), 73, 143; White, *A Philadelphia Perspective*, 83.

17. White, *A Philadelphia Perspective*, 87.

18. Sarah H. Killikelly, *The History of Pittsburgh: Its Rise and Progress* (Pittsburgh, Pa.: B.C. & Gordon Montgomery Co., 1906), 423–424; Eric Ledell Smith, ed., "The Civil War Letters of Quartermaster Sergeant John C. Brock, 43rd Regiment, United States Colored Troops," in *Making and Remaking: Pennsylvania's Civil War*, eds. William Blair and William Pencak (University Park: Pennsylvania State University Press, 2001), 143.

19. "The Colored Philadelphians Forming Regiments," *Philadelphia Press*, April 22, 1861.

20. James M. McPherson, *The Negro's Civil War: How American Blacks Felt and Acted During the War for the Rebellion* (New York: Vintage Books, 1965), 32.

21. Ibid.

22. "Formation of Colored Regiments," *Weekly Anglo-African*, October 26, 1861.

23. "Philadelphian Affairs," *Weekly Anglo-African*, November 2, 1861.

24. Leon Gardiner Collection of American Negro Historical Society Records, *Collection 0008: Correspondence and Personal Papers, Box 9G, Folders 3–10*, Historical Society of Pennsylvania.

25. "We Should Not Drill," *Weekly Anglo-African*, October 12, 1861.

26. The 1862 Militia Act revised the earlier 1792 Militia Act that restricted the military to white men only. Henry Wilson, the Massachusetts Republican Senator, envisioned that the 1862 law would allow African American men to perform

various forms of military labor for the U.S. Army. Paul D. Escott, *Paying Freedom's Price: A History of African Americans in the Civil War* (New York: Rowman & Littlefield, 2017), 22–33; Joseph P. Reidy, *Illusions of Emancipation: The Pursuit of Freedom and Equality in the Twilight of Slavery* (Chapel Hill: University of North Carolina Press, 2020), 293–294; Vitor Izecksohn, *Slavery and War in the Americas: Race, Citizenship, and State Building in the United States and Brazil, 1861–1870* (Charlottesville: University of Virginia Press, 2014), 46–49; Elizabeth R. Varon, *Armies of Deliverance: A New History of the Civil War* (Oxford: Oxford University Press, 2019), 185–189.

27. Jonathan M. Steplyk, *Fighting Means Killing: Civil War Soldiers and the Nature of Combat* (Lawrence: University Press of Kansas, 2015), 41–57.

28. White, *A Philadelphia Perspective*, 196.

29. Edward A. Miller Jr., *The Black Civil War Soldiers of Illinois: The Story of the Twenty-Ninth U.S. Colored Infantry* (Columbia: University of South Carolina Press, 1998), 5.

30. Ibid., 10.

31. Ibid., 23.

32. Taylor, *"The Most Complete Political Machine Ever Known,"* 43–44.

33. Allan Nevins, ed., *Diary of the Civil War, 1860–1865, George Templeton Strong* (New York: Macmillan Company, 1962), 347.

34. Ibid.

35. Cultural citizenship, as previously noted, refers to an individual or communal belief in belonging to a community or even a nation-state.

36. "A Great Festival of Freedom," *Weekly Anglo-African*, January 3, 1863; "Meeting at Shiloh Church," *Weekly Anglo-African*, April 25, 1863.

37. Douglass, "Another Word to Black Men."

38. Ibid.

39. "Colored Man Must Fight," *Weekly Anglo-African*, May 16, 1863; "War Meeting in Philadelphia," *Weekly Anglo-African*, July 4, 1864; Kelly D. Mezurek, *For Their Own Cause: The 27th United States Colored Troops* (Kent, Ohio: Kent State University Press, 2016), 41.

40. James G. Mendez, *A Great Sacrifice: Northern Black Soldiers, Their Families, and the Experience of Civil War* (New York: Fordham University Press, 2019), 30.

41. Leslie A. Schwalm, *Emancipation's Diaspora: Race and Reconstruction in the Upper Midwest* (Chapel Hill: University of North Carolina Press, 2009), 107.

42. Historian Paul Taylor asserts that the ULP's endorsement of African American enlistment was due to the United States' revised war aims and a "healthy competitive spirit" with the Union League Club of New York. Taylor, *"Most Complete Political Machine,"* 79–81, 90–91, 183.

43. Hereafter, Supervisory Committee. Maxwell Whiteman, *Gentlemen In Crisis: The First Century of the Union League of Philadelphia 1862–1962* (Philadelphia: Union League of Philadelphia, 1974), 28–36.

44. Whiteman, *Gentlemen In Crisis*, 32–33; Taylor, "*Most Complete Political Machine*," 104–107.

45. "Formation of Colored Troops," *Weekly Anglo-African*, September 28, 1861; "Philadelphia Affairs," *Weekly Anglo-African*, April 15, 1862.

46. George H. Boker, *Washington and Jackson on Negro Soldiers. Gen. Banks on the Bravery of Negro Troops. Poem—The Second Louisiana* (Philadelphia: Printed for gratuitous distribution, 1863), 1.

47. Spurgeon, *Soldiers in the Army of Freedom*, 68–69.

48. Neither African American Massachusetts regiment was a USCT regiment. Douglas R. Egerton, *Thunder At The Gates: The Black Civil War Regiments That Redeemed America* (New York: Basic Books, 2016), 70–71; Ira Berlin, Joseph P. Reidy, and Leslie S. Rowland, eds., *Freedom: A Documentary History of Emancipation, 1861–1867*, vol. 1, *The Black Military Experience: Series II,* 2 vol., paperback ed. (Cambridge: Cambridge University Press, 2010), 75.

49. Deposition of Mary Williamson, on April 8, 1884, in Benjamin Davis, Sixth USCI, pension file, National Archives and Records Administration, Washington, D.C. (hereafter pension file).

50. Reid Mitchell, *The Vacant Chair: The Northern Soldier Leaves Home* (Oxford: Oxford University Press, 1993), 29–30.

51. Nicole Etcheson, *A Generation at War: The Civil War Era in a Northern Community* (Lawrence: University Press of Kansas, 2011), 124–125.

52. This early spike in Philadelphian-born enlisting runs counter to historian J. Matthew Gallman's assertion that there was an ebb and flow of recruits coming from in and outside of the Quaker State. J. Matthew Gallman, *Mastering Wartime: A Social History of Philadelphia During the Civil War* (Philadelphia: University of Pennsylvania Press, 1990), 49.

53. "Our Colored Soldiers," *Weekly Anglo-African*, April 4, 1863.

54. Virginia M. Adams, ed., *On the Altar of Freedom: A Black Soldier's Civil War Letters from the Front* (Amherst: University of Massachusetts Press, 1991), 14.

55. *Address at a Meeting for the Promotion of Colored Enlistments, Philadelphia* (Philadelphia: n.p., 1863), 4.

56. Ibid., 2.

57. Reid Mitchell, "Soldiering, Manhood, and Coming of Age: A Northern Volunteer," in *Divided Houses: Gender and the Civil War*, eds. Catherine Clinton and Nina Silber (Oxford: Oxford University Press, 1992), 45; Paul Cimbala and Randall M. Miller, *The Northern Home Front During the Civil War* (Santa Barbara, Calif.: Praeger, 2017), 39.

58. Aaron Sheehan-Dean, *Why Confederates Fought: Family and Nation in Civil War Virginia* (Chapel Hill: University of North Carolina Press, 2007), 25.

59. 1850 U.S. Census, M432; Deposition of William H. Parker, on March 7, 1910, in Robert G. Parker, Third USCI, pension file.

60. Thavolia Glymph, *The Women's Fight: The Civil War's Battles for Home, Freedom, and Nation* (Chapel Hill: University of North Carolina Press, 2020), 135.

61. 1866 claim for widow's pension for Martha Jackson, and 1865 copy of marriage certificate, in Jacob G. Jackson, Eighth USCI, pension file.

62. Compiled Military Service Records of Volunteer Union Soldiers Who Served with the United States Colored Troops (Washington, D.C.: National Archives and Records Administration, n.d.), accessed via *Ancestry.com* (hereafter Compiled Military Service Records), M1821, roll 8, reel 674.

63. 1881 widow's application, in Solomon Hoff, Eighth USCI, pension file.

64. A brief in Hannah Deets 1864 widow's pension, 1870 original pension of minor children, marriage certificate, in Charles Deets, Sixth USCI, pension file.

65. 1870 original pension of minor children, Charles Deets pension file.

66. Brian Matthew Jordan, *Marching Home: Union Veterans and Their Unending Civil War* (New York: Liveright Publishing Corporation, 2014), 154; Megan J. McClintock, "Binding up the Nation's Wounds: Nationalism, Civil War Pensions, and American Families, 1861–1890" (PhD diss., Rutgers University, 1994), 35.

67. William Blair, "We Are Coming, Father Abraham—Eventually: The Problem of Northern Nationalism in the Pennsylvania Recruiting Drives of 1862," in *The War Was You and Me: Civilians in the American Civil War*, ed. Joan E. Cashin (Princeton: Princeton University Press, 2002), 189; Ira Berlin and Leslie S. Rowland, eds., *Families and Freedom: A Documentary History of African-American Kinship in the Civil War Era* (New York: The New Press, 1997), 79–80.

68. W. E. B. Du Bois, *The Philadelphia Negro* (Philadelphia: University of Pennsylvania Press, 1899; rpt., 1996), 27–29; Daniel R. Biddle and Murray Dubin, *Tasting Freedom: Octavius Catto and the Battle for Equality in Civil War America* (Philadelphia: Temple University Press, 2010), 99–100, 297.

69. Blair, "We Are Coming," 192.

70. William Marvel, *Lincoln's Mercenaries: Economic Motivation Among Union Soldier During the Civil War* (Baton Rouge: Louisiana State University Press, 2018), 123, 164; Brian P. Luskey, *Men Is Cheap: Exposing the Frauds of Free Labor in Civil War America* (Chapel Hill: University of North Carolina Press, 2020), 72, 80.

71. Mendez, *A Great Sacrifice*, 67.

72. Paul A. Cimbala, *Soldiers North and South: The Everyday Experiences of the Men Who Fought America's Civil War* (New York: Fordham University Press, 2010), 44–46.

73. "Display Ad 10," *New York Times*, July 10, 1863.

74. "Flag Presentation at Camp William Penn," *Christian Recorder*, September 5, 1863.

75. Jessica Zapiro, "Northern Women, the State, and Wartime Mobilization," in *Women and the American Civil War: North and South Counterpoints*, eds. Judith Giesberg and Randall M. Miller (Kent, Ohio: Kent State University Press, 2018), 71.

76. Glymph, *The Women's Fight*, 160.

77. Ash, *Firebrand of Liberty*, 37; Richard M. Reid, *Freedom for Themselves: North*

Carolina's Black Soldiers in the Civil War Era (Chapel Hill: University of North Carolina Press, 2008), 32.

78. Chandra Manning, *What This Cruel War Was Over: Soldiers, Slavery, and the Civil War* (New York: Alfred A. Knopf, 2007), 160.

79. Compiled Military Service Records: M1820, roll 72, reel 1496.

80. Compiled Military Service Records: M1820, roll 72, reel 1496; M1820, roll 68, reel 1252; M1820; roll 80, reel 644; M1820, roll 70, reel 1577.

81. *U.S., Statutes at Large, Treaties, and Proclamations of the United States* (Boston, n.p., 1866), 13:126–130.

82. Mendez, *A Great Sacrifice*, 67, 70; Marvel, *Lincoln's Mercenaries*, 169.

83. Lorien Foote, *The Gentlemen and the Roughs: Violence, Honor, and Manhood in the Union Army* (New York: New York University Press, 2010), 132.

84. "Colored Men, Be On Your Guard," *Weekly Anglo-African*, January 16, 1864; "War Meeting in Philadelphia," *Weekly Anglo-African*, July 4, 1863; Marvel, *Lincoln's Mercenaries*, 61, 157.

85. Earl F. Mulderink III, *New Bedford's Civil War* (New York: Fordham University Press, 2012), 103.

86. Mezurek, *For Their Own Cause*, 65.

87. *"To Men of Color"* (Philadelphia: Steam-Power Job Printing Establishment, 1863), 1.

88. There is no record of any of the men examined here receiving payments directly from the ULP. Gallman, *Mastering Wartime*, 49.

89. New York State Archives, Albany, New York, Town Clerks' Registers of Men Who Served in the Civil War, ca. 1861–1865, collection number (N-Ar)13774: box 61, roll 33, reel 29; box 29, roll 17, reel 12, accessed via *Ancestry.com*.

90. Clarence D. Long, "Wages by Occupational and Individual Characteristics," in *Wages and Earnings in the United States, 1869–1890*, ed. Clarence D. Long (Princeton: Princeton University Press, 1960), 95–99.

91. Mezurek, *For Their Own Cause*, 61; Blair, "We Are Coming," 194–196.

92. "Formation of New York Colored Regiments," *Weekly Anglo-African*, September 26, 1863.

93. "Display Ad 10," *New York Times*, July 4, 1863.

94. Luskey, *Men Is Cheap*, 168.

95. Berlin, Reidy, and Rowland, *Freedom*, 12.

96. It is possible that some of the Canadian-born USCT enlistees were actually born in the United States but later fled for their safety. Richard M. Reid, *African Canadians in Union Blue: Volunteering for the Cause in the Civil War* (Kent, Ohio: Kent State University Press, 2014), 29–30,46–49.

97. Reidy, *Illusions of Emancipation*, 51.

98. Brian Taylor, "A Politics of Service: Black Northerners' Debates over Enlistment in the American Civil War," *Civil War History* 58, no. 4 (December 2012), 463, 467.

99. Long, "Wages by Occupational and Individual Characteristics," 95–99.

100. Etcheson, *A Generation at War*, 125.

101. Taylor, "A Politics of Service," 466.

102. "For the Christian Recorder. Camp of the 3rd Regt. United States," *Christian Recorder*, November 7, 1863.

103. Peter S. Carmichael, *The War for the Common Soldier: How Men Thought, Fought, and Survived in Civil War Armies* (Chapel Hill: University of North Carolina Press, 2018), 9, 124, 126, 136.

104. Lesley J. Gordon, "Armies and Discipline," in *The Cambridge History of The American Civil War*, ed. Aaron Sheehan-Dean, vol. 2, *Affairs of the State* (Cambridge: Cambridge University Press, 2019), 161.

105. Mezurek, *For Their Own Cause*, 90; Christian G. Samito, *Becoming American under Fire: Irish Americans, African Americans, and the Politics of Citizenship During the Civil War Era* (Ithaca, N.Y.: Cornell University Press, 2009), 84.

106. Benedict Anderson, *Imagined Communities* (London: Verso, 1991), 144.

107. Foote, *The Gentlemen and the Roughs*, 163.

108. Joseph T. Glatthaar, *Forged in Battle: The Civil War Alliance of Black Soldiers and White Officers* (Baton Rouge: Louisiana State University Press, 1990), 109–110; Michael C. C. Adams, *Living Hell: The Dark Side of the Civil War* (Baltimore: Johns Hopkins University Press, 2014), 35.

109. Foote, *The Gentlemen and the Roughs*, 127; Glatthaar, *Forged in Battle*, 85.

110. James C. Scott, *Domination and the Arts of Resistance: Hidden Transcripts* (New Haven, Conn.: Yale University Press, 1992), 183–191; Robin D. G. Kelley, *Race Rebels: Culture, Politics, and the Black Working Class* (New York: Free Press, 1994), 18.

111. Mendez, *A Great Sacrifice*, 45; *U.S., Statutes at Large, Treaties, and Proclamations of the United States of America* (Boston, [n.p.] 1863), 12:597–600.

112. Noah Andre Trudeau, ed., *Voices of the 55th Massachusetts Volunteers, 1861–1865* (Dayton, Ohio: Morningside House, 1996), 81.

113. Compiled Military Service Records: M1801, roll 14, reel 789–790, 792–793.

114. Mendez, *A Great Sacrifice*, 46; Mezurek, *For Their Own Cause*, 63.

115. *U.S., Statutes at Large, Treaties, and Proclamations of the United States* (Boston: Little, Brown & Company, 1866), 13:126–130.

116. Lieutenant Colonel Louis F. Wagner to Assistant Adjutant General C. W. Foster, June 6, 1864, RG110, *Records of the Provost Marshal General Pennsylvania: Camp William Penn*, Entry 3595, *Letters Received, 1863–1865*, box 1, National Archives and Records Administration, Washington, D.C.

117. "The Pay of Colored Soldiers," *Christian Recorder*, December 26, 1863.

118. Taylor, "A Politics of Service," 473, 475.

119. Letter to Sarah Reeves, composed on March 25, 1864, in Andrew White, Sixth USCI, pension file.

120. LeeAnn Whites, "Written on the Heart: Soldiers' Letters, the Household Supply Line, and the Relational War," in *Household War: How Americans Lived and*

Fought the Civil War, eds. Lisa Tendrich Frank and LeeAnn Whites (Athens: University of Georgia Press, 2020), 119.

121. Deposition of Theresa Thomas and Horace Potter, on March 6, 1865, in Alexander Robinson, Sixth USCI, pension file.

122. Reid, *Freedom for Themselves*, 102; Donald Yacovone, ed., *A Voice of Thunder: The Civil War Letters of George E. Stephens* (Urbana: University of Illinois Press, 1997), 325; Mendez, *A Great Sacrifice*, 48–50.

123. Ginette Aley, "Inescapable Realities: Rural Midwestern Women and Families During the Civil War," in *Union Heartland: The Midwestern Home Front During the Civil War*, eds. Ginette Aley and J. L. Anderson (Carbondale: Southern Illinois University Press, 2013), 126–127.

124. Mendez, *A Great Sacrifice*, 49–50, 58–59, 67; Marshall Myers and Chris Pope, "'I Don't Fear Nothing in the Shape of Man': The Civil War and Texas Border Letters of Edward Francis, United States Colored Troops," *Register of the Historical Society* 101, no. 4 (Autumn 2004), 473, 477.

125. Jonathan W. White, Katie Fisher, and Elizabeth Wall, "The Civil War Letters of Tillman Valentine, Third U.S. Colored Troops," *Pennsylvania Magazine of History and Biography* 139, no. 2 (April 2015), 183–184.

126. Compiled Military Service Records: M1820, roll 27, reels 598, 609, 612.

127. George C. Rable, "Heath and Home at Fredericksburg," in *The War Was You and Me: Civilians in the American Civil War*, ed. Joan E. Cashin (Princeton: Princeton University Press, 2002, 91–92; Etcheson, *A Generation at War*, 135.

128. White, Fisher, and Wall, "The Civil War Letters of Tillman Valentine," 185; Marvel, *Lincoln's Mercenaries*, 75, 80.

129. Myers and Pope, "'I Don't Fear Nothing,'" 462.

130. Mezurek, *For Their Own Cause*, 203.

CHAPTER 3. The Idealism versus the Realism of Military Service

1. Brian Taylor, "A Politics of Service: Black Northerners' Debates over Enlistment in the American Civil War," *Civil War History* 58, no. 4 (December 2012), 455.

2. Reid Mitchell, *The Vacant Chair: The Northern Soldier Leaves Home* (Oxford: Oxford University Press, 1993), 56–59; Anna C. Rose, *Victorian America and the Civil War* (Cambridge: Cambridge University Press, 1992), 187; Carole Emberton, *Beyond Redemption: Race, Violence, and the American South after the Civil War* (Chicago: University of Chicago Press, 2013), 127–128, 131, 154.

3. Lorien Foote, *The Gentlemen and the Roughs: Violence, Honor, and Manhood in the Union Army* (New York: New York University Press, 2010), 119, 128, 146, 152, 158.

4. Compiled Military Service Records of Volunteer Union Soldiers Who Served with the United States Colored Troops (Washington, D.C.: National Archives and Records Administration, n.d.), accessed via *Ancestry.com* (hereafter Compiled Military Service Records), M1820, roll 70, reels 881, 1574, 1674.

5. Compiled Military Service Records: M1820, roll 69, reels 766–773.

6. Compiled Military Service Records: M1820, roll 22, reels 1006, 1008.

7. Compiled Military Service Records: M1820, roll 22, reel 984.

8. Lesley J. Gordon, "Armies and Discipline," in *The Cambridge History of The American Civil War*, ed. Aaron Sheehan-Dean, vol. 2, *Affairs of the State* (Cambridge: Cambridge University Press, 2019), 163–164; Susannah J. Ural, "Citizen Soldiers," in *The Cambridge History of The American Civil War*, ed. Aaron Sheehan-Dean, vol. 3, *Affairs of the People* (Cambridge: Cambridge University Press, 2019), 166.

9. Compiled Military Service Records: M1820, roll 20, reel 886; roll 21, reel 385; roll 23, reel 1196; roll 28, reel 297; roll 68, reel 1252; roll 69, reel 757; roll 70, reel 1515; roll 71, reel 843; roll 75, reel 318; roll 77, reel 1055; roll 78, reel 71; M1821, roll 5, reel 1068; roll 10, reel 1369; roll 16, reel 1271; roll 16, reel 976; roll 23, reel 1017.

10. Peter S. Carmichael, *The War for the Common Soldier: How Men Thought, Fought, and Survived in Civil War Armies* (Chapel Hill: University of North Carolina Press, 2018), 178–179.

11. Ella Lonn, *Desertion During the Civil War* (Lincoln: University of Nebraska Press, 1998), 127–130; Keith P. Wilson, *Campfires of Freedom: The Camp Life of Black Soldiers During the Civil War* (Kent, Ohio: Kent State University Press, 2002), 21–22.

12. Carmichael, *The War of the Common Soldier*, 177.

13. Compiled Military Service Records: M1820, roll 23, reels 1017, 1026.

14. *Records of the Adjutant General's Office: Book Records of the Volunteer Union Organizations: 20th* USCT *Infantry*, Regimental Descriptive Book, Companies A–K, National Archives and Records Administration, Washington, D.C. (hereafter Descriptive Book Companies), PI-17, vol. 2, RG 94; *26th* USCT *Infantry*, Descriptive Book Companies A–K, PI-17, vol. 2, RG 94; *31st* USCT *Infantry*, Descriptive Book Companies A–K, PI-17, vol. 2, RG 94.

15. Guard Report from March 13, 1864, Guard Report from September 25, 1864, *Records of the Provost Marshal General Pennsylvania: Camp William Penn*, Entry 3602, National Archives and Records Administration, Washington, D.C., Guard Reports, 9/15/1863–5/19/1865, box 2, RG 110.

16. Ibid.

17. Diane Miller Sommerville, "'A Burden Too Heavy to Bear": War Trauma, Suicide, and Confederate Soldiers," *Civil War History Journal* 59, no. 4 (December 2013), 459–460.

18. Diane Miller Sommerville, *Aberration of Mind: Suicide and Suffering in the Civil War–Era South* (Chapel Hill: University of North Carolina Press, 2018), 27–47.

19. Sommerville, "'A Burden Too Heavy to Bear,'" 472, 475.

20. Twenty-six officers and 365 enlisted men successfully committed suicide in the U.S. Army. David Silkenat, *Moments of Despair: Suicide, Divorce, and Debt in Civil War Era North Carolina* (Chapel Hill: University of North Carolina Press,

2011), 40–41; Michael R. Gilchrist, "Disease and Infection in the American Civil War," in *American Biology Teacher* 60, no. 4 (April 1998), 258.

21. Ian Michael Spurgeon, *Soldiers in the Army of Freedom: The 1st Kansas Colored, the 63–64, The Civil War's First African American Combat Unit* (Norman: University of Oklahoma Press, 2014), 116–117.

22. Virginia M. Adams, ed., *On the Altar of Freedom: A Black Soldier's Civil War Letters from the Front* (Amherst: University of Massachusetts Press, 1991), 7.

23. Michael C. C. Adams, *Living Hell: The Dark Side of the Civil War* (Baltimore: Johns Hopkins University Press, 2014), 27; Thomas R. Kemp, "Community and War: The Civil War Experience of Two New Hampshire Towns," in *Toward a Social History of the American Civil War*, ed. Maris A. Vinoviskis (Cambridge: Cambridge University Press, 1990), 72.

24. Richard M. Reid, *Freedom for Themselves: North Carolina's Black Soldiers in the Civil War Era* (Chapel Hill: University of North Carolina Press, 2008), 232–242; Joseph T. Glatthaar, *Soldiering in the Army of Northern Virginia: Statistical Portrait of the Troops Who Served Under Robert E. Lee* (Chapel Hill: University of North Carolina Press, 2014), 14–16; Jeffrey W. McClurken, *Take Care of the Living: Reconstructing Confederate Veteran Families in Virginia* (Charlottesville: University of Virginia Press, 2009), 37.

25. Dora L. Costa and Matthew E. Kahn, *Heroes and Cowards: The Social Face of War* (Princeton: Princeton University Press, 2008), 78; Jonathan Lande, "Trials of Freedom: African American Deserters during the U.S. Civil War," *Journal of Social History* 49, no. 3 (Spring 2016), 699–701; Steven J. Ramold, *Baring the Iron Hand: Discipline in the Union Army* (Dekalb: Northern Illinois University Press, 2010), 219–220, 253–255.

26. Ira Berlin, Joseph P. Reidy, and Leslie S. Rowland, eds., *Freedom: A Documentary History of Emancipation, 1861–1867*, vol. 1, *The Black Military Experience: Series II,* 2 vol., paperback ed. (Cambridge: Cambridge University Press, 2010). 449–451.

27. *Sixth* USCT *Infantry*, Regimental Descriptive Book Companies, vol. 1, PI-17, RG 94.

28. Spurgeon, *Soldiers in the Army of Freedom*, 113; Carmichael, *War of the Common Soldier*, 181.

29. Adams, *Altar of Freedom*, 92.

30. Compiled Military Service Records: M1820, roll 27, reel 1508.

31. Compiled Military Service Records: M1820, roll 20, reel 1548; roll 22, reel 1006; roll 25, reel 1649; roll 15, reel 1494; roll 16, reel 824.

32. Compiled Military Service Records: M1820, roll 27, reel 959.

33. Compiled Military Service Records: M1820, roll 18A, reels 1403–1404.

34. Historian Jonathan W. White calculates that 2,000 U.S. Army soldiers received court-martials for sleeping at their post. Ninety of those soldiers were issued a death sentence, but President Abraham Lincoln commuted all of them. Jonathan W. White, *Midnight in America: Darkness, Sleep, and Dreams During the Civil War* (Chapel Hill: University of North Carolina Press, 2017), 4–7.

35. Cecilia Elizabeth O'Leary, *To Die For: The Paradox of American Patriotism* (Princeton, N.J.: Princeton University Press, 1999), 26–27.

36. Jonathan M. Steplyk, *Fighting Means Killing: Civil War Soldiers and the Nature of Combat* (Lawrence: University Press of Kansas, 2015), 90–91.

37. Ibid., 154, 164–165, 172, 182, 190, 201, 205–212; Carmichael, *War for the Common Soldier*, 246–247.

38. Berlin, Reidy, and Rowland, *Freedom*, 501–502.

39. Correspondence to Sarah Reeves, undated, in Andrew White, Sixth USCI, pension file, National Archives and Records Administration, Washington, D.C. (hereafter pension file).

40. Berlin, Reidy, and Rowland, *Freedom*, 502.

41. Ibid., 385.

42. Ibid., 502.

43. Eric Ledell Smith, "The Civil War Letters of Quartermaster Sergeant John C. Brock, 43rd Regiment, United States Colored Troops," in *Making and Remaking: Pennsylvania's Civil War*, eds. William Blair and William Pencak (University Park: Pennsylvania State University Press, 2001), 155.

44. Margaret Humphreys, *Intensely Human: The Health of the Black Soldier in the American Civil War* (Baltimore: Johns Hopkins University Press, 2008), 82.

45. 1891 medical examination, in James Burk, Eighth USCI, pension file.

46. Deposition of Absolom Watson, on November 19, 1898, in Samuel Derry, Third USCI, pension file.

47. Deposition of William Ingram, on November 28, 1888, in John Short, Sixth USCI, pension file.

48. Deposition of John Burton, on September 21, 1887, John Short pension file.

49. Brian Steel Willis, *Inglorious Passages: Noncombat Deaths in the American Civil War* (Lawrence: University Press of Kansas, 2017), 125.

50. Compiled Military Service Records: M1820, roll 25, reel 174.

51. Deposition of John A. Cooper, on October 28, 1868, in Joseph Perkins, Third USCI, pension file.

52. Ricardo Herrera, *For Liberty and the Republic: The American Citizen as Soldiers, 1775–1861* (New York: New York University Press, 2015), 155–157; Foote, *The Gentlemen and the Roughs*, 57, 78–79.

53. David W. Blight, "No Desperate Hero: Manhood and Freedom in a Union Soldiers Experience," in *Divided Houses: Gender and the Civil War*, eds. Catherine Clinton and Nina Silber (Oxford: Oxford University Press, 1992), 63–65; Reid Mitchell, "The Northern Soldier and His Community," in *Toward a Social History of the American Civil War*, 84.

54. The Third USCI participated in military engagements at Forts Wagner and Gregg, Charleston. It also took part in expeditions throughout Florida. While in Virginia (December 1863–December 1864), the Sixth USCI took part in numerous military operations, including expeditions to New Kent Court House,

Williamsburg, Bailor's Farm, Petersburg, Richmond, King County, and Queen County, and Matthews County. Additionally, it participated in City Point's capture and was involved in conflicts at Fort Converse, Chapin's Farm, New Market Heights, Fort Harrison, and Fair Oaks. The Eighth USCI spent time in Virginia, where it stayed until April 1865. In Virginia the regiment took part in conflicts at Chapin's Farm, New Market Heights, Fort Harrison, Darbytown Road, Fair Oaks, and Petersburg; military operations at Deep Bottom and Hatcher's Run; and the pursuit of Confederate general Robert E. Lee to the Appomattox Court House. "United States Colored Troops: 6th Regiment, United States Colored Infantry," National Park Service, https://www.nps.gov/civilwar/search-battle-units-detail.htm?battleUnitCode=UUS0006RI00C; "United States Colored Troops: 8th Regiment, United States Colored Infantry," National Park Service, https://www.nps.gov/civilwar/search-battle-units-detail.htm?battleUnitCode=UUS0008RI00C; "United States Colored Troops: 3rd Regiment, United States Colored Infantry," National Park Service, https://www.nps.gov/civilwar/search-battle-units- detail.htm?battleUnitCode=UUS0003RI01C; "From the Sixth Regiment U.S. Colored Troops," *Weekly Anglo-African*, February 20, 1864; "From the Sixth Regiment U.S. Colored Troops," *Weekly Anglo-African*, July 2, 1864; "From the 3d Regt. U.S.C.T.," *Weekly Anglo-African*, April 22, 1865.

55. In historian Frank H. Taylor's study, he only tabulated information on the soldiers of the Sixth USCI and the Eighth USCI who had wounds, deaths, became prisoners, or went missing. The National Park Service website on the Third USCI provides no data on the wounded or dead for the regiment. It is quite possible that the percentage that I have given would be much lower with information on the Third USCI. Perhaps a future scholar will be able to fill this historical gap. Frank H. Taylor, *Philadelphia In The Civil War* (Philadelphia: n.p., 1913), 189–191; "United States Colored Troops: 3rd Regiment, United States Colored Infantry," National Park Service, https://www.nps.gov/civilwar/search-battle-units-detail.htm?battleUnitCode=UUS0003RI01C.

56. Dudley Taylor Cornish, *The Sable Arm: Black Troops in the Union Army, 1861–1865* (Lawrence: The University of Kansas, 1987), 288; James M. McPherson, *The Negro's Civil War: How American Blacks Felt and Acted During the War for the Rebellion* (New York: Vintage Books, 1965), 237.

57. Franny Nudelman, *John Brown's Body: Slavery, Violence, and the Culture of War* (Chapel Hill: University of North Carolina Press, 2004), 39.

58. Nicole Etcheson, *A Generation at War: The Civil War Era in a Northern Community* (Lawrence: University Press of Kansas, 2011), 146.

59. Allison M. Johnson, *The Scars We Carve: Bodies and Wounds in Civil War Print Culture* (Baton Rouge: Louisiana State University Press, 2019), 73.

60. Ibid., 61.

61. Ibid., 76.

62. "Battle of Olustee Facts and Summary," American Battlefield Trust, https://www.battlefields.org/learn/civil-war/battles/olustee.

63. Winsboro, "Give Them Their Due," 338–339.

64. 1865 examining surgeon certificate, in Ephraim Maloney, Sixth USCI, pension file.

65. Compiled Military Service Records: M1821, roll 14, reel 1220.

66. Letter from Joseph Anderson, composed on February 3, 1898, in Joseph Anderson, Third USCI, pension file.

67. 1867 pension document, in George Henderson, Third USCI, pension file.

68. 1866 examining surgeon's certificate, in Charles Brant, Eighth USCI, pension file; 1878 examining surgeon's certificate, in Hezekiah Wilson, Sixth USCI, pension file.

69. Compiled Military Service Records: M1820, roll 20, reel 1556.

70. 1875 medical examination and 1879 medical examination in George Roland, Sixth USCI, pension file.

71. Brian Craig Miller, *Empty Sleeves: Amputation in the Civil War South* (Athens: University of Georgia Press, 2015), 24.

72. Deposition of Joshua James, on December 9, 1879, in George H. Buck, Third USCI, pension file.

73. Deposition of James Brown, on June 14, 1895, in Lorenzo George, Third USCI, pension file.

74. Deposition of James H. Royal, on November 12, 1894, Lorenzo George pension file.

75. Compiled Military Service Records: M1820, roll 21, reel 1131.

76. Humphreys, *Intensely Human*, 20–21, 57–77; Jane E. Schultz, *Women at the Front: Hospital Workers in Civil War America* (Chapel Hill: University of North Carolina Press, 2004), 136.

77. Taylor, *Reminiscences of Life in Camp*, 34.

78. Margaret Humphreys, *Marrow of Tragedy: The Health Crisis of the American Civil War* (Baltimore: Johns Hopkins University Press, 2013), 31–33.

79. Dr. Beck performed at least six surgeries on September 19, 1862. "Letters of a Civil War Surgeon," *Indiana Magazine of History* 27, no. 2 (June 1931), 145; Ansley Herring Wegner, "Phantom Pain: Amputation and North Carolina's Maimed Veterans," *North Carolina Historical Review* 75, no. 3 (July 1998), 280.

80. Shauna Devine, *Learning from the Wounded: The Civil War and the Rise of American Medical Science* (Chapel Hill: University of North Carolina Press, 2014), 94–95, 98, 141–142, 202–203.

81. Ibid., 209.

82. Miller, *Empty Sleeves*, 52–59.

83. 1868 Adjutant General's Office document, in Jacob Thornton, Third USCI, pension file.

84. Compiled Military Service Records: M1820, roll 69, reel 1424.

85. Devine, *Learning from the Wounded*, 206–207.

86. Compiled Military Service Records: M1820, roll 79, reel 721; roll 80, reel 1551.

87. Undated correspondence from Eugene M. Williams, in Robert Johnson, Sixth USCI, pension file.

88. Dillon Jackson Carroll, "The Case of Napoleon Perkins," in *Life and Limb: Perspectives on the American Civil War*, eds. David Seed, Stephen C. Kenny, and Chris Williams (Liverpool: Liverpool University Press, 2015), 116; Miller, *Empty Sleeves*, 43, 72, 80, 84.

89. Johnson, *The Scars We Carve*, 57.

90. W. H. Whitley, Clarence E. Mitcham, and Harry Forrest Lupold, "Civil War Letters," *Register of the Kentuckian Historical Society* 72, no. 3 (July 1974), 265, 270, 272–273; Spurgeon, *Soldiers in the Army of Freedom*, 245.

91. Deposition of John Marshall, on February 18, 1890, in William Brown, Sixth USCI, pension file.

92. Compiled Military Service Records: M1821, roll 14, reel 1220; roll 15, reel 1506; M1820, roll 18A, reel 768, 778; roll 27, reel 269.

93. Adams, *Living Hell*, 51.

94. Reid, *Freedom for Themselves*, 69.

95. Edwin Redkey, ed., *A Grand Army of Black Men: Letters from African-American Soldiers in the Union Army, 1861–1865* (Cambridge: Cambridge University Press, 1992), 180.

96. Adams, *Living Hell*, 49; Taylor, *Reminiscences of Life in Camp*, 33.

97. 1885 invalid pension application in Thomas C. King Sr., Third USCI, pension file.

98. W. Stephen McBride, "From the Bluegrass to the Rio Grande: Kentucky's U.S. Colored Troops on the Border, 1865–1867," in *The Civil War on the Rio Grande, 1846–1876*, eds. Roseanna Bacha-Garza, Christopher L. Miller, and Russell K. Skowronek (College Station: Texas A&M University Press, 2019), 199–205.

99. Humphreys, *Intensely Human*, 82, 98.

100. Depositions of James Deacon, on March 21, 1896, and deposition of James B. Davis, on November 15, 1892, Lorenzo George pension file.

101. 1898 invalid pension application, Samuel Derry pension file.

102. 1889 pension document, and 1890 pension document, in John Thompson, Third USCI, pension file.

103. USCT soldiers were only able to rectify the issue after purchasing canteens supplied by Mexicans with water out of the Rio Grande River for ten cents a canteen. Isaac J. Hill, *A Sketch of the 29th Regiment of Connecticut Colored Troops* (Baltimore: Daugherty, Maguire & Co., 1867), 34.

104. Humphreys, *Intensely Human*, 117.

105. Compiled Military Service Records: M1820, roll 17, reel 115; roll 21, reel 941; roll 23, reel 252; roll 27, reel 1107; roll 25, reel 1464; roll 77, reel 269; roll 74, reel 660; roll 78, reel 1502.

106. Kelly D. Mezurek, *For Their Own Cause: The 27th United States Colored Troops* (Kent, Ohio: Kent State University Press, 2016), 177.

107. Humphreys, *Intensely Human*, 84.

108. Deposition of Edward Brown, on January 31, 1888, in Edward Brown, Third USCI, pension file.

109. Spurgeon, *Soldiers in the Army of Freedom*, 252; Jeremiah Marion Mickley, *The Forty-Third Regiment United States Colored Troops* (Gettysburg, Pa.: J. E. Wible, printer, 1866), 84.

110. Willis, *Inglorious Passages*, 4–5, 48.

111. Adams, *Altar of Freedom*, 47–48.

112. Leslie A. Schwalm, *Emancipation's Diaspora: Race and Reconstruction in the Upper Midwest* (Chapel Hill: University of North Carolina Press, 2009), 125.

113. Berlin, Reidy, and Rowland, *Freedom*, 514.

114. Frank H. Taylor, *Philadelphia in the Civil War 1861–1865* (Philadelphia: n.p., 1913), 189–191.

115. Compiled Military Service Records: M1820, roll 25, reel 1464; roll 27, reel 1107.

116. "Consumption," *Scientific American* 32, no. 26 (June 26, 1875), 406; Theodore Fisher, "The Causation of Pleurisy," *British Medical Journal* 2, no. 2310 (April 8, 1905), 802.

117. Humphreys, *Intensely Human*, 53.

118. Mezurek, *For Their Own Cause*, 187.

119. Lorien Foote, "Prisoners of War," in *The Cambridge History of The American Civil War*, 2:297–298, 301; Lauren K. Thompson, *Friendly Enemies: Soldier Fraternization throughout the American Civil War* (Lincoln: University of Nebraska Press, 2020), 7–8, 132–133.

120. Reid Mitchell, *Civil War Soldiers: Their Expectations and Their Experiences* (New York: Viking Books, 1998), 47–49.

121. "A Confederate Private at Fort Donelson, 1862," *American Historical Review* 31, no. 3 (April 1926), 482; Tommy Thompson, "'Dying Like Rotten Sheepe': Camp Randall as a Prisoner of War Facility during the Civil War," *Wisconsin Magazine of History* 92, no. 1 (Autumn 2008), 12; Joseph L. Eisendrath Jr., "Chicago's Camp Douglas, 1861–1865," *Journal of the Illinois State Historical Society* 53, no. 1 (Spring 1960), 62.

122. David Silkenat, *Raising the White Flag: How Surrender Defined the American Civil War* (Chapel Hill: University of North Carolina Press, 2019), 933–94, 104–105; Glenn M. Robins, "Race, Repatriation, and Galvanized Rebels: Union Prisoners and the Exchange Question in Deep South Prison Camps," *Civil War History Journal* 53, no. 2 (June 2007), 121, 123, 130, 137, 139.

123. Angela M. Zombek, *Penitentiaries, Punishment, and Military Prisons: Familiar Responses to an Extraordinary Crisis during the American Civil War* (Kent, Ohio: Kent State University Press, 2018), 81, 93.

124. Steplyk, *Fighting Means Killing*, 172; Robins, "Race, Repatriation, and Galvanized Rebels," 119.

125. "Prisoners of War," National Park Service, https://www.nps.gov/parkhistory/online_books/civil_war_series/2/sec19.htm.

126. Howard C. Westwood, "Captive Black Union Soldiers in Charleston—What to Do?," *Civil War History Journal* 28, no. 1 (March 1982), 37.

127. Christopher Barr, "Loathsome Disease and Principle: Conceptualizing Race and Slavery in Civil War Prisons," in *Crossing the Deadlines: Civil War Prisons Reconsidered*, ed. Michael P. Gray (Kent, Ohio: Kent State University Press, 2018), 107–109; Kelly D. Mezurek, "'De Bottom Rails on Top Now': Black Union Guards and Confederate Prisoners of War," in *Crossing the Deadlines*, 127–128.

128. Reid, *Freedom for Themselves*, 93; *Personal Narratives of Events in the War of the Rebellion, Being Papers Read Before the Rhode Island Soldiers and Sailors Historical Society. Fifth Series—No. 1* (Providence: Providence Press, 1894), 30; Caroline Wood Newhall, "'Under the Rebel Lash': Black Prisoners of War in the Confederate South" (PhD diss., University of North Carolina at Chapel Hill, 2020), 9–11.

129. Westwood, "Captive Black Union Soldiers in Charleston," 38–44.

130. John Cimprich, "The Fort Pillow Massacre: Assessing the Evidence," in *Black Soldiers in Blue: African American Troops in the Civil War Era*, ed. John David Smith (Chapel Hill: University of North Carolina Press, 2002), 150–156.

131. Silkenat, *Raising the White Flag*, 101–103, 156–159; Kevin M. Levin, *Remembering the Battle of the Crator: War as Murder* (Lawrence: University of Kansas Press, 2012), 20–21.

132. Gregory J. W. Urwin, "'We cannot treat negroes . . . as prisoners of war': Racial Atrocities and Reprisals in Civil War Arkansas," *Civil War Military History* 42, no. 3 (June 1996), 203.

133. Ibid.

134. The details of James Robinson's prisoner experiences remain unknown. Deposition of James Robinson, on October 15, 1864, in Benjamin Davis, Sixth USCI, pension file.

135. Don Pettijohn, "African Americans at Andersonville," National Park Service, https://www.nps.gov/ande/learn/historyculture/african_americans.htm; Evan A. Kutzler, *Living By Inches: The Smells, Sounds, Tastes, and Feeling of Captivity in Civil War Prisons* (Chapel Hill: University of North Carolina Press, 2019), 21, 24–25, 38–39.

136. Compiled Military Service Records: M1821, roll 5, reel 1116.

137. Barr, "Loathsome Disease and Principles," 109.

138. Deposition of James Robinson, on October 5, 1865, deposition of Eliza Bryant, on April 2, 1884, and deposition of Robert Davis, on March 31, 1884, Benjamin Davis pension file.

139. Russell L. Johnson, "'Not one Jot or Tittle of Evidence': The Civil War Pension Files," *Australasian Journal of American Studies* 30, no. 2 (December 2011), 78, 83.

140. John P. Resch, "Politics and Public Culture: The Revolutionary War Pension Act of 1818," *Journal of the Early Republic* 8, no. 2 (Summer 1998), 142.

141. Nineteen African and African American men received a pension in the first year of the program's existence. John P. Resch, "Federal Welfare for Revolu-

tionary War Veterans," *Social Science Review* 56, no. 2 (June 1983), 171–172; "The Black Men in the Revolution, and the War of 1812," *Christian Recorder*, September 13, 1862.

142. Congress spent close to $2 million in the program's first year. Resch, "Politics and Public Culture," 152.

143. William Henry Glasson, *Federal Military Pensions in the United States* (Oxford: Oxford University Press, 1918), 124–125.

144. Ibid., 125.

145. Ibid., 125–126.

146. Ibid., 125–129.

147. Ibid., 125–129; Megan J. McClintock, "Civil War Pensions and the Reconstruction of Union Families," *Journal of American History* 83, no. 2 (September 1996), 457–464.

148. Theda Skocpol, *Protecting Soldiers and Mothers: The Political Origins of Social Policy in the United States* (Cambridge, Mass.: Belknap Press of Harvard University Press, 1992), 106.

149. Resch, "Politics and Public Culture," 157.

150. Skocpol, *Protecting Soldiers and Mothers*, 106.

151. James Marten, *Sing Not War: The Lives of Union and Confederate Veterans in Gilded Age America* (Chapel Hill: University of North Carolina Press, 2011), 205.

152. "Coming Home to Plague Them," *Vincennes Weekly Western Sun*, January 17, 1867.

153. John Resch, *Suffering Soldiers: Revolutionary War Veterans, Moral Sentiment, and Political Culture in the Early Republic* (Amherst: University of Massachusetts Press, 1999), 143, 168–169.

154. Donald R. Shaffer, "'I Do Not Suppose That Uncle Sam Looks at the Skin,'" in *The Civil War Veteran: A Historical Reader*, eds. Larry M. Logue and Michael Barton (New York: New York University Press, 2007), 201–203; Larry M. Logue and Peter Blanck, *Race, Ethnicity, and Disability: Veterans and Benefits in Post–Civil War America* (Cambridge: Cambridge University Press, 2010), 32–37.

155. Brandi Clay Brimmer, *Claiming Union Widowhood: Race, Respectability, and Poverty in the Post-Emancipation South* (Durham, N.C.: Duke University Press, 2020), 6–7.

156. Robert I. Golerel and Michael F. Rhode, "From Individual Trauma to National Policy: Tracking the Uses of Civil War Veteran Medical Records," in *Disabled Veterans in History*, rev. ed., ed. David A. Gerber (Ann Arbor: University of Michigan Press, 2012, 167.

157. Donald Shaffer, *After the Glory: The Struggles of Black Civil War Veterans* (Lawrence: University of Kansas Press, 2004), 122–129; Logue and Blanck, *Race, Ethnicity, and Disability*, 32–33, 42, 53, 65, 111–114.

158. Shaffer, *After the Glory*, 126–134; Sven E. Wilson, "Prejudice and Policy: Racial Discrimination in the Union Army Disability Pension System, 1865–1906," *American Journal of Public Health* 10, no. S1 (2010), 56–58; Brimmer, *Claiming Union Widowhood*, 123–125.

159. Logue and Blanck, *Race, Ethnicity, and Disability*, 69–70.

160. 1879 medical examination, George Roland pension file; Undated pension slip, in William Butler, Sixth USCI, pension file; Undated pension document, in Nathaniel Logan Sr., Sixth USCI, pension file; 1865 pension slip, Ephraim Maloney pension file; 1884 original invalid claim, in James Crippen, Sixth USCI, pension file; Undated pension slip, in Henry Thompson, Eighth USCI, pension file; Claim for an invalid pension, John Short pension file; Undated pension slip, Hezekiah Wilson pension file.

161. Skocpol, *Protecting Soldiers and Mothers*, 109.

162. Ibid., 106–107; John William Oliver, "History of the Civil War Military Pensions, 1861–1885" (PhD diss., University of Wisconsin, 1915), 16.

163. 1870 United States Federal Census (Washington, D.C.: National Archives and Records Administration, n.d.), accessed via *Ancestry.com* (hereafter 1870 U.S. Census), M593.

164. 1879 medical examination, George Roland pension file.

165. By 1870 a teamster could earn almost two dollars per day. Since most people worked six days a week, as the eight-hour workday and forty-hour work week movement had not yet become universally supported in the United States, my calculations reflect that tabulation. Clarence D. Long, "Wages by Occupational and Individual Characteristics," in *Wages and Earnings in the United States, 1869–1890*, ed. Clarence D. Long (Princeton: Princeton University Press, 1960), 98.

166. Russell L. Johnson, *Warriors into Workers: The Civil War and the Formation of Urban-Industrial Society in a Northern City* (New York: Fordham University Press, 2003), 281; Larry M. Logue, *To Appomattox and Beyond: The Civil War Soldier in War and Peace* (Chicago: Ivan R. Dee, 1996), 133.

167. Letter from George A. Armes, on January 25, 1868, Jacob Thornton pension file.

168. Ibid.

CHAPTER 4. Familial Hardships during the Civil War

1. Deposition of Mary Craig, on April 1, 1884, in Benjamin Davis, Sixth USCI, pension file, National Archives and Records Administration, Washington, D.C. (hereafter pension file).

2. Paul A. Cimbala and Randall M. Miller, *The Northern Home Front During the Civil War* (Santa Barbara, Calif.: Praeger, 2017), 47; Douglas R. Egerton, *Thunder At The Gates: The Black Civil War Regiments That Redeemed America* (New York: Basic Books, 2016), 87.

3. Special Order 31, issued by Lieutenant Colonel Louis F. Wagner on April 6, 1864, *Records of the Provost Marshal General Pennsylvania: Camp William Penn*, Entry 3598, Special Orders, 1863–1865, National Archives and Records Administration, Philadelphia, RG 110.

4. This daily schedule comes from General Order No. 5 for the Sixth USCI

issued on September 8, 1863. James M. Paradis, *Strike the Blow for Freedom: The 6th United States Colored Infantry in the Civil War* (Shippensburg, Pa.: White Mane Books, 1998), 15.

5. Deposition of Rachel Dilton, on April 3, 1884, Benjamin Davis pension file.

6. Deposition of Lydia Marsh, on April 3, 1884, Benjamin Davis pension file.

7. Nicole Etcheson, *A Generation at War: The Civil War Era in a Northern Community* (Lawrence: University Press of Kansas, 2011), 129–130, 134.

8. Deposition of Mary Gaines, on April 3, 1884, Benjamin Davis pension file.

9. J. Matthew Gallman, *Defining Duty in the Civil War: Personal Choice, Popular Culture, and the Union Home Front* (Chapel Hill: University of North Carolina Press, 2015), 190.

10. Judith Giesberg, *Army at Home: Women and the Civil War on the Northern Home Front* (Chapel Hill: University of North Carolina Press, 2009), 65.

11. Judith Giesberg, *Sex and the Civil War: Soldiers, Pornography, and the Making of American Morality* (Chapel Hill: University of North Carolina Press, 2017), 36, 72–73; Lawrence R. Murphy, "The Enemy among Us: Venereal Disease among Union Soldiers in the Far West, 1861–1865," *Civil War History Journal* 31, no.3 (September 1985), 260–264.

12. Keith P. Wilson, *Campfires of Freedom: The Camp Life of Black Soldiers During the Civil War* (Kent, Ohio: Kent State University Press, 2002), 19.

13. Kate Masur, *An Example for All the Land: Emancipation and the Struggle Over Equality in Washington, D.C.* (Chapel Hill: University of North Carolina Press, 2010), 109.

14. Elizabeth Strodeur Pryor, *Colored Travelers: Mobility and the Fight for Citizenship before the Civil War* (Chapel Hill: University of North Carolina Press, 2016), 79; Richard Archer, *Jim Crow North: The Struggle for Equal Rights in Antebellum New England* (Oxford: Oxford University Press, 2017), 92–93.

15. M. P. Jones, *The Rights of Railway Travelers and the Rights of Railway Companies in Their Various Capacities as a Common Carrier. Being Facts of Importance to Those Versed in Railway Law-Based upon Common Law, Special Acts and Legal Decisions* (Lancaster, Pa.: Pearsol & Geist, 1859), 45–46; Giesberg, *Army at Home*, 96–98; "The Colored People and the City Railways," *Christian Recorder*, July 23, 1864; "The Passenger Cars of Philadelphia," *Christian Recorder*, December 26, 1863.

16. Pryor, *Colored Travelers*, 26–27, 44–45; Robin D. G. Kelley, *Race Rebels: Culture, Politics, and the Black Working Class* (New York: Free Press, 1994), 57, 59–60; Giesberg, *Army at Home*, 95; Geoff D. Zylstra, "Whiteness, Freedom, and Technology: The Racial Struggle over Philadelphia's Streetcars, 1859–1867," *Technology and Culture* 52, no. 4 (October 2011), 679–684; Philip S. Foner, "The Battle to End Discrimination Against Negroes on Philadelphia Streetcars: Background and Beginning of the Battle," pt. 1, *Pennsylvania History: A Journal of Mid-Atlantic Studies* 40, no. 3 (July 1973), 269–278.

17. Pryor, *Colored Travelers*, 61–62, 70.

18. Deposition of Mary Gaines, on April 3, 1884, Benjamin Davis pension file.

19. Giesberg, *Army at Home*, 95.

20. Archer, *Jim Crow North*, 96

21. Deposition of Jerome Davis, on April 14, 1884, Benjamin Davis pension file.

22. Ibid.

23. Ibid.

24. Deposition of Mary Williamson, on April 8, 1884, Benjamin Davis pension file.

25. Etcheson, *A Generation at War*, 141.

26. Deposition of John J. Brown, on April 2, 1892, in Solomon Wilson, Thirty-First USCI, pension file.

27. William Blair, "We Are Coming, Father Abraham—Eventually: The Problem of Northern Nationalism in the Pennsylvania Recruiting Drives of 1862," in *The War Was You and Me: Civilians in the American Civil War*, ed. Joan E. Cashin (Princeton: Princeton University Press, 2002), 190.

28. Drew Gilpin Faust, *The Republic of Suffering: Death and the American Civil War* (New York: Alfred A. Knopf, 2008), 125, 146, 165, 228; Sean A. Scott, "'Good Children Die Happy': Confronting Death during the Civil War," in *Children and Youth during the Civil War*, ed. James Marten (New York: New York University Press, 2012), 93.

29. Karsonya Wise Whitehead, ed., *Notes from a Colored Girl: The Civil War Pocket Diaries of Emilie Frances Davis* (Columbia: The University of South Carolina Press, 2014), 44.

30. Deposition of Amelia Jannis, on April 9, 1884, Benjamin Davis pension file.

31. Jeffrey W. McClurken, *Take Care of the Living: Reconstructing Confederate Veteran Families in Virginia* (Charlottesville: University of Virginia Press, 2009), 15, 28.

32. Peter Badaglio, "The Children of Jubilee: African American Children in Wartime," in *Divided Houses: Gender and the Civil War*, eds. Catherine Clinton and Nina Silber (Oxford: Oxford University Press, 1992), 224; Kelly D. Mezurek, *For Their Own Cause: The 27th United States Colored Troops* (Kent, Ohio: Kent State University Press, 2016), 72.

33. Joseph P. Reidy, *Illusions of Emancipation: The Pursuit of Freedom and Equality in the Twilight of Slavery* (Chapel Hill: University of North Carolina Press, 2020), 138.

34. Egerton, *Thunder at the Gates*, 288–289, 292, 296–297, 303.

35. Joseph T. Glatthaar, *Forged in Battle: The Civil War Alliance of Black Soldiers and White Officers* (Baton Rouge: Louisiana State University Press, 1990), 209–210.

36. Noah Trudeau, *Like Men of War: Black Troops in the Civil War, 1862–1865* (Boston: Little, Brown, & Company, 1998), 461–462.

37. W. Stephen McBride, "From the Bluegrass to the Rio Grande: Kentucky's

U.S. Colored Troops on the Border, 1865–1867," in *The Civil War on the Rio Grande, 1846–1876*, eds. Roseanna Bacha-Garza, Christopher L. Miller, and Russell K. Skowronek (College Station: Texas A&M University Press, 2019), 214.

38. McClurken, *Taking Care of the Living*, 41; Gregory P. Downs, *After Appomattox: Military Occupation and the Ends of War* (Cambridge, Mass.: Harvard University Press, 2015), 23.

39. Evan C. Rothera, "The Men Are Understood to Have Been Generally Americans, in the Employ of the Liberal Government: Civil War Veterans and Mexico, 1865–1867," in *The War Went On: Reconsidering the Lives of Civil War Veterans*, eds. Brian Matthew Jordan and Evan C. Rothera (Baton Rouge: Louisiana State University, 2020), 37–39.

40. McBride, "From the Bluegrass to the Rio Grande," 214.

41. Richard M. Reid, *Freedom for Themselves: North Carolina's Black Soldiers in the Civil War Era* (Chapel Hill: University of North Carolina Press, 2008), 230–231; Amy Murrell Taylor, *Embattled Freedom: Journeys through the Civil War's Slave Refugee Camps* (Chapel Hill: University of North Carolina Press, 2018), 144–145.

42. Edwin Redkey, ed., *A Grand Army of Black Men: Letters from African-American Soldiers in the Union Army, 1861–1865* (Cambridge: Cambridge University Press, 1992), 179.

43. Ira Berlin, Joseph P. Reidy, and Leslie S. Rowland, eds., *Freedom: A Documentary History of Emancipation, 1861–1867*, vol. 1, *The Black Military Experience: Series II,* 2 vol., paperback ed. (Cambridge: Cambridge University Press, 2010), 680–681.

44. Ibid., 680–681.

45. Ibid., 668.

46. Ibid., 666. Assistant Adjutant-General C. W. Foster notified Lucy Bailey on May 16, 1865, stating no other information on John Bailey's military service.

47. Cimbala and Miller, *The Northern Home Front during the Civil War*, 41, 58–59, 61.

48. McClurken, *Take Care of the Living*, 35.

49. Mark E. Neely, "Lincoln, Slavery, and the Nation," *Journal of American History* 96, no. 2 (September 2009), 457.

50. Sarah Handley-Cousins, *Bodies in Blue: Disability in the Civil War North* (Athens: University of Georgia Press, 2019), 36

51. Compiled Military Service Records of Volunteer Union Soldiers Who Served with the United States Colored Troops (Washington, D.C.: National Archives and Records Administration, n.d.), accessed via *Ancestry.com* (hereafter Compiled Military Service Records), M1820, roll 23, reels 1196, 1200.

52. Handley-Cousins, *Bodies in Blue*, 24–29.

53. Compiled Military Service Records: M1820, roll 74, reel 670.

54. Compiled Military Service Records: M1820, roll 69, reel 1002.

55. Compiled Military Service Records: M1820, roll 71, reel 1171.

56. 1903 pension document, in James Ellsbury, Sixth USCI, pension file.

57. Steven J. Ramrold, *Across the Divide: Union Soldiers View the Northern Home Front* (New York: New York University Press, 2013), 47.

58. Cimbala and Miller, *The Northern Home Front*, 88–89.

59. "Flag Presentation at Camp William Penn," *Liberator*, September 11, 1863.

60. "Presentation of a Stand of Colors to the Twenty-Sixth Regiment U.S.C.T.," *Weekly Anglo-African*, March 28, 1864.

61. Michael J. Bennett, "The Black Flag and Confederate Soldiers: Total War from the Bottom Up?," in *This Distracted and Anarchical People: New Answers for Old Questions about the Civil War–Era North*, eds. Andrew L. Slap and Michael Thomas Smith (New York: Fordham University Press, 2013), 143, 153.

62. R. J. M. Blackett, ed., *Thomas Morris Chester, Black Civil War Correspondent: His Dispatches from the Virginia Front* (New York: Da Capo Press, 1989), 109.

63. Drew Gilpin Faust, *The Republic of Suffering: Death and the American Civil War* (New York: Alfred A. Knopf, 2008), 48.

64. Noah Andre Trudeau, ed. *Voices of the 55th Massachusetts Volunteers, 1861–1865* (Dayton, Ohio: Morningside House, 1996), 51.

65. Ibid.

66. Ford Risley, *Civil War Journalism* (Santa Barbara, Calif.: 2012), 18.

67. Ramrold, *Across the Divide*, 18–19; Andrew S. Bledsoe, "Technology and War," in *The Cambridge History of The Civil War,* ed. Aaron Sheehan-Dean, vol. 2, *Affairs of the State* (Cambridge: Cambridge University Press, 2019), 143.

68. McClurken, *Take Care of the Living*, 33; Allison M. Johnson, *The Scars We Carve: Bodies and Wounds in Civil War Print Culture* (Baton Rouge: Louisiana State University Press, 2019), 128, 132.

69. Johnson, *The Scars We Carve*, 142–143.

70. Deposition of Rachel Dilton, on April 3, 1884, Benjamin Davis pension file.

71. Letter from Thomas R. Rockhold, on August 27, 1863, in Alfred Rothwell, Third USCI, pension file.

72. Undated pension slip, Alfred Rothwell pension file.

73. Faust, *The Republic of Suffering*, 17; Shannon Bontrager, *Death at the Edges of Empire: Fallen Soldiers, Cultural Memory, and the Making of an American Nation, 1863–1921* (Lincoln: University of Nebraska Press, 2020), 12–16.

74. Reid Mitchell, *The Vacant Chair: The Northern Soldier Leaves Home* (Oxford: Oxford University Press, 1993), 143.

75. Faust, *The Republic of Suffering*, 17.

76. Mitchell, *The Vacant Chair*, 143–145.

77. Jennifer Terry, "'When Dey 'Listed Colored Soldiers': Paul Laurence Dunbar's Poetic Engagement with the Civil War, Masculinity, and Violence," *African American Review* 41, no. 2 (Summer 2007), 270.

78. Historian Drew Gilpin Faust does not provide information about how

much time society deemed appropriate for brothers and fathers to lament a male relative's demise. Perhaps no one considered a mourning time either necessary or appropriate for men. Faust, *The Republic of Suffering*, 148.

79. Ibid., 148–149, 163, 165, 227–228, 247–248.

80. Drew Gilpin Faust, "Death and Dying," National Park Service, https://www.nps.gov/nr/travel/national_cemeteries/Death.html.

81. Brandi Clay Brimmer, "All Her Rights and Privileges: Women and the Politics of Civil War Widows' Pensions" (PhD diss., University of California–Los Angeles, 2006), 32–33, 117; Megan J. McClintock, "Impact of the Civil War on Nineteenth-Century Marriages," in *Union Soldiers and the Northern Home Front: Wartime Experiences, Postwar Adjustments*, eds. Paul A. Cimbala and Randall Miller (New York: Fordham University Press, 2002), 398–399.

82. Though historian Jeffrey E. Vogel states that ex-Confederates who were also Mexican–American War veterans or their nuclear dependents eventually had their pensions restored after the passage of an 1885 pension law, long after white reconciliation engrossed the nation. Jeffrey E. Vogel, "Redefining Reconciliation: Confederate Veterans and the Southern Responses to Federal Civil War Pensions," *Civil War History Journal* 51, no. 1 (March 2005), 71, 73–74.

83. This number includes the previously mentioned eleven soldiers who died from combat wounds.

84. Emily J. Harris, "Sons and Soldiers: Deerfield, Massachusetts, and the Civil War," in *Civil War History Readers*, ed. J. Matthew Gallman, vol. 4, *Citizens and Communities* (Kent, Ohio: Kent State University Press, 2015), 135.

85. Copy of marriage certificate, in Robert Streets, Eighth USCI, pension file.

86. Tera W. Hunter, *Bound in Wedlock: Slave and Free Black Marriage in the Nineteenth Century* (Cambridge, Mass.: Belknap Press of Harvard University Press, 2017), 142–143, 162–164, 200, 224–225.

87. "The Pension Act.; Important Instructions Regarding Its Details," *New York Times*, August 31, 1864.

88. Historian Brandi Clay Brimmer notes that the 1864 Pension Law was in response to the horrific events at the Fort Pillow Massacre to provide some economic stability to deceased USCT soldiers' dependents. Brandi Clay Brimmer, *Claiming Union Widowhood: Race, Respectability, and Poverty in the Post-Emancipation South* (Durham, N.C.: Duke University Press, 2020), 9.

89. Brimmer, "All Her Rights and Privileges," 22–23, 113, 117.

90. Megan J. McClintock, "Impact of the Civil War on Nineteenth-Century Marriages," in *Union Soldiers and the Northern Home Front*, 397; Donald Shaffer, *After the Glory: The Struggles of Black Civil War Veterans* (Lawrence: University of Kansas Press, 2004), 99–101.

91. Etcheson, *A Generation at War*, 200.

92. Elizabeth Regosin, *Freedom's Promise: Ex-Slave Families and Citizenship in the Age of Emancipation* (Charlottesville: University of Virginia Press, 2002), 120–121.

93. Brimmer, "All Her Rights and Privileges," 34.

94. Deposition of James Turner, on April 11, 1884, and deposition of Mary Craig, on April 1, 1884, Benjamin Davis pension file.

95. Deposition of Robert Davis, on May 10, 1882, Benjamin Davis pension file.

96. McClintock, "The Impact of the Civil War on Nineteenth-Century Marriages," 398–399; Jordan, *Marching Home*, 154.

97. Deposition of Jane Robinson, on March 6, 1865, in Alexander Robinson, Sixth USCI, pension file.

98. Deposition of Sarah Reeves, on January 31, 1884, in Andrew White, Sixth USCI, pension file.

99. Undated pension slip, in George Henderson, Third USCI, pension file.

100. Nicole Etcheson, "Women and Family in the North," in *Women and the American Civil War: North and South Counterpoints*, eds. Judith Giesberg and Randall M. Miller (Kent, Ohio: Kent State University Press, 2018), 200.

CHAPTER 5. Reconstructing the Northern African American Family

1. For scholarship on formerly enslaved families in the Reconstruction era, please refer to the following texts: Heather Andrea Williams, *Help Me Find My People: The African American Search for Family Lost in Slavery* (Chapel Hill: University of North Carolina Press, 2012); Leslie A. Schwalm, *A Hard Fight for We: Women's Transition from Slavery to Freedom in South Carolina* (Urbana: University of Illinois Press, 1997); Eugene D. Genovese, *Roll, Jordan, Roll: The World the Slaves Made* (New York: Vintage Books, 1976).

2. Jacqueline Jones, *American Work: Four Centuries of Black and White Labor* (New York: W. W. Norton & Company, 1998), 286.

3. Kelly D. Mezurek, "'The Colored Veteran Soldiers Should Receive the Same Tender Care': Soldiers' Homes, Race, and the Post–Civil War Midwest," in *The War Went On: Reconsidering the Lives of Civil War Veterans*, eds. Brian Matthew Jordan and Evan C. Rothera (Baton Rouge: Louisiana State University, 2020), 230–231.

4. Adam H. Domby, *The False Cause: Fraud, Fabrication, and White Supremacy in Confederate Memory* (Charlottesville: University of Virginia Press, 2020), 13–44, 104–131; Nina Silber, *This War Ain't Over: Fighting the Civil War in New Deal America* (Chapel Hill: University of North Carolina Press, 2018), 13–33; Kevin M. Levin, *Searching for Black Confederates: The Civil War's Most Persistent Myth* (Chapel Hill: University of North Carolina Press, 2019), 70–87.

5. William B. Holberton, *Homeward Bound: The Demobilization of Union and Confederate Armies, 1865–1866* (Mechanicsburg, Pa.: Stackpole Books, 2001), 140–141.

6. "United States Colored Troops: 6th Regiment, United States Colored Infantry," National Park Service, https://www.nps.gov/civilwar/search-battle-units

-detail.htm?battleUnitCode=UUS0006RI00C; "United States Colored Troops: 8th Regiment, United States Colored Infantry," National Park Service, https://www.nps.gov/civilwar/search-battle-units- detail.htm?battleUnitCode =UUS0008RI00C; "United States Colored Troops: 3rd Regiment, United States Colored Infantry," National Park Service, https://www.nps.gov/civilwar/search -battle-units- detail.htm?battleUnitCode=UUS0003RI01C;

7. Larry M. Logue, *To Appomattox and Beyond: The Civil War Soldier in War and Peace* (Chicago: Ivan R. Dee, 1996), 85–86.

8. Paul A. Cimbala, *Veterans North and South: The Transition from Soldier to Civilian after the American Civil War* (Santa Barbara, Calif.: Praeger, 2015), 24.

9. Kelly D. Mezurek, *For Their Own Cause: The 27th United States Colored Troops* (Kent, Ohio: Kent State University Press, 2016), 226; James Marten, *Sing Not War: The Lives of Union and Confederate Veterans in Gilded Age America* (Chapel Hill: University of North Carolina Press, 2011), 49.

10. Larry M. Logue and Peter Blanck, *Heavy Laden: Union Veterans, Psychological Illness, and Suicide* (Cambridge: Cambridge University Press, 2018), 14.

11. "Our Soldiers," *Weekly Anglo-African*, May 27, 1865.

12. Sven Beckert, *The Monied Metropolis: New York City and the Consolidation of the American Bourgeoisie, 1850–1896* (Cambridge: Cambridge University Press, 2001), 115–120.

13. James F. Farley, *Making Arms in The Machine Age: Philadelphia's Frankford Arsenal, 1816–1870* (University Park: Pennsylvania State University Press, 1994), 78, 83, 85, 87.

14. Daniel B. Thorp, *Facing Freedom: An African American Community in Virginia from Reconstruction to Jim Crow* (Charlottesville: University of Virginia Press, 2017), 41.

15. Brian Matthew Jordan, *Marching Home: Union Veterans and Their Unending Civil War* (New York: Liveright Publishing Corporation, 2014), 56–57.

16. 1889 Health Office document, in William Brown, Sixth USCI, pension file, National Archives and Records Administration, Washington, D.C. (hereafter pension file); 1860 United States Federal Census (Washington, D.C.: National Archives and Records Administration, n.d.), accessed via *Ancestry.com* (hereafter 1860 U.S. Census), M593; 1870 United States Federal Census (Washington, D.C.: National Archives and Records Administration, n.d.), accessed via *Ancestry.com* (hereafter 1870 U.S. Census), M593; 1900 United States Federal Census (Washington, D.C.: National Archives and Records Administration, n.d.), accessed via *Ancestry.com* (hereafter 1900 U.S. Census), M1469; Deposition of Alice King, on April 29, 1903, in Thomas C. King Sr., Third USCI, pension file.

17. Undated pension slip, in James Ellsbury, Sixth USCI, pension file; 1870 U.S. Census, M593.

18. James G. Mendez, *A Great Sacrifice: Northern Black Soldiers, Their Families, and the Experience of Civil War* (New York: Fordham University Press, 2019), 180.

19. Darius J. Young, "Henry S. Harmon: Pioneer African American Attorney

in Reconstruction-Era Florida," *Florida Historical Quarterly* 85, no. 2 (Fall 2006), 183–188.

20. Mendez, *A Great Sacrifice*, 85.

21. Richard M. Reid, *Freedom for Themselves: North Carolina's Black Soldiers in the Civil War Era* (Chapel Hill: University of North Carolina Press, 2008), 315–316; Ian Michael Spurgeon, *Soldiers in the Army of Freedom: The 1st Kansas Colored, the 63–64, The Civil War's First African American Combat Unit* (Norman: University of Oklahoma Press, 2014), 267–268; Edward A. Miller Jr., *The Black Civil War Soldiers of Illinois: The Story of the Twenty-Ninth U.S. Colored Infantry* (Columbia: University of South Carolina Press, 1998), 175–176.

22. Roger Lane, *William Dorsey's Philadelphia and Ours: On the Past and Future of the Black City in America* (Oxford: Oxford University Press, 1991), 57.

23. W. E. B. Du Bois, *The Philadelphia Negro* (Philadelphia: University of Pennsylvania Press, 1899; rpt., 1996), 39.

24. Joe Trotter Jr., *Workers on Arrival: Black Labor in the Making of America* (Oakland: University of California Press, 2021), 55, 64; *Judith Wellman, Brooklyn's Promised Land: The Free Black Community of Weeksville, New York* (New York: New York University Press, 2014), 133–134.

25. Barbara J. Beeching, *Hopes and Expectations: The Origins of the Black Middle Class in Hartford* (New York: SUNY Press, 2017), 163.

26. Gerald G. Eggert, "'Two Steps Forward, a Step-and-a-Half Back': Harrisburg's African American Community in the Nineteenth Century," in *African Americans in Pennsylvania: Shifting Historical Perspectives*, eds. Joe William Trotter Jr. and Eric Ledell Smith (University Park: Pennsylvania State University Press, 1997), 228.

27. Du Bois, *Philadelphia Negro*, 345; Thomas H. O'Connor, *Civil War Boston: Home Front and Battlefield* (Boston: Northeastern University Press, 1997), 238–240.

28. Gretchen Long, *Doctoring Freedom: The Politics of African American Medical Care in Slavery and Emancipation* (Chapel Hill: University of North Carolina Press, 2012), 162.

29. David E. Goldberg, *The Retreats of Reconstruction: Race, Leisure, and the Politics of Segregation at the New Jersey Shore, 1865–1920* (New York: Fordham University Press, 2017), 13, 18, 27, 53.

30. 1870 U.S. Census, M593.

31. Du Bois, *Philadelphia Negro*, 345.

32. Records do not reveal any information on the USCT veteran barbers' clientele. "Our Opinion Wanted," *Christian Recorder*, March 4, 1865; "Barber Shops," *Christian Recorder*, March 4, 1865.

33. Lane, *William Dorsey's Philadelphia*, 115–116.

34. Ibid., 119.

35. Deposition of Arretta Davis, on December 15, 1896, in Edward Davis, Sixth USCI, pension file.

36. W. Jeffrey Bolster "'To Feel Like a Man': Black Seamen in the Northern States, 1800–1860," in *A Question of Manhood*, eds. Darlene Clark Hine and Earnestine Jenkins, vol. 1, *"Manhood Rights": The Construction of Black Male History and Manhood, 1750–1870* (Bloomington: Indiana State Press, 1999), 359–361.

37. Deposition of Arretta Davis, on December 15, 1896, Edward Davis pension file.

38. Elmo P. Hohman, "Wages, Risk, and Profits in the Whaling Industry," *Quarterly Journal of Economics* 40, no. 4 (August 1926), 646; Bolster "'To Feel Like a Man,'" in *A Question of Manhood*, 1:361.

39. Earl F. Mulderink III, *New Bedford's Civil War* (New York: Fordham University Press, 2012), 188.

40. Letter from Edward Davis to Arretta Davis, on April 26, 1873, Edward Davis pension file.

41. Deposition of Charles H. Lee, on December 26, 1896, Edward Davis pension file.

42. Letter from Edward Davis to Arretta Davis, on April 26, 1873, Edward Davis pension file.

43. Allison Dorothy Fredette, *Marriage on the Border: Love, Mutuality, and Divorce in the Upper South during the Civil War* (Lexington: University Press of Kentucky, 2020), 29.

44. Deposition of John Brisco, on January 23, 1897, and deposition of Sarah Jane Hayes, on December 28, 1896, Edward Davis pension file.

45. Deposition of James Jackson, on December 19, 1896, Edward Davis pension file.

46. Letter from Edward Davis to Arretta Davis, on April 26, 1873, Edward Davis pension file.

47. Deposition of Arretta Davis, on December 15, 1896, Edward Davis pension file.

48. Jaqueline Jones, *Labor of Love, Labor of Sorrow: Black Women, Work, and the Family from Slavery to the Present* (New York: Basic Books, 1985), 75.

49. This number may be much higher, but there is limited to no documentation on many USCT veterans' postwar lives.

50. John A. Casey Jr., *New Men: Reconstructing the Image of the Veteran in Late-Nineteenth-Century American Literature and Culture* (New York: Fordham University Press, 2015), 50.

51. "To Have the Pay of the Laborer, Equal the Pay of the Artisan," *Christian Recorder*, June 26, 1873.

52. Laurie and Schmitz, "Manufacturing and Productivity," in *Philadelphia: Work, Space, Family, and Group Experience in the 19th Century*, ed. Theodore Hershberg (Oxford: Oxford University Press, 1981), 44.

53. Jonathan W. White, ed., *A Philadelphia Perspective: The Civil War Diary of Sidney George Fisher* (New York: Fordham University Press, 2007), 271.

54. Lane, *William Dorsey's Philadelphia*, 63.

55. 1865 examining certificate and 1869 surgeon examination for increase of a pension, in Hezekiah Wilson, Sixth USCI, pension file.

56. 1867 invalid application, in Charles Tobias, Third USCI, pension file.

57. Deposition of Charles H. Freeman, on August 17, 1864, in Samuel Derry, Third USCI, pension file.

58. Brian Matthew Jordan, "'Living Monuments': Union Veteran Amputees and the Embodied Memory of the Civil War," *Civil War History Journal* 57, no. 2 (June 2011), 127.

59. 1879 Invalid Application, in James Crippen, Sixth USCI, pension file; Deposition of A. S. Redstreak, on February 13, 1868, in George Henderson, Third USCI, pension file.

60. Deposition of George Stiles, on March 3, 1886, in George Stiles, Eighth USCI, pension file.

61. Declaration for the increase of an invalid pension, George Stiles pension file.

62. Deposition of Joseph Preston and William Summers, on May 23, 1891, in Edward Brown, Third USCI, pension file.

63. 1905 declaration for the increase of an invalid pension, Edward Brown pension file.

64. Letter from Edward Purnell Jr., undated, in John Thompson, Third USCI, pension file.

65. Deposition of Charles H. Freeman, on August 17, 1864, and deposition of Henry Anderson, on October 31, 1865, Samuel Derry pension file.

66. Deposition of William Ingraham, on November 28, 1888, in John Short, Sixth USCI, pension file.

67. Sarah H. Rose, *"No Right to Be Idle": The Invention of Disability, 1840s–1930s* (Chapel Hill: University of North Carolina Press, 2017), 51, 111.

68. Elizabeth D. Leonard, *Men of Color to Arms!: Black Soldiers, Indian Wars, and the Quest for Equality* (New York: W. W. Norton & Company, 2010), 40–41.

69. William A. Dobak, "Fort Riley's Black Soldiers, and the Army's Changing Role in the West, 1867–85," in *Buffalo Soldiers in the West: A Black Soldier's Anthology*, eds. Bruce A. Glasurd and Michael N. Searles (College Station: Texas A&M University Press, 2007), 36.

70. Le'Trice D. Donaldson, *Duty Beyond the Battlefield: African American Soldiers Fight for Racial Uplift, Citizenship, and Manhood, 1879–1920* (Carbondale: Southern Illinois University Press, 2020), 14–17, 22, 35.

71. William R. Shafter, "Black Troops, and the Opening of the Llano Estacado, 1870–75," in *Buffalo Soldiers in the West*, 52; James N. Leiker, *Racial Borders: Black Soldiers along the Rio Grande* (College Station: Texas A&M University Press, 2002), 67.

72. "Buffalo Soldiers," National Parks Service, https://www.nps.gov/chyo/learn/historyculture/buffalo-soldiers.htm.

73. Thomas H. O'Connor, *Civil War Boston: Home Front and Battlefield* (Boston: Northeastern University Press, 1993), 166.

74. Cimbala, *Veterans North and South*, 26.

75. Leonard, *Men of Color to Arms!*, 53.

76. Douglas C. McChristian, "'Dress on the Colors, Boys!' Black Noncommissioned Officers in the Regular Army, 1866–98," in *Buffalo Soldiers in the West*, 85.

77. James M. Leiker, *Racial Borders: Black Soldiers Along the Rio Grande* (College Station: Texas A&M University Press, 2010), 184–185.

78. Deposition of Lorenzo George, on December 14, 1895, in Lorenzo George, Third USCI, pension file.

79. Ibid.

80. Leiker, *Racial Borders*, 75–76.

81. Deposition of Alexander W. Brown, on June 21, 1898, in Francis Hawkins, Third USCI, pension file.

82. Deposition of John H. Little, on February 10, 1899, Francis Hawkins pension file.

83. Leiker, *Racial Borders*, 184.

84. Leonard, *Men of Color to Arms!*, 53; W. E. B. Du Bois, *Black Reconstruction, in America, 1860–1880* (New York: Free Press, 1992), 106.

85. Edward D. Coffman, *The Regulars: The American Army, 1898–1941* (Cambridge, Mass.: Belknap Press of Harvard University, 2004), 127, 132; James N. Leiker, "Black Soldiers at Fort Hayes, Kansas, 1867–69," in *Buffalo Soldiers in the West*, 162–163.

86. Coffman, *The Regulars*, 132.

87. Andrew F. Lang, *In the Wake of War: Military Occupation, Emancipation, and Civil War* (Baton Rouge: Louisiana State University Press, 2017), 145, 176, 198–202.

88. Deposition of Lorenzo George, on December 14, 1895, Lorenzo George pension file.

89. Christen Jensen, "The Pardoning Power in the American States" (PhD diss., University of Chicago, 1922), 117.

90. Deposition of Lorenzo George, on December 14, 1895, Lorenzo George pension file.

91. Under the policy, deserters had to return by January 1, 1874. The federal government stated that 2,007 men were eligible to have their charges forgiven. Fred T. Wilson, *Digest of Laws, Rulings, and Decisions Governing the Military Crime of Desertion. To Which Added a Compendium of the Disabilities Attaching to Desertion as Regards Claims Against the United States, Citizenship, Etc., Etc.* (Washington, D.C.: Government Printing Office, 1882), 217.

92. Deposition of Lorenzo George, on December 14, 1895, Lorenzo George pension file.

93. Ibid.

94. Ibid.

95. Ibid.

96. Erica Armstrong Dunbar, *A Fragile Freedom: African American Women and Emancipation in the Antebellum City* (New Haven, Conn.: Yale University Press, 2008), 127–131.

97. 1897 special examiner's notes, Edward Davis pension file.

98. Alice Kessler-Harris, *Women Have Always Worked: A Concise History* (Urbana: University of Illinois Press, 2018), 13–18.

99. Deposition of Mary Taylor, on July 3, 1895, in Henry Thompson, Eighth USCI, pension file.

100. Megan Kate Nelson, *Ruin Nation: Destruction and the American Civil War* (Athens: University of Georgia Press, 2012), 171–175, 181–182.

101. Massachusetts Vital Records, 1840–1911, New England Historic Genealogical Society, Boston, Massachusetts, accessed via *Ancestry.com*.

102. A church marriage meant exchanging vows with a clergyman overseeing the ceremony. However, in the case of the examples here, these marriages were also legally documented. Tera W. Hunter, *Bound in Wedlock: Slave and Free Black Marriage in the Nineteenth Century* (Cambridge, Mass.: Belknap Press of Harvard University Press, 2017), 142, 162–164, 200, 211–214, 221–226, 293–296.

103. "Marriages," *Christian Recorder*, October 16, 1873; "Marriages," *Christian Recorder*, August 7, 1873; "A Happy Marriage," *Christian Recorder*, November 9, 1873.

104. Julius Bailey, *Around the Family Altar: Domesticity in the African Methodist Episcopal Church, 1865–1900* (Gainesville: University Press of Florida, 2005), 10–11, 14, 36, 47, 67; Thorp, *Facing Freedom*, 61.

105. "LIVE LIKE LOVERS. Married people should treat each li," *Christian Recorder*, July 3, 1873.

106. Deposition of Mary M. Parker, on March 8, 1900, in Robert G. Parker, Third USCI, pension file.

107. Deposition of William H. Parker, on March 7, 1910, Robert G. Parker pension file.

108. Dennis W. Brandt, *Pathway to Hell: A Tragedy of the American Civil War* (Lincoln: University of Nebraska Press, 2008), 147.

109. Deposition of Sarah A. Fisher, on August 21, 1901, in Wilson Day, Third USCI, pension file.

110. Deposition of Mary Elizabeth Crawford and Sarah A. Fisher, on November 12, 1902, Wilson Day pension file.

111. Ibid.

112. Ibid.

113. Deposition of Sarah A. Fisher, on March 3, 1902, Wilson Day pension file.

114. Eric T. Dean Jr., "Post-Traumatic Stress," in *The Civil War Veteran: A Historical Reader*, eds. Larry M. Logue and Michael Barton (New York: New York University Press, 2007), 135.

115. Logue and Blanck, *Heavy Laden*, 160.

116. Judith Giesberg, ed., *Emilie Davis's Civil War: The Diaries of a Free Black*

Woman in Philadelphia, 1863–1865 (University Park: Pennsylvania State University Press, 2014), 80.

117. Gross, *Colored Amazons*, 89; McClurken, *Take Care of the Living*, 66–67; Robin C. Sager, *Marital Cruelty in Antebellum America* (Baton Rouge: Louisiana State University Press, 2016), 56–57.

118. Cimbala, *Veterans North and South*, 90; Dean, "Post-Traumatic Stress," 137–138.

119. Diane Miller Sommerville, "'A Burden Too Heavy to Bear': War Trauma, Suicide, and Confederate Soldiers," *Civil War History Journal* 59, no. 4 (December 2013), 483–484.

120. Deposition of Joshua James, on December 9, 1879, in George H. Buck, Third USCI, pension file.

121. Deposition of January Felder, on May 24, 1881, and deposition of William E. Livingston, on December 27, 1880, George H. Buck pension file.

122. Records do not reveal the exact length of his stay in each facility.

123. Deposition of Porter Dobbins, on May 8, 1903, Wilson Day pension file.

124. The Blockley Almshouse was initially built in 1739 to provide aid to the poor and disabled. In 1804 the Dauphin County Almshouse began operation. Ian Charlton, "Philadelphia General Hospital (Old Blockley): Philadelphians 'Ain't Goin' to no Bellevue,'" http://www.philaplace.org/story/897/; Deposition of Margaret Day, on February 26, 1903, and deposition of Porter Dobbins, on May 8, 1903, and correspondence from the Bureau of Pensions, composed November 22, 1902, Wilson Day pension file; Luther Reily Kelker, *History of Dauphin County Pennsylvania* (New York: The Lewis Publishing Company, 1907), 1:109.

125. Deposition of Susan Gray, on April 19, 1900, in William F. Gray, Third USCI, pension file.

126. Stephen Anthony Klips, "Institutionalizing the Poor: The New York City Almshouse, 1825–1860" (PhD diss., City University of New York, 1980), 269.

127. Catherine Ruth Huggins, "Out of Mind: The Institutionalized Insane in Nineteenth Century Philadelphia," (PhD diss., Bryn Mawr College, 1986), 72.

128. Ibid., 74–75.

129. Catherine Jean Whitaker, "Almshouses and Mental Institutions in Michigan, 1871–1930" (PhD diss., University of Michigan, 1986), 8–9.

130. Helen W. Munson, "The Care of the Sick in Almshouses," *American Journal of Nursing* 30, no. 1 (October 1930), 1227–1228.

131. Ella F. Harris, "Charity Functions of the Pennsylvania County," *Annals of the American Academy of Political and Social Sciences* 47 (May 1913), 175.

132. Munson, "The Care of the Sick in Almshouses," 1229.

133. Ibid., 1230.

134. James Marten, "Nomads in Blue: Disabled Veterans and Alcohol at the National Home," in *Disabled Veterans in History*, rev. ed., ed. David A. Gerber (Ann Arbor: University of Michigan Press, 2012), 277.

135. On February 28, 1865, Congress passed a bill establishing the NHDVS,

an institution that provided long-term medical care to veterans. The NHDVS Central Branch opened in 1867. "History of the National Home for Disabled Volunteer Soldiers," National Parks Service, https://www.nps.gov/articles/history-of-disabled-volunteer-soldiers.htm#:~:text=First%20established%20in%201876%20as,members%20after%20World%20War%20I; "Central Branch Dayton, Ohio," National Parks Service, https://www.nps.gov/nr/travel/veterans_affairs/Central_Branch.html; 1869 Application for a Transfer, in William Butler, Sixth USCI, pension file.

136. 1895 invalid pension increase, Lorenzo George pension file; 1904 invalid application, in Samuel Brown, Third USCI, pension file.

137. Mezurek, *For Their Own Cause*, 229.

138. Judith Gladys Cetina, "A History of Veterans' Homes in the United States, 1811–1930" (PhD diss., Case Western Reserve University, 1977), 128.

139. Ibid., 173.

140. Ibid., 283.

141. Marten, "Nomads in Blue," 286.

142. Marten, *Sing Not War*, 77; Marten, "Nomads in Blue," 286–287.

143. Shaffer, *After the Glory*, 136–138.

144. The Southern branch, in Hampton, Virginia, was the only known branch that practiced full racial integration in their facility. Cetina, "A History of Veterans' Homes," 112, 173; Kelly, "Creating a National Home," 180.

145. Marten, *Sing Not War*, 187.

146. Mezurek, "'Same Tender Care,'" 230–231, 234–235, 240.

147. Steven A. Reich, *A Working People: A History of African American Workers since Emancipation* (New York: Rowman & Littlefield Publishers, 2013), 45–46; 1870 U.S. Census, M593.

148. Lane, *William Dorsey's Philadelphia*, 76–77; Tera W. Hunter, *To 'Joy My Freedom: Southern Black Women's Lives and Labor after the Civil War* (Cambridge, Mass.: Harvard University Press, 1997), 50–52, 107.

149. 1870 U.S. Census, M593.

150. Ibid.

151. Ibid.

152. Marten, *Sing Not War*, 34, 53; Casey, *New Men*, 61.

153. Lara Vapnek, *Breadwinners: Working Women and Economic Independence, 1865–1920* (Urbana: University of Illinois Press, 2009), 11–16.

154. Daniel R. Biddle and Murray Dubin, *Tasting Freedom: Octavius Catto and the Battle for Equality in Civil War America* (Philadelphia: Temple University Press, 2010), 431.

155. Lane, *William Dorsey's Philadelphia*, 72.

156. 1870 U.S. Census, M593.

157. Rebecca Sharpless, *Cooking in Other Women's Kitchens: Domestic Workers in the South, 1865–1960* (Chapel Hill: University of North Carolina Press, 2010), 15, 44, 61, 67.

158. 1870 U.S. Census, M593.

159. Cimbala, *Veterans North and South*, 49, 51.

160. Glasson, *Federal Military Pensions*, 123–129.

161. Ibid., 130–131.

162. Murray N. Rothbard, "Beginning the Welfare State: Civil War Veterans' Pensions," *Quarterly Journal of Austrian Economics* 22, no. 1 (Spring 2019), 70

163. Peter David Blanck and Michael Millender, "Before Disability Civil Rights: Civil War Pensions and the Politics of Disability of America," *Alabama Law Review* 5, no. 1 (Fall 2000), 8.

164. Glasson, *Federal Military Pensions*, 126–127.

165. Ibid., 139.

166. 1874 invalid pension increase, in Jacob Thornton, Third USCI, pension file; 1866 pension document, in Robert Johnson, Sixth USCI, pension file; 1876 original invalid pension application, George Stiles pension file.

167. Letter from Loren Burrit, composed on June 12, 1867, in Charles Brant, Eighth USCI, pension file.

168. Deposition of E. H. Baily, on February 8, 1868, Charles Tobias pension file.

169. Undated Pension document, in Nathaniel Logan Sr., Sixth USCI, pension file.

170. 1870 U.S. Census, M593.

171. Douglass, "Another Word to Black Men," *Weekly Anglo-African*, March 17, 1863; James M. McPherson, *The Negro's Civil War: How American Blacks Felt and Acted During the War for the Rebellion* (New York: Vintage Books, 1965), 32.

172. W. Fitzhugh Brundage, "Black Veterans Recall the Civil War," in *The Civil War Veteran*, 425–426, 430, 432; David W. Blight, *Beyond the Battlefield: Race, Memory, and the American Civil War* (Amherst: University of Massachusetts Press, 2002), 143.

173. Mezurek, *For Their Own Cause*, 237–238; Anderson, *Imagined Communities*, 4–7, 144–145.

174. Copy of marriage record, in Jacob G. Jackson, Eighth USCI, pension file.

175. 1863 Camp William Penn document, Jacob G. Jackson pension file.

176. Deposition of Samuel Dill and John Clark, on January 25, 1867, in George Glascow, Sixth USCI, pension file.

177. Undated pension slip, George Glascow pension file.

178. 1866 claim for increase of widow's pensions, Jacob G. Jackson pension file.

179. Declaration of guard of minor children for pension, in Jeremiah Griggs, Sixth USCI, pension file.

180. Brandi Clay Brimmer, *Claiming Union Widowhood: Race, Respectability, and Poverty in the Post-Emancipation South* (Durham, N.C.: Duke University Press, 2020), 87.

181. Brandi Clay Brimmer, "'All Her Rights and Privileges': Women and the

Politics of Civil War Widows' Pensions" (PhD diss., University of California–Los Angeles, 2006), 22–23, 113, 117.

182. 1867 claim for minor's pension with two dollars per month additional, Jeremiah Griggs pension file.

183. Catherine A. Jones, *Intimate Reconstruction: Children in Postemancipation Virginia* (Charlottesville: University of Virginia Press, 2015), 133–140.

CHAPTER 6. USCT Families in an Industrializing Nation

1. Jacqueline Jones, *American Work: Four Centuries of Black and White Labor* (New York: W. W. Norton & Company, 1998), 256.

2. Roger Lane, *William Dorsey's Philadelphia and Ours: On the Past and Future of the Black City in America* (Oxford: Oxford University Press, 1991), 58.

3. Bruce Laurie and Mark Schmitz, "Manufacturing and Productivity: The Making of an Industrial Base, Philadelphia, 1850–1880," in *Philadelphia: Work, Space, Family, and Group Experience in the 19th Century*, ed. Theodore Hershberg (Oxford: Oxford University Press, 1981), 48.

4. Theodore Hershberg, Harold E. Cox, Dale B. Light Jr., and Richard R. Greenfield, "The 'Journey-to-Work,'" in *Philadelphia: Work, Space, Family, and Group Experience in the 19th Century*, 142; Lane, *William Dorsey's Philadelphia*, 64–71.

5. Roger Lane, *Roots of Violence in Black Philadelphia, 1860–1900* (Cambridge, Mass.: Harvard University Press, 1986), 39; Joe Trotter Jr., *Workers on Arrival: Black Labor in the Making of America* (Oakland: University of California Press, 2021), 65.

6. For information on the struggles of the laborers' right movement in the late nineteenth century, see David R. Roediger and Elizabeth D. Esch, *The Production of Difference: Race and the Management of Labor in U.S. History* (Oxford: Oxford University Press, 2014); Peter Krause, *The Battle for Homestead, 1880–1892: Politics, Culture, and Steel* (Pittsburgh, Pa.: University of Pittsburgh Press, 1992); Theresa A. Case, *The Great Southwest Railroad Strike and Free Labor* (College Station: Texas A&M University Press, 2010).

7. Lane, *Roots of Violence*, 39.

8. Lane, *William Dorsey's Philadelphia*, 65; Lane, *Roots of Violence*, 39.

9. Maureen Elgersman Lee, *Black Bangor: African Americans in a Maine Community, 1880–1950* (Durham: University of New Hampshire, 2005), 25–26; Walter Licht, *Getting Work: Philadelphia, 1840–1950* (Philadelphia: University of Pennsylvania Press, 1999), 126, 138–139, 141.

10. W. E. B. Du Bois, *The Philadelphia Negro* (Philadelphia: University of Pennsylvania Press, 1899; rpt., 1996), 98.

11. Jones, *American Work*, 306; Charlotte Hinger, *Nicodemus: Post-Reconstruction Politics and Racial Justice in Western Kansas* (Norman: University of Oklahoma Press, 2016), 61.

12. Lane, *William Dorsey's Philadelphia*, 119.

13. 1900 United States Federal Census (Washington, D.C.: National Archives and Records Administration, n.d.), accessed via *Ancestry.com* (hereafter 1900 U.S. Census), M1457; Deposition of Thomas C. King Sr., in Thomas C. King Sr., Third USCI, pension file, National Archives and Records Administration, Washington, D.C. (hereafter pension file).

14. Deposition of Charles Brown, on January 14, 1899, in Charles Brown, Sixth USCI, pension file; Letter from Jacob Thornton, composed on June 29, 1887, in Jacob Thornton, Third USCI, pension file; Du Bois, *Philadelphia Negro*, 100, 133.

15. 1880 United States Federal Census (Washington, D.C.: National Archives and Records Administration, n.d.), accessed via *Ancestry.com* (hereafter 1880 U.S. Census), M789, M1114, M1171, M1180, M1183; 1900 U.S Census, M1469; Darius J. Young, "Henry S. Harmon: Pioneer African American Attorney in Reconstruction-Era Florida," *Florida Historical Quarterly* 85, no. 2 (Fall 2006), 192–194.

16. Marne L. Campbell, *Making Black Los Angeles: Class, Gender, and Community, 1850–1917* (Chapel Hill: University of North Carolina Press, 2016), 94; Daniel B. Thorp, *Facing Freedom: An African American Community in Virginia from Reconstruction to Jim Crow* (Charlottesville: University of Virginia Press, 2017), 102–103.

17. Jones, *American Work*, 303–304, 306.

18. Lee, *Black Bangor*, 40.

19. Du Bois, *Philadelphia Negro*, 116; Douglas Walter Bristol Jr., *Knights of the Razor: Black Barbers in Slavery and Freedom* (Baltimore: Johns Hopkins University Press, 2009), 121–122.

20. Bristol, *Knights of the Razor*, 128, 131.

21. Ibid., 141.

22. Deposition of Sarah Hawkins, on February 23, 1894, and deposition of Francis Hawkins, on December 1, 1893, in Francis Hawkins, Third USCI, pension file.

23. Deposition of Francis Hawkins, on December 1, 1893, Francis Hawkins pension file.

24. Deposition of William H. James, on December 1, 1898, Francis Hawkins pension file.

25. Deposition of Francis Hawkins, on December 1, 1893, Francis Hawkins pension file.

26. Ibid.

27. Ibid.

28. Vicki Howard, "The Courtship Letters of an African American Couple: Race, Gender, Class, and the Cult of True Womanhood," in *A Question of Manhood*, eds. Ernestine Jenkins and Darlene Clark Hines, vol. 2, *The 19th Century: From Emancipation to Jim Crow* (Bloomington: Indiana University Press, 2001), 238.

29. Deposition of Sarah Hawkins, on February 23, 1894, Francis Hawkins pension file.

30. 1880 U.S. Census, M789, M1171; 1924 declaration for pension, Francis Hawkins pension file.

31. 1910 United States Federal Census (Washington, D.C.: National Archives and Records Administration, n.d.), accessed via *Ancestry.com* (hereafter 1910 U.S. Census), M624_1388; 1880 U.S. Census, M1171.

32. John E. Bodnar, "The Impact of the 'New Immigration' on the Black Worker: Steelton, Pennsylvania, 1880–1920," in *African American in Pennsylvania: Shifting Historical Perspectives*, eds. Joe William Trotter Jr. and Eric Ledell Smith (University Park: Pennsylvania State University Press, 1997), 263.

33. 1880 U.S. Census, M1170.

34. Ibid., M1180.

35. Susie J. Shorter, "Our Trip to the Land of Flowers. (Concluded)," *Christian Recorder*, April 2, 1891; "A Bill Cheating a Commission of Colored Men to Look into the Condition of the Colored Race of the South, and Report the Same to the Next Regular Session of Congress. By Reb. A.J. Chambers," *Christian Recorder*, February 14, 1878.

36. E. H. Fairchild, "What Are for the Negro?," *Christian Recorder*, July 4, 1878.

37. Young, "Henry S. Harmon," 193–194.

38. Ibid.

39. Deposition of Grace Brown, on July 26, 1929, Charles Brown pension file; Copy of marriage license, in Edward Purnell Jr., Third USCI, pension file; 1913 special examiner's notes, in Henry Harley, Third USCI, pension file; 1915 Bureau of Pensions document, Francis Hawkins pension file; Deposition of John Thompson, on April 14, 1910, in William H. Parker, Third USCI, pension file; Young, "Henry S. Harmon," 194; 1880 U.S. Census, M919; Undated pension slip, in Franklin Viney, Sixth USCI, pension file.

40. Deposition of Mary Purnell, on April 21, 1897, Edward Purnell Jr. pension file.

41. 1900 pension document, in George Henderson, Sixth USCI, pension file; Deposition of Joseph Woodson, on April 3, 1915, in Joseph Woodson, Eighth USCI, pension file.

42. Andrew L. Slap, "'No Regular Marriage': African American Veterans and Marriage Practices after Emancipation," in *This Distracted and Anarchical People: New Answers for Old Questions about the Civil War–Era North*, eds. Andrew L. Slap and Michael Thomas Smith (New York: Fordham University Press, 2013), 172, 180; Tyler D. Parry, *Jumping the Broom: The Surprising Multicultural Origins of a Black Wedding Ritual* (Chapel Hill: University of North Carolina Press, 2020), 38–39, 58–59.

43. 1880 U.S. Census, M789.

44. Ibid.

45. "The Marriage Relation," *Christian Recorder*, November 29, 1888; Belle B. Dorce, "Happy Homes—the Hearts That Make Them," *Christian Recorder*, July 11, 1889.

46. 1880 U.S. Census, M1170.

47. Ibid.

48. Rebecca Sharpless, *Cooking in Other Women's Kitchens: Domestic Workers in the South, 1865–1960* (Chapel Hill: University of North Carolina Press, 2010), 15, 67–68, 77.

49. 1880 U.S. Census, M1183.

50. Thorp, *Facing Freedom*, 62.

51. 1900 U.S. Census, M1469

52. Ibid.

53. J. C. Ayler, "Education," *Christian Recorder*, January 24, 1889.

54. M. Louise Taylor, "The Importance of an Education," *Christian Recorder*, October 9, 1884.

55. 1880 U.S. Census, M1114.

56. "Send the Children to School," *Christian Recorder*, September 14, 1899.

57. Jaqueline Jones, *Labor of Love, Labor of Sorrow: Black Women, Work, and the Family from Slavery to the Present* (New York: Basic Books, 1985), 63.

58. Deposition of William Washington, on May 18, 1894, in William Woodson, Eighth USCI, pension file; Deposition of W. D. Sanborn, on September 20, 1907, in John Poulson, Third USCI, pension file; Deposition of Elias Hickman and Levi Shimmers, on February 23, 1893, Franklin Viney pension file; Deposition of Sarah Brown, on February 17, 1890, in William Brown, Sixth USCI, pension file; Deposition of Anna Elizabeth Fausett, on January 27, 1896, in Francis Fausett, Sixth USCI, pension file; Deposition of Arretta Davis, in Edward Davis, Sixth USCI, pension file; Deposition of Perry Cisco, on May 23, 1889, in Isaac Bynard, Third USCI, pension file; Deposition of Robert Butler and Mary J. Mickey, on October 25, 1900, in Wilson Day, Third USCI, pension file; Deposition of George K. Wilson and William Woodyard, on April 26, 1905, in Isaac Becket Jr., Third USCI, pension file; Deposition of Lucille J. Thornton, on August 21, 1902, Jacob Thornton pension file; Deposition of Julia Stiles, on March 6, 1891, in George Stiles, Eighth USCI, pension file; Deposition of Cecilia Simon, on March 5, 1910, in Robert G. Parker, Sixth USCI, pension file; Deposition of Elizabeth Matthews and Emery Johnson, on July 20, 1896, Edward Purnell Jr. pension file; Deposition of Grace Brown, on July 26, 1929, Charles Brown pension file; Deposition of James P. Levin, on February 9, 1895, deposition of Esebella Blacker, on September 20, 1895, and deposition of John Wright, on August 9, 1895, in George H. Buck, Third USCI, pension file.

59. Deposition of Mary E. Baynard, Isaac Bynard pension file; Jennifer Jensen Wallach, *Getting Ourselves What We Need: How Food Has Shaped African American Life* (Lanham, Md.: Rowman & Littlefield Publishing, 2019), 67–69.

60. Tera W. Hunter, *To 'Joy My Freedom: Southern Black Women's Lives and Labor after the Civil War* (Cambridge, Mass.: Harvard University Press, 1997), 56–57.

61. Stuart McConnell, *Glorious Contentment: The Grand Army of the Republic, 1865–1900* (Chapel Hill: University of North Carolina Press, 1992), 125–160.

62. Theda Skocpol, "America's First Social Security System," in *The Civil War Veteran: A Historical Reader*, eds. Larry M. Logue and Michael Barton (New York: New York University Press, 2007), 190.

63. Brian Matthew Jordan, *Marching Home: Union Veterans and Their Unending Civil War* (New York: Liveright Publishing Corporation, 2014), 162–163.

64. Ibid., 161.

65. Ibid., 164; John M. Taylor, "Cleveland Loses the Battle of Rebel Flags," *Washington Times*, August 27, 2004.

66. William Seraile, *New York's Black Regiments During the Civil War* (New York: Routledge, 2001), 117.

67. Deposition of George Stiles, on February 4, 1885, George Stiles pension file.

68. Undated pension slip, in John Short, Sixth USCI, pension file.

69. 1884 original invalid claim, in James Crippen, Sixth USCI, pension file.

70. Undated Pension slip and 1887 declaration for the increase of an invalid pension, in George Roland, Sixth USCI, pension file.

71. 1886 declaration for the increase of an invalid pension, in Henry Thompson, Eighth USCI, pension file.

72. 1890 declaration for the increase for an invalid pension, Henry Thompson pension file.

73. 1888, 1891, 1892, 1905, 1924, 1926, and 1927 invalid pension applications, in Nathaniel Logan Sr., Sixth USCI, pension file.

74. 1891 invalid pension application, Nathaniel Logan Sr. pension file.

75. 1900 U.S. Census, M1469.

76. William Henry Glasson, *Federal Military Pensions in the United States* (Oxford: Oxford University Press, 1918), 238, 258–263.

77. Deposition of C. Arthur Scott, on September 13, 1927, Nathaniel Logan Sr. pension file.

78. Theda Skocpol, *Protecting Soldiers and Mothers: The Political Origins of Social Policy in the United States* (Cambridge, Mass.: Belknap Press of Harvard University Press, 1992), 127.

79. Deposition of Thomas C. King Sr., on June 20, 1885, Thomas C. King Sr. pension file.

80. Undated pension slip, Thomas C. King Sr. pension file.

81. 1902 increase invalid pension, Thomas C. King Sr. pension file.

82. 1887 pension slip, 1890 invalid application, 1894 invalid application, 1898 invalid application, 1912 invalid application, in Edward Brown, Third USCI, pension file.

83. 1905 invalid increase, in Lorenzo George, Third USCI, pension file.

84. Larry M. Logue, "The Reality of Veterans' Voting," in *The Civil War Veteran*, 312.

85. Jordan, *Marching Home*, 164–165; McConnell, *Glorious Contentment*, 152.

86. Mary F. Berry, "Reparations for Freedom, 1890–1916: Fraudulent Practices or Justice Deferred?," *Journal of Negro History* 57, no. 3 (July 1972), 221.

87. Larry M. Logue and Peter Blanck, "'Benefit of the Doubt': African-American Civil War Veterans and Pensions," *Journal of Interdisciplinary History* 38, no. 3 (Winter 2008), 378.

88. Glasson, *Federal Military Pensions*, 236–237.

89. Russell L. Johnson, "'Great Injustice': Social Status and the Distribution of Military Pensions after the Civil War," *Journal of the Gilded Age and Progressive Era* 10, no. 2 (April 2011), 159.

90. Brandi C. Brimmer, "'Her Claim for Pension Is Lawful and Just': Representing Black Union Widows in Late–Nineteenth Century North Carolina," *Journal of the Civil War Era* 1, no. 2 (June 2011), 221.

91. Russell L. Johnson, "'Not One Jot or Title of Evidence': The Civil War Pension Files," *Australasian Journal of American Studies* 30, no. 2 (December 2011), 77.

92. Skocpol, *Protecting Soldiers and Mothers*, 109.

93. Peter David Blanck and Michael Millender, "Before Disability Civil Rights: Civil War Pensions and the Politics of Disability of America," *Alabama Law Review* 5, no. 1 (Fall 2000), 26.

94. Glasson, *Federal Military Pensions*, 250, 253–254.

95. Skocpol, *Protecting Soldiers and Mothers*, 109.

96. Undated pension slip, in Marshall Price, Sixth USCI, pension file; 1890 invalid pension application, Henry Harley pension file; 1914 invalid payment, William H. Parker pension file; 1890 invalid pension, Charles Brown pension file; 1909 pension document, Robert G. Parker pension file.

97. Larry M. Logue and Peter Blanck, *Race, Ethnicity, and Disability: Veterans and Benefits in Post–Civil War America* (Cambridge: Cambridge University Press, 2010), 114.

98. Glasson, *Federal Military Pensions*, 234.

99. Undated pension slip, in William Tallman, Sixth USCI, pension file.

100. 1891 invalid application; 1892 invalid application, Franklin Viney pension file.

101. Undated Pension slip, George Henderson pension file.

102. Letter from John B. Nedary, composed on October 24, 1905, George Henderson pension file.

103. Letter from Joseph Anderson, composed on October 6, 1898, in Joseph Anderson, Third USCI, pension file.

104. 1890 invalid pension application and undated pension slip, in Joseph Harris, Sixteenth USCI, pension file.

105. Undated pension slip, Joseph Woodson pension file; 1908 pension document, in Charles Penn, Third USCI, pension file.

106. 1893 medical examination notes, Marshall Price pension file.

107. James Marten, "Those Who Have Borne the Battle: Civil War Veterans, Pension Advocacy, and Politics," *Marquette Law Review* 93, no. 4 (Summer 2010), 1410.

108. 1907 increase invalid pension, Henry Harley pension file.

109. Deposition of Francis Hawkins, on June 30, 1897, Francis Hawkins pension file.

110. 1920 invalid increase document, Francis Hawkins pension file.

111. Deposition of Francis Hawkins, on October 15, 1924, Francis Hawkins pension file.

112. 1927 invalid increase, Nathaniel Logan Sr. pension file.

113. Larry M. Logue and Peter Blanck, *Heavy Laden: Union Veterans, Psychological Illness, and Suicide* (Cambridge: Cambridge University Press, 2018), 115, 145.

114. Richard Reid, "USCT Veterans in Post–Civil War North Carolina," in *The Civil War Veteran*, 163.

115. Eric T. Dean Jr., "The Fate of the Civil War Veteran," in *The Civil War Veteran*, 262; Sarah H. Rose, *No Right to Be Idle: The Invention of Disability, 1840s–1930s* (Chapel Hill: University of North Carolina Press, 2017), 53.

116. Claire Prechtel-Kluskens, "'A Reasonable Degree of Promptitude': Civil War Pension Application Processing, 1861–1865," *Prologue Magazine* 42, no. 1 (Spring 2010), https://www.archives.gov/publications/prologue/2010/spring/civilwarpension.html.

117. Logue and Blanck, *Heavy Laden*, 113–114.

118. Margaret Humphreys, *Marrow of Tragedy: The Health Crisis of the American Civil War* (Baltimore: Johns Hopkins University Press, 2013), 30–38, 88–92; Aaron Sheehan-Dean, *The Calculus of Violence: How Americans Fought the Civil War* (Cambridge, Mass.: Harvard University Press, 2018), 150, 160, 241; Dean, "Post-Traumatic Stress," in *The Civil War Veteran*, 127–137; Diane Miller Sommerville, "'A Burden Too Heavy to Bear': War Trauma, Suicide, and Confederate Soldiers," *Civil War History Journal* 59, no. 4 (December 2013), 467.

119. Jonathan S. Jones, "Opium Slavery: Civil War Veterans and Opiate Addiction," *Journal of the Civil War Era* 10, no. 2 (June 2020), 188–192.

120. Diane Miller Sommerville, *Aberration of Mind: Suicide and Suffering in the Civil War–Era South* (Chapel Hill: University of North Carolina Press, 2018), 80; Michael C. C. Adams, *Living Hell: The Dark Side of the Civil War* (Baltimore: Johns Hopkins University Press, 2014), 59.

121. 1922 reimbursement document, in James Ellsbury, Sixth USCI, pension file.

122. Special examiner letter, composed on March 18, 1878, in Alexander Robinson, Sixth USCI, pension file.

123. 1888 pension document, in Andrew White, Sixth USCI, pension file.

124. Deposition of H. Powell, on October 8, 1883, Andrew White pension file.

125. Deposition of Henry Gamble, on January 31, 1884, Andrew White pension file.

126. Undated pension slip, Andrew White pension file.

127. 1889 widow's pension, William Brown pension file.

128. Undated pension slip, in Daniel Brown, Third USCI, pension file.

129. 1893 pension document, Daniel Brown pension file.

130. Deposition of Samuel Benson, on April 10, 1890, and deposition of Edward Purnell Jr., on August 14, 1890, Daniel Brown pension file.

131. 1882 declaration for a mother's pension, in Hiram Waters, Third USCI, pension file.

132. Deposition of Anna G. Waters, on April 9, 1891, Hiram Waters pension file.

133. Undated pension document, in Solomon Hoff, Third USCI, pension file.

134. Deposition of Joshua James, on December 9, 1879, and deposition of George W. Green, on May 24, 1880, George H. Buck pension file.

135. Undated Bureau of Pensions document, George H. Buck pension file.

136. Undated pension slip, George H. Buck pension file.

137. Donald Shaffer, *After the Glory: The Struggles of Black Civil War Veterans* (Lawrence: University of Kansas Press, 2004), 129; Donald R. Shaffer, "'I Do Not Suppose That Uncle Sam Looks at the Skin,'" in *The Civil War Veteran*, 208–209.

138. Deposition of James P. Levin, on February 9, 1895, George H. Buck pension file.

139. Ibid.

140. Deposition of John Wright, on August 9, 1895, George H. Buck pension file.

141. Deposition of Flowers Dorsey, on February 24, 1891, George H. Buck pension file.

142. Deposition of Reuben Gardner, on September 20, 1895, George H. Buck pension file.

143. Deposition of Susie Battle, on September 20, 1895, George H. Buck pension file.

144. 1895 Bureau of Pensions document, George H. Buck pension file.

145. 1895 special examiner's notes, George H. Buck pension file.

146. Deposition of Susan Gray, on April 19, 1900, in William F. Gray, Third USCI, pension file.

147. Deposition of Rebecca Dolliver, on April 2, 1900, William F. Gray pension file.

148. Kelly D. Mezurek, *For Their Own Cause: The 27th United States Colored Troops* (Kent, Ohio: Kent State University Press, 2016), 243.

149. "The Dependent Pension Act," *New York Times*, June 29, 1890.

150. 1911 pension slip, in George Stiles pension file; undated pension slip, in Solomon Flemmer, Sixth USCI, pension file; Undated pension slip, Franklin Viney pension file; 1890 pension slip, Francis Fausett pension file.

151. Deposition of Anna L. Fausett, on November 13, 1896, Francis Fausett pension file.

152. Undated pension slip, Franklin Viney pension file.

153. Undated pension slip, in James Gray, Third USCI, pension file.

154. 1890 pension slip, in William Smallwood, Sixth USCI, pension file; Undated pension slip, in Robert Johnson, Sixth USCI, pension file.

155. 1892, 1893, 1895, 1896, 1897, 1898, 1899, and 1901 pension documents, in Joseph Thomas, Third USCI, pension file.

156. Deposition of Sarah Hawkins, on February 23, 1894, Francis Hawkins pension file.

157. Undated pension slip, Isaac Baynard pension file; Undated pension slip, Charles Brown pension file; 1909 widow's application, Robert G. Parker pension file; Undated pension slip, Joseph Woodson pension file; 1900 declaration for widow's pension, Wilson Day pension file; Deposition of Elizabeth Matthews and Emery Johnson, Edward Purnell Jr. pension file; Undated pension slip, Thomas C. King Sr. pension file; Undated pension slip, in Alfred Rothwell, Third USCI, pension file.

158. Deposition of Alice King, on April 29, 1903, Thomas C. King Sr. pension file.

159. Letter from Elizabeth Poulson, composed on August 9, 1917, John Poulson pension file.

160. Ibid., 1917 Bureau of Pensions document.

161. Undated pension slip, Alfred Rothwell pension file.

162. Deposition of Alice King, on April 29, 1903, Thomas C. King Sr. pension file.

163. Deposition of Elizabeth M. Becket, on August 6, 1906, Isaac Becket Jr. pension file.

164. Deposition of Elizabeth Anderson, on December 3, 1903, Alfred Rothwell pension file; 1899 Bureau of Pensions document, Isaac Baynard pension file.

165. Letter from Margaret Parker, on October 25, 1923, William H. Parker pension file.

166. Letter from Margaret Parker, on October 25, 1923, William H. Parker pension file.

167. Letter from Margaret Parker, on February 4, 1924, William H. Parker pension file.

168. Ibid.

169. 1921 special examiner's notes, William H. Parker pension file.

170. Special examiner's letters, composed on January 23, 1897, and March 1, 1897, Henry Harley pension file.

171. 1903 special examiner's notes, Wilson Day pension file.

172. Ibid.

173. Deposition of Mary M. Parker, on March 8, 1910, Robert G. Parker pension file.

174. Deposition of Ida Rebecca Nola, on March 4, 1910, Robert G. Parker pension file.

175. Deposition of William H. Parker, on March 7, 1910, Robert G. Parker pension file.

176. Deposition of Mary M. Parker, on March 8, 1910, Robert G. Parker pension file.

177. Brandi Clay Brimmer, *Claiming Union Widowhood: Race, Respectability, and Poverty in the Post-Emancipation South* (Durham, N.C.: Duke University Press, 2020), 7–13.

178. Shaffer, *After the Glory*, 101–112.

179. Larry M. Logue, *To Appomattox and Beyond: The Civil War Soldier in War and Peace* (Chicago: Ivan R. Dee, 1996), 134.

EPILOGUE

1. "Databases, Tables & Calculators by Subject," U.S. Bureau of Labor Statistics, https://data.bls.gov/timeseries/LFU21000100&series_id=LFU22000100&from_year=1929&to_year=1939&periods_option=specific_periods&periods=Annual+Data.

2. Charles Pete Banner-Haley, "Philadelphia Tribune and the Persistence of Black Republicanism during the Great Depression," *Pennsylvania History: A Journal of Mid-Atlantic Studies* 65, no. 2 (Spring 1998), 193.

3. Christopher Klein, "Last Hired, First Fired: How the Great Depression Affected African Americans," *History.com*, https://www.history.com/news/last-hired-first-fired-how-the-great-depression-affected-african-americans.

4. William McKee Evans, *Open Wound: The Long View of Race in America* (Champaign: University of Illinois Press, 2009), 208; Fran Burke, "Eleanor Roosevelt, October 11, 1884–November 7, 1962—She Made a Difference," *Public Administration Review* 44, no. 5 (September–October 1984), 370.

5. Letter from Edmonia Woodson to Eleanor Roosevelt, composed on September 18, 1939, in William Woodson, Eighth USCI, pension file, National Archives and Records Administration, Washington, D.C. (hereafter pension file).

6. Ibid.

7. 1897 widow's pension application, William Woodson pension file.

8. Letter from Edmonia Woodson to Eleanor Roosevelt, composed on September 18, 1939, William Woodson pension file.

9. Letter from the Veterans Administration to Edmonia Woodson, composed on September 25, 1939, William Woodson pension file.

10. There is no record in William Woodson's pension file coming directly from Eleanor Roosevelt. Perhaps Edmonia kept those letters for herself.

11. Letter from Edmonia Woodson to Eleanor Roosevelt, composed on October 3, 1939, William Woodson pension file.

12. Ibid.

13. Letter from the VA to the White House, undated, and letter from E. L. Bailey to Edmonia Woodson, composed on October 17, 1939, William Woodson pension file.

14. 1897 widow's pension application, William Woodson pension file.

15. Deposition of Mary Williamson, on April 8, 1884, in Benjamin Davis, Sixth USCI, pension file.

APPENDIX I. Methodology

1. Nancy Folbre and Marjorie Abel, "Women's Work and Women's Households: Gender Bias in the U.S. Census," *Social Research* 56, no. 3 (Autumn 1989), 547–549; Margaret Coleman, "Homemaker as Worker in the United States," *Challenge* 41, no. 6 (November–December 1998), 76–79.

2. Jeanne Boydston, *Home and Work: Housework, Wages, and the Ideology of Labor in the Early Republic* (New York: Oxford University Press, 1990), 16–17, 20, 38, 40, 97, 123, 126; Seth Rockman, "Women's Labor, Gender Ideology, and Working-Class Households in Early Republic Baltimore," *Pennsylvania History: A Journal of Mid-Atlantic Studies* 66 (1999), 175, 185.

3. For examples of studies on Civil War pensions, see Larry M. Logue and Peter Blanck, *Race, Ethnicity, and Disability: Veterans and Benefits in Post–Civil War America* (Cambridge: Cambridge University Press, 2010); Elizabeth Regosin, *Freedom's Promise: Ex-Slave Families and Citizenship in the Age of Emancipation* (Charlottesville: University of Virginia Press, 2002); Noralee Frankel, *Freedom's Women: Black Women and Families in Civil War Era Mississippi* (Bloomington: Indiana University Press, 1999).

4. For studies that highlight the importance of Civil War pensions to understanding the lives of USCT veterans, see William Seraile, *New York's Black Regiments During the Civil War* (New York: Routledge, 2001); Megan J. McClintock, "Civil War Pensions and the Reconstruction of Union Families," *Journal of American History* 83, no. 2 (September 1996), 457–464; Elizabeth A. Regosin and Donald R. Shaffer, eds., *Voices of Emancipation: Understanding Slavery, the Civil War, and Reconstruction through the U.S. Pension Bureau Files* (New York: New York University Press, 2008), 1–7; Brandi Clay Brimmer, *Claiming Union Widowhood: Race, Respectability, and Poverty in the Post-Emancipation South* (Durham, N.C.: Duke University Press, 2020).

5. *The Weekly Anglo-African*, previously branded as *The Anglo-African*, began publishing in 1859. Thomas and Robert Hamilton both ran the paper, which ceased publishing in late 1865. The Hamilton brothers published their paper in New York City, New York. The African Methodist Episcopal Church, in 1852, began publishing *The Christian Recorder*. Mitch Kachun, "Interrogating the Silences: Julia C. Collins, 19th-Century Black Readers and Writers, and the '*Christian Recorder*,'" *African American Review* 40, no. 4 (Winter 2006), 649–650; "Notice," *Christian Recorder*, December 21, 1861; "Resignation," *Christian Recorder*, December 28, 1861; "For the *Christian Recorder*," *Christian Recorder*, March 23, 1861; Veralle F. Washington, *Eagles on Their Buttons: A Black Infantry Regiment in the Civil War* (Columbia: University of Missouri Press, 1999), 11.

6. David R. Brown, "From the 31st Regiment U.S. Colored Troops," *Weekly Anglo-African*, December 16, 1864; William B. Johnson, "Florida Correspondence. Battery Myrick, Jacksonville, FLA," *Christian Recorder*, January 14, 1865.

INDEX

abolitionists, as school teachers, 24
addiction, 133
African Fire Association (AFA), 25
Allen, Josiah, employment, 31
Allen, Mary, 119
almshouses, 105–107
Ames, John A., on deserters, 55
amputations, 61–62, 71–72, 97, 107
Anderson, Elizabeth, 139
Anderson, Henry, 98
Anderson, Joseph: injuries of, 60; pension, denied, 131; postwar employment, 97
Anderson, Robert, pension, 139
Andersonville prison, 66
Armes, George A., 72
Army Appropriation Bill (1864), 44, 49
Army Reorganization Act (1866), 98

bachelorhood, 30–33; wages to support family, 49–50
Bailey, E. L., 144
Bailey, John, 78–79
Bailey, Lucy, 78–79
Battle, Susie, 137
Baynard, Isaac, pension, 139
Beck, E. W. B., 61
Becket, Elizabeth M., 139
Becket, Isaac, Jr.: pension, 139; postwar family and employment, 94, 110
Benn, Daniel, 120
Benson, Samuel: postwar employment, 118; testimony of, 135
Bird, Malachi, enlistment bounty, 44
Black, Anna Lamberson, 27
Black, Richard: employment, 31; marriage, 27
Blockley Almshouse, 105–107
Boker, George H., 39–40
Bond, Elizabeth, 28
Brant, Charles: injuries of, 60; pension, 111–112
Brock, John C., 57
Brown, Alexander W., 100
Brown, Annie, 135
Brown, Charles: marriage and children, 119; postwar employment, 96, 116
Brown, Daniel, pension, 135
Brown, Edward: illness of, 64; pension, 127, 128, 129; postwar employment, 97, 98
Brown, Grace, 119
Brown, John: family composition, 19; theft and, 53
Brown, Lee Othello (Solomon Wilson), enlistment, 76–77
Brown, Margaret, 135
Brown, Marion, 135
Brown, Mary (Charles Brown's daughter), 119
Brown, Mary (John Brown's mother), 19
Brown, Mary (John Brown's sister), 19
Brown, Samuel: employment and income, 29; NHDVS and, 107; postwar employment, 94
Brown, Sarah, 135
Brown, William: furlough for, 79–80; on military marches, 62–63; pension, 135
Brown, William Wells, 8–9
Bryant, Jacob, 31

Bryant, John, death of, 82
Bryant, Richard, 31
Buck, George H.: injuries of, 60, 105; mental illness and, 105; pension, 136–137; postwar employment, 94
Buck, Patience, 123, 136–137
Bureau of Pensions. *See* pensions
Burk, James, injuries of, 57
Burritt, Loren, 111
Burrows, John L., 20
Burton, John, 58
Butler, William: amputation and, 61–62; fictive kin and, 109; NHDVS and, 107–108; pension, 71–72

Camden Court House, 59
Carter, Hannah, 121
Carter, John, 121
Carter, Richard: childhood employment, 25; postwar family, 121
Cary, Mary Ann Shadd, 39
casualties, 59, 80–83. *See also* illnesses, diseases, and disabilities; pensions
Catto, Octavius, 39
Charleston, S.C., 58–59, 60
Chester, Thomas Morris, 81
churches, 103–104
Church Hill, Va., 60
citizenship: cultural citizenship, 10; education and schooling and, 22; military service and, 35–36, 38–40; pensions and, 10, 67; women and sacrifice and, 112–113
Civil Rights Act (1866), 163–164n41
Clark, John, 113
Clayton, Elizabeth, 21
Clayton, Hannah, 21
Clayton, Jacob, 21
Clayton, Susanna, 21
Cleveland, Grover, 124, 128
Colored Public School, 23
Colored School Number 2 (Weeksville, N.Y.), 24
Connor, Bull, 143
Cooper, Ann Eliza, 31
Cooper, John, 58
Cooper, Sarah, 31
Cooper, William, employment, 31
Costa, Emma, 29, 108
Craig, Mary, 73–74
Crawford, Mary Elizabeth, 104
Crawford, Samuel, postwar family and employment, 92, 110
Crippen, Allen, 120
Crippen, Carrie, 120
Crippen, Ellen, 120
Crippen, James: children's schooling, 122–123; family, extended kin, 120; pension, 71, 112, 125; postwar employment, 97, 118
Crook, Eva, 121–122
Crook, Isabella H., 121–122
Crook, John, 121–122
Crook, Mary, 121–122
Curtin, Andrew, 35

Dauphin County Almshouse, 105
Davis, Arretta, 94–96, 123, 140
Davis, Benjamin: death of, 82; enlistment, 40, 77; family of, 28, 76; insubordination and, 53; pension, 1, 76, 85; as prisoner-of-war, 66–67
Davis, Edward: enlistment bounty, 44; marriage, common-law, 102; pension, 140; postwar employment, 94–96
Davis, Emilie, 77
Davis, Jefferson, on African American combatants, 65–66
Davis, Jerome, 1, 40, 76, 85
Davis, Mary Leighton (Williamson), 28, 40, 76, 85, 145
Day, Kate, 140
Day, Margaret, 104–105, 140
Day, Wilson: marriage, 28, 104–105; mental illness, 107; pension, 140
Deep Bottom, Va., 58, 66–67
Deets, Charles, 42
Deets, Ella Irene, 42, 85
Deets, Hannah, 42
Department of Disability (1890), 127, 128–132, 136
Department of Veterans Affairs (Va.), 144
Derry, Samuel: infractions, 56; injuries and illness of, 57–58, 63; postwar employment, 96, 97, 98
desertion, 53–55, 79, 100–102, 144–145
Dill, Samuel, 113
Dilton, John, family of, 74, 82
Dilton, Rachel, 74, 82
divorce, 28, 120

Dix-Hill Cartel, 65–66
Dolliver, Rebecca, 137
Donnelly (teacher), 23
Dorsey, Flowers, 137
Douglass, Frederick: on citizenship, path to, 34; military service, support of, 38–39
draft, 37
Duffy, Charles, 30
Duffy, Charlotte, 30
Duffy, Isabella, 29–30
Duffy, Pauline, 30
Duffy, Richard: childhood of, 21; children of, 30; employment, 29–30

Eakin, John R., 66
Edson, Nathan, 25
education and schooling, 20–26, 31–32, 122, 123
Edwards, William, death of, 66
Elligood, Alexander, 109
Elligood, Jane, 109
Ellsbury, Catherine Harrison, 28–29, 80, 108
Ellsbury, James: furlough for, 79–80; marriage and children, 28–29; pension and death, 134; postwar employment, 92; postwar family, 108
Ellsbury, Katherine, 134
Ellsbury, William, 29
Emancipation Proclamation, 37
employment: apprenticeships, 20, 25; bachelorhood and, 31–33; of children, 20, 21, 24–25; gender roles and, 17; manhood and masculinity and, 91, 109; men's wage earning, 17–18, 29–33; opportunities as limited, 13–15; racial discrimination and, 31–33, 108, 143; racial violence over competition for, 25; as "scab" workers during strikes, 115–116; semiskilled and skilled professions, 14–15; women's wage earning, 9, 16–17, 19–20, 31, 108–109. *See also* postwar employment
enlistment bounties, 43–47, 55
enlistment into military service: African American recruitment for, 38–39; enlistment bounties, 43–47; family reaction to, 76–77; family's finances and, 43, 76–77; motivation for enlistment, 40, 42, 45; motivation to abstain from enlisting, 46–47; in Pennsylvania, 40–41; Pennsylvanians enlistment numbers, 46; Pennsylvanians enlistment with other states, 40, 46; ULP recruitment efforts, 39–40; whites' racism and support for, 37–38
Enrollment Act (1863), 37

families: extended family networks, 17–18, 42, 120–122; fictive kin, 6, 17, 18–21, 30, 108–109; postwar restructuring of, 80–83, 108–109, 120–122. *See also* marriages; pensions
Fausett, Anna, 123, 138
Fausett, Francis: pension, 138; postwar employment, 92
feme sole, 27–28
Fifty-Fourth Massachusetts: financial concerns and, 55; illness and disease, 64; Pennsylvanians' service in, 40, 163n37; as prisoners of war, 66
First Kansas Colored Infantry, 40, 55, 64
Fisher, Sarah A., 104
Fisher, Sidney George, 36, 37, 97
Flemmer, Solomon: pension, 138; postwar employment, 93
Fort Gregg, 58–59
Fort Pillow Massacre, 66, 194n88
Fort Wagner, 58–59, 60
Fourteenth Amendment, 163–164n41
Fourteenth United States Colored Heavy Artillery, 93
Francis, Edward, 51
Francis, Liza, 51
Francis, Sarah, 138
Frankford Arsenal, 91
Frederick, Michael R., 28
Freeman, Charles H., 98
friendly gunfire, 58
furloughs, 79

Gamble, Henry, 135
Garmin family, 109
Garner, Reuben, 137
George, Lorenzo: illness, injuries, and disability of, 60–61, 63, 99–100, 101–102; NHDVS and, 107; pension, 127, 128; postwar family, 120; postwar

George, Lorenzo (*continued*)
reenlistment in military, 99–100, 101–102
Gilmore, Charity, 102, 140
Glascow, George: marriage, 27; pension, 113
Glascow, Margaret (daughter), 113
Glascow, Margaret Clark (wife), 27, 113
Glasgow, William, 30
"good death," 82–83
Gooding, James Henry: on camp diseases, 64; on combat, eagerness for, 57; on desertion, 55; on recruitment efforts by women, 41
Grand Army of the Republic (GAR), 124, 128
Grant, Ulysses S., 101
Gray, Henderson, 19, 138
Gray, James: family composition, 19; pension, 138
Gray, Louisa, 106
Gray, Rachel, 20–21
Gray, Susan, 137
Gray, William F.: mental illness, 106; pension, 137–138
Great Depression, 143
Green, Alfred M., 36–37
Green, George W., 136
Green, Joseph: fictive kin and, 109; postwar employment, 96
Green, William L. (Lorenzo George), 101. *See also* George, Lorenzo
Griffin, William, enlistment bounty for, 44
Griggs, Emeretta, 114
Griggs, Maria Louisa, 114
Griggs, Mary E., 84, 113–114
Gross, Wealthy, mother's pension, 86

Hamilton, Robert, 215n5
Hamilton, Rosana, 19
Hamilton, Thomas, 215n5
Hammond, William R., 79–80
Hardy, Crawford, injuries of, 60
Harley, Henry: pension, 129, 132, 140; postwar employment, 97
Harley, Rose, 140
Harmon, Henry S., 81; on military training, 47–48; postwar employment, 92, 119
Harris, Joseph, pension, denied, 131
Harrison, Benjamin, 128
Hatfield, Rachel, 137
Hawkins, Francis: education of, 13, 24; family, postwar separation, 117–118; pension, 118, 131, 132, 138; postwar employment, 117; postwar reenlistment in military, 99–100
Hawkins, Sarah, 117–118
Hayes, Francis, 32–33
Hayes, Sarah Jane, 95
Hemenway, Stacey, 63
Henderson, Anna, 20–21
Henderson, Florence, 20–21
Henderson, Frances, 20–21
Henderson, George: employment, 32; pension, denied, 131; pension for mother, 86; postwar employment, 97
Henderson, Isaac D.: family of origin, 20–21; postwar employment, 96
Henderson, Sophia, 20–21
Henry, Mary, employment, 16
Henry, William: mother's employment, 16; postwar employment, 94
Hill, Isaac J., 9
Hoff, Anna Elizabeth, 42, 136
Hoff, George, 42
Hoff, Solomon: employment and income, 29; family of, 42; pension, 136
Hogan, James, injuries of, 61
Hooper, Joseph, mother's employment, 16
Hopkins, Henry, 33
House of Refuge for Colored Children (HRCC), 20
Howard, Charles, bachelorhood, 30

illnesses, diseases, and disabilities, 63–65, 66, 102–103. *See also* pensions
imagined community term, use of, 12
immigrants, European, 14, 18; military service and, 35–36
Ingraham, William, 98
Institute for Colored Youth (ICY), 22, 23–24
Invalid Corps, 79
Irish Americans, 93, 97

Jackson, Jacob G.: enlistment and family, 42; pension, 113

Jackson, James, 95–96
Jackson, John W., furlough for, 79–80
Jackson, Martha Ann, 42, 113; widow's pension, 85
Jackson, Victoria, 42, 113
Jacksonville, Fla., 59
James, Joshua, 105, 136
James, William, 117
Jannis, Amelia, 77
Jay, John, 80–81
John, Malinda Orr, 103
John, Richard, marriage, 103
Johnson, Henry, postwar employment, 93
Johnson, Jesse, 21
Johnson, Robert: amputation and, 62; pension, 72, 111, 112, 138
Johnson, Thomas, employment, 32
Johnston, William B.: on demobilization of USCT, 78; on infections disease, 63; theft and, 53
Jones, Anna, 121
Jones, Charles W.: postwar employment, 118; postwar family, 120–121
Jones, Robert, Jr., 120–121
Jones, Robert, Sr., 120–121
Jones, Sarah, 120

Kate (common-law union with Day), 28
Kelley, Edward, 94–96
Kelley, William D., 41–42
Kelly, Adaline, 109
Kelly, E., 27
King, Alice, 122, 139
King, Earl, 122
King, Thomas, Jr., 122
King, Thomas C., Sr.: children's schooling, 122–123; illness of, 63; pension, 127, 139; postwar employment, 94, 116

labor organizations, 14, 93, 115–116
Langston, John Mercer, 39
Lee, Charles H., 95
Lee, Robert E., surrender, news of, 77, 79–80
Leighton, Mary (Williamson), 28, 40, 76, 85, 145
Levin, James P., 136–137
Lieber Code, 66
life insurance, 139
Little, John H., 100
Logan, Mary, 109, 122
Logan, Nathaniel, Sr.: family and employment of, 112; medical care for, 132–133; pension, 71, 112, 126–127; postwar family, 108–109, 122
Logan, R. P., 122

malnutrition, 63
Maloney, Ephraim: injuries of, 60; pension, 71; postwar employment, 97
Maloney, Solomon, 110
Maloney, Wesley: postwar employment, 94; postwar family and employment, 110
manhood and masculinity: conformity and, 107; death and sacrifice and, 80–83; desertion and, 100; disabilities and, 61–62, 97, 98; employment and income and, 29–30, 91, 109; through marriage, 26–27; military service and, 36, 38–40, 41–42, 52–53, 56–57, 58–62; pensions and, 69, 112; prisoners-of-war and, 66–67; white notions of, 2
marriages: children and, 28–29; churches and, 103–104; legal versus common-law, 26–30, 42–43, 102–105, 119–120, 137; legal versus common-law, pensions, 68–69, 84–85; pensions and, 27, 67–69, 112–114; as Victorian ideal, 26; wages of soldiers and, 50–51; wives' writing to come home, 78–79. *See also* families; pensions
Marsh, Lydia, 74
Marsh, Peter, family of, 74
Marshall, John, on military marches, 62–63
Mason, John, desertion of, 54
mental health, 104–107, 133–134
Midvale Steel, 115
military medical treatment, 61–62
military service: African American exclusion from, 35–37; amputations and, 61–62; citizenship and, 35–36, 38–40; combat, 58–62; demobilization of, delayed, 77–80; disciplinary action and, 53–56; enlistment numbers of, 3; fatigue duty, 56–58; illnesses, diseases, and disabilities, 63–65, 71–72, 99–100, 101–102; manhood and masculinity

military service (*continued*)
and, 36, 38–40, 41–42, 52–53, 56–57, 58–62; marches and, 62–63; military training, 47–48; pensions and, 70–72; as prisoners-of-war, 65–67, 81, 194n88; racial discrimination and, 48–51, 77–80; resistance to military service, 36–37, 48; scholarship on, 7–10; veterans' regimental histories, 9; wages, 47, 48–51, 54–56; white officers and racism, 48
Militia Act (1792), 173–174n26
Militia Act (1862), 37, 48
minié ball, 60–61
Monroe, James, 67
Moore, Ann, 21
Moore, Sarah, 21
Moore, William, 21
Morel, Junius C., 24, 47
Morris Island, S.C., 57–58
mourning, 83
Murray, Emeline, 104, 140

National Home for Disabled Volunteer Soldiers (NHDVS), 89, 107–108
Native American removal, 98–99
Nedary, John B., 131
Nelson, Jones, 54
Newton, Alexander Heritage, 9
Nolan, Ida Rebecca, 140

Parker, Margaret, 139–140
Parker, Mary M., 104, 140
Parker, Miles: education of, 21; family of origin, 21
Parker, Robert G.: enlistment with family, 42; pension, 129–130, 140; postwar family and employment, 94, 104, 110
Parker, Sarah, 120
Parker, Susan, 17
Parker, William, 17
Parker, William H.: brother Robert and, 42, 104, 140; family, extended kin, 120; pension, 129–130; postwar family and employment, 110, 118
Penn, Charles: family of origin and childhood, 20; pension, 131; postwar reenlistment in military, 99
Pension Act (1861), 67–68
Pension Act (1862), 68, 71, 83–87
Pension Act (1864), 71, 84
Pension Act (1866), 110
Pension Act (1873), 110–112
Pension Act (1878), 130
Pension Act (1887), 124
Pension Act (1890), 127, 128–132, 136
Pension Act (1907), 130
pensions: for children of veterans, 1, 68–69, 76, 83–85, 111, 113–114, 129, 134–135, 138; citizenship and, 10, 67; as Civil War memorialization, 11, 90, 112, 114, 117–118, 128, 130, 134; for Confederate soldiers, revoked, 84; eligibility and applications, 11, 70, 84–87, 89–90, 112–114; eligibility and applications, as invasive, 119, 136–138; eligibility and applications, difficulties and denials, 89–90, 124–128, 135–138, 139–141; eligibility and applications, liberalization of, 111–112, 128–132, 138–139; for fathers, 138; manhood and masculinity, 69, 112; for mothers or sisters, 68–69, 83, 85, 111, 129, 134–135, 138; for nonphysical disabilities, 133–134; opposition to, 69–70, 124, 128–132; origins of, 67; pay increases, 110–111; racial discrimination and, 2–3, 70, 90; widows' pensions, 111, 112–114, 129, 135–141, 143–145; widows' pensions, legal versus common-law marriages, 42–43, 84–85, 119–120, 137–141
Perkins, Elizabeth, 30
Perkins, Joseph: death of, 58; employment, 31; fictive kin and, 30
Pinney, Alfred W., 51
politics of respectability, 15, 103
Pollack, James, 22
Porter, Jane, 23
postwar employment: disabilities and, 97–98; men's wage earning, 116–119; military reenlistment, 98–102; racial discrimination and, 93–97; segregation of industries, 115; women's wage earning, 121–122, 123–124
Potter, Horace, 32
Poulson, Elizabeth, 139
Poulson, John, pension, 139
Powell, H., 135
Preston (colonel), 118

Preston, Joseph, 98
Price, Emily, 121–122
Price, Marshall: pension, 129, 131–132; postwar family, 121–122
prisoners of war (POWs), 65–67, 81, 194n88; Confederates, release of, 78
prostitution, 74
public transportation, 75–76
Purnell, Edward, Jr.: employment, 32; pension, 119, 127–128; testimony of, 98, 135
Purnell, Jacob: children's schooling, 122–123; injuries of, 58; postwar employment, 96
Purnell, Mary, 123

Rawley, Nimrod, on combat, eagerness for, 56–57
Reagan, Maggie, 109
real estate ownership, 19
Reconstruction Acts (1867), 92
Reeves, George, 135
Reeves, James, 32–33, 134–135
Reeves, Sarah, 86, 134–135
Revolutionary War Pension Act (1818), 67
rheumatic pain, 62–63
Richardson, Henry: financial dependence of, 31; insubordination and, 53
Richardson, Margaret, 31
Richmond, James, postwar employment, 96
Robinson, Alexander: employment, 32; on military wages, 50; pension, 86, 134
Robinson, James, as prisoner of war, 66
Robinson, Jane, 86, 134
Rockhold, Thomas R., 82
Roland, George: injuries of, 60; pension, 71, 125; postwar employment, 93, 97
Roosevelt, Eleanor, 143–144
Roosevelt, Franklin Delano, 143
Rothwell, Alfred: death of, 82; pension, 139
Rothwell, Elizabeth: husband's death, 82; widow's pension, 85

Schneck, Moses, death of, 64–65
Scott, Madeline, 19
Scott, Rachel, 19
Scott, Theodore, 19
Seddon, James, 65–66
segregation, 75–76, 106, 108, 115–116
Seventy-Ninth USCI, 93
Sewell, Charles W., insubordination and, 53
Sheridan, Philip Henry, 77
Short, John: injuries of, 58; pension, 71, 112, 125; postwar employment, 97, 98
Shorter, George M.: amputation and, 62; education of, 24–25
Shorter, John, 24–25
Simmons, William J., 9
sit-ins, 75–76
Sixth Street Colored School, 24
Smallwood, William: pension, 138; postwar employment, 96
Smith, Grant, 122
Smith, John, children's schooling, lack of, 122
Smith, Richard, 109
South Mills, N.C., 59
Stanton, Edwin, on pay equalization, 49
Stevens, Thaddeus, 49
Stiles, George: pension, 111, 125, 138; postwar employment, 97–98
Streets, Charlotte, 84, 85
Stringham, Thomas, 54
Strong, George Templeton, 38
suicide, 54, 105, 133
Summers, William, 98
Supervisory Committee, 74

Tallman, William: enlistment bounty for, 44; pension, denied, 131
Taylor, Charles W., desertion and, 55
Taylor, Mary, 102
Taylor, M. Louise, 122
Taylor, Susie King, 9, 61
textile industry, 115
Thomas, Hannah, 138
Thomas, Henry, injuries of, 60
Thomas, John, illness of, 63
Thomas, Joseph, pension, 138
Thomas, Theresa, 32
Thomas, William, 54
Thompson, Elizabeth, 120
Thompson, Hannibal, 17
Thompson, Henry: disability and marriage, 102–103; pension, 71, 126, 127; postwar employment, 93
Thompson, James, 17

Thompson, John: family household composition, 17, 42, 120; mother's employment, 16; pension, 127; postwar employment, 97, 98, 118

Thompson, Robert E., family, extended kin, 120

Thornton, Jacob: amputation of, 61; pension, 72, 111; postwar employment, 116; postwar reenlistment in military, 99

Tobias, Caroline, 19

Tobias, Charles: family of origin, 19–21; pension, 111–112; postwar family and employment, 97, 110

Tobias, Zeholar, 19

Tunnel, Ann, 28

Turner, John, amputation and, 62

Tyler, Benjamin L., 113–114

Union League Club of New York, 80–81

Union League of Philadelphia (ULP), 39–40, 45

United States Colored Infantry (USCI) units: Third, 41, 46–47, 58–59; Sixth, 1, 41, 44, 46–47, 59, 64, 80; Eighth, 46–47, 59, 64; Thirteenth, 163n37; Twenty-Ninth, 93, 163n37; Thirty-Third, 9; Thirty-Fifth, 93; Thirty-Sixth, 93; Thirty-Seventh, 93; Forty-First, 163n37; Forty-Third, 64; Sixty-Second, 64; Sixty-Fifth, 64; Sixty-Seventh, 64

U.S. Navy, African American service in, 35

Valentine, Annie Elizabeth, 50

Valentine, Tillman, on military wages, 50

Vandermark, Peter, enlistment bounty of, 45

veterans: employment and racial discrimination, 88–89; employment opportunities, 109–110; employment opportunities, improvement in, 92, 118–119; families, 119–124; families, extended kin, 120–122; families, fictive kin, 108–109; marriages, 102–105, 119–120; pension eligibility and applications, 89–90, 124–128, 129–141; pensions for widows, 143–145; reenlistment in military, 98–102; school for children and, 122–123. *See also* pensions

Viney, Alphonso, 138

Viney, Franklin: pension, 138; pension, denied, 131

Wagner, Louis F., 44, 49, 74, 80

Walker, Amelia, 19

Walker, Joseph H., 49

water contamination, 63–64, 66, 100, 135

Waters, Etta, 78

Waters, Hiram: pension, 135; postwar employment, 97; wages docked, 55–56

Waters, Priscilla, 135

Watkins, Joseph, deaths of, 64–65

Wears, Isaiah C., 37

Webster, Thomas B., 59, 74

Welch, Isiah H., 81

westward expansion, 98

Westwood, Charles W., 122

Westwood, U. E., 122, 127, 132–133

White, Andrew: on combat, eagerness for, 57; employment, 32–33; on military wages, 49–50; pension, 86, 134–135

White, Anna, 30

White, George, wages docked, 55

White, Hannah, 30

White, Jacob C., Jr., on education, 22

White, James, fictive kin and, 30

Williams, Charles, 18

Williams, Frank, 119

Williams, George Washington, 9

Williams, Samuel, 17–18, 120

Williams, Thomas, family household composition, 17–18

Williamson, Mary Leighton (Davis), 1, 28, 40, 76, 85, 145

Wilson, Henry, 173–174n26

Wilson, Hezekiah: injuries of, 60; pension, 70; postwar employment, 97

Wilson, Joseph T., 9

Wilson, Solomon, enlistment, 76–77

women: citizenship and sacrifice, 112–113; education and schooling gender dynamics, 25–26; employment at military camps, 9, 73–75; motherhood and, 15–17, 19–21; racial discrimination, 74–76; recruitment efforts of, 39, 41–42; sacrifice, public display of, 74;

war widows, creation of, 84 (*see also* pensions). *See also* families
Woodson, Edmonia, 143–145
Woodson, Joseph: family of origin, 19, 20; marriage and children of, 120; pension, 131
Woodson, Julia, 144–145
Woodson, Margaret, 19, 20
Woodson, Mattie, 120
Woodson, William: desertion, 144–145; pension, 143–145; postwar employment, 96
Woodyard, Henrietta, 137
Wright, John, 137

UNCIVIL WARS

Weirding the War: Stories from the Civil War's Ragged Edges
edited by Stephen Berry

Ruin Nation: Destruction and the American Civil War
by Megan Kate Nelson

America's Corporal: James Tanner in War and Peace
by James Marten

The Blue, the Gray, and the Green: Toward an Environmental History of the Civil War
edited by Brian Allen Drake

Empty Sleeves: Amputation in the Civil War South
by Brian Craig Miller

Lens of War: Exploring Iconic Photographs of the Civil War
edited by J. Matthew Gallman and Gary W. Gallagher

The Slave-Trader's Letter-Book: Charles Lamar, the Wanderer, and Other Tales of the African Slave Trade
by Jim Jordan

Driven from Home: North Carolina's Civil War Refugee Crisis
by David Silkenat

The Ghosts of Guerrilla Memory: How Civil War Bushwhackers Became Gunslingers in the American West
by Matthew Christopher Hulbert

Beyond Freedom: Disrupting the History of Emancipation
edited by David W. Blight and Jim Downs

The Lost President: A. D. Smith and the Hidden History of Radical Democracy in Civil War America
by Ruth Dunley

Bodies in Blue: Disability in the Civil War North
by Sarah Handley-Cousins

Visions of Glory: The Civil War in Word and Image
edited by Kathleen Diffley and Benjamin Fagan

Household War: How Americans Lived and Fought the Civil War
edited by Lisa Tendrich Frank and LeeAnn Whites

Buying and Selling Civil War Memory in Gilded Age America
edited by James Marten and Caroline E. Janney

The War after the War: A New History of Reconstruction
by John Patrick Daly

The Families' Civil War: Black Soldiers and the Fight for Racial Justice
by Holly A. Pinheiro Jr.